STILL-WATER
ANGLING

RICHARD WALKER

Still-Water Angling

*Revised fourth edition with
an additional chapter on zander
by Doctor Barrie Rickards*

DAVID & CHARLES

NEWTON ABBOT   LONDON   NORTH POMFRET (VT)

British Library Cataloguing in Publication Data
Walker, Richard, *1918–*
Still-water angling.—Rev. 4th ed.
1. Fishing—Great Britain
I. Title
799.1'2   SH605
ISBN 0–7153–7074–X

FIRST PUBLISHED 1953
SECOND EDITION 1955
THIRD EDITION 1960
REPRINTED 1962
FOURTH, FULLY REVISED EDITION 1975
SECOND IMPRESSION 1978
THIRD IMPRESSION 1979
FOURTH IMPRESSION 1984

Printed and bound in Great Britain by
Redwood Burn Limited, Trowbridge, Wilts
for David & Charles (Publishers) Limited
Brunel House   Newton Abbot   Devon

Published in the United States of America
by David & Charles Inc.
North Pomfret   Vermont 05053   USA

CONTENTS

ILLUSTRATIONS

The author would like to express his gratitude to Mrs David Forbes for permission to use her late husband's fine illustration of the carp on page 114.

PREFACE TO THE SECOND EDITION

THE only changes of importance in this second edition are in the illustrations, twelve of which I have replaced with what I hope will be considered to be better photographs. The changes in the text have for the most part been added as notes at the end of pages and at the end of chapters. These do, I think, bring the book as nearly up-to-date as an angling book can be.

Although few of them are likely to read this preface, I should like to thank my many correspondents for their letters, so many of which have been interesting and useful to me.

R. W.

May, 1955.

Diagrams and photographs (except where stated to the contrary) are by the author

PREFACE TO THE FOURTH EDITION

W HEN it became known that I had been asked to produce a fourth edition of this book, many of my friends told me forcefully that I ought on no account to re-write it. They felt that it would be far preferable to retain the original text and expand, where necessary, by means of additional notes at the end of each chapter. Accordingly, that is what I have done under the sub-headings FURTHER NOTES.

I have discarded altogether the chapter on trout that appeared in the earlier editions, for since the book was written there has been a vast expansion of still-water trout-fishing facilities, of which anglers have not been slow to take advantage. New rods, reels, lines, nets, leaders and flies have been developed for it, so that not only has my chapter on trout become obsolete, it has also become impossible to replace it with anything short of a complete book, which I am in process of writing.

Also since the first edition, the European pike-perch or zander has spread widely through the Great Ouse system of waterways, and it is also to be found in a number of lakes and ponds. As it will inevitably spread to many more, I think it right that this book should include a chapter about it.

As my own experience with zander is limited—despite the fact that I rented the fishing rights on a lake that holds plenty—I have asked my friend Doctor Barrie Rickards to contribute a chapter on this species.

I have also decided to delete the chapter on still-water fisheries. Since 1953, there has been much more interest shown in the management of fisheries of this kind, and the services of Mr. Eric Birch, as a consultant, are available to anyone who wants to know how to run a fishery properly.

There are still too many people who continue to pour thousands of stunted, worthless fish into waters already grossly overstocked, but I have given up hoping they will ever see sense.

Many people have been kind enough to say that the publication of *Still-Water Angling* in 1953 had some influence upon angling progress, in that it not only advanced the claim of still waters to be able to provide splendid sport, but it also convinced anglers that the capture of exceptionally large fish need not be a rare event dependent mainly upon luck. Whether the book had as much influence as has been suggested, I don't know, but it is true that in the twenty years or so that have elapsed since it was first published, a cult among anglers has grown up which has come to be called specimen-hunting. Its protagonists seek only exceptionally large fish.

This in itself is good, but it seems to me regrettable that it should lead to two aspects of the game which detract from its enjoyment.

One is over-ambition. Young men nowadays feel positively cheated if they are not catching 20 lb. carp or pike, or correspondingly large fish of other species, regularly. 'How many double-figure carp must I wade through,' asked one, 'before I get a twenty?' To him, a carp of 18 or 19 lb. was an insignificant fish, a positive nuisance.

Anglers often say to me 'Of course, I've never caught a carp that was big by *your* standards—the best I've ever had was only 28 lb.!'

Now this is quite ridiculous. The hardest scrap I ever had with a carp was with a fish of $9\frac{1}{2}$ lb. Any fish that requires a landing net to put it on the bank is worth catching.

When I put forward the view that big fish could be caught in fair numbers by the use of methods designed for that purpose, I didn't mean that anglers ought to feel cheated unless they regularly caught fish of 70 or 80 per cent of record size.

The notion that a carp of 20 lb. 1 oz. is a great triumph, while one of 19 lb. 15 oz. is a mere tiddler of which its captor should be ashamed, is manifestly ridiculous. We have come to a pretty pass in standard-setting if our pleasure is dependent on whether or not a fish drops an ounce or two of shit on its way to the landing net.

The arbitrary figures that anglers are apt to lay down as distinguishing between credit and discredit are all the more ridiculous when one realises that they are dependent upon our weighing in pounds avoirdupois. If 10 Kg. replaces 20 lb. as the 'magic figure' (as has been suggested), quite a few anglers whose biggest carp are over 20 lb. but under 22 lb. will have to alter their sense of values or go and hang themselves from sheer disappointment!

The other aspect of the game of big-fish catching that I deplore is competition, and I don't mean match-fishing. Organised fishing matches are fine; although by the very nature of things it is never possible to give each contestant equal opportunity, the organisers can and do try to achieve fairness. It is frank and honest competition and good luck to it, say I.

What I don't like is the one-upmanship attitude. 'How many "doubles" did you catch last season? Only twenty-nine? I had forty-three!'

'How many rod-hours is it necessary to put in to qualify for membership of the Muddypool Specimen Group?'

I am proud to say that I don't know how many fish, eligible to be considered as 'specimens', I have caught. All I know is that I enjoyed catching them, I enjoyed seeing friends catch big fish, I enjoyed the surroundings in which they were caught, and I hope to go on enjoying all this till I die. Which is more, I know why I enjoy it.

It has taken some 15 million years from the time when man first stood upright, for him to evolve into what he is today. For all of that time, except for the last 10,000 years or so, his survival was totally dependent upon his hunting ability, and in the case of some races, it still is. Man developed, but he still needed to preserve the instinct to hunt—without it he would have become extinct. That instinct, so essential for survival through millions of years, has not been lost in the few years during which it has not been strictly necessary; thus fishing is a way of fulfilling a basic need and the pleasure we feel in catching a good fish should be sufficient reward in itself.

Primitive man combined with his fellows in hunting bands. Members of those bands did not compete with one another. It was all for each and each for all. In modern fishing, a band of friends gains the greatest pleasure from its collective success. It matters not whether Tom, Dick or Harry caught the biggest fish, or the most big fish.

In the preface to the first edition, I expressed my thanks to a long list of people without whose help, in various ways, writing the book would have been impossible. Now, twenty years later, the list would be altogether too long to include. To all those, therefore, who know well enough how they have helped me, I now extend my thanks, while expressing my sorrow that so many fine men whose names appeared when this book was first published, are no longer with us.

Those excellent publications, *The Fishing Gazette* and *The Anglers' News*, are also gone, though we are fortunate in having the finest angling press of any country in the world.

What future there is for angling is hard to decide. With most, if not all of the governments of the world devoted to the philosophy that a sufficiency of material possessions and synthetic entertainment will guarantee human happiness, the outlook is bleak. Where politicians are concerned, conservation is something about which they are prepared to lie and mouth platitudes, but is not yet a cause they wish to espouse with sincerity. They talk gravely about the importance of conservation while they permit rivers and streams to be destroyed by abstraction, pollution and indiscriminate dredging, and still waters to be destroyed by back-filling with domestic refuse, industrial waste, and often enough deadly poisons.

I therefore dedicate the fourth edition of this book to the memory of the late Bernard Donovan, who led a protest march of anglers to the House of Commons; a man who, right up until he died, never ceased to fight against all the evils that conspire to destroy not only the lakes, rivers and ponds of Britain but all the wildlife they support.

May, 1975.   RICHARD WALKER.

ON CATCHING BIG FISH

Most anglers regard the catching of 'specimen' fish—big fish—as something which hardly ever happens. Some think it is a matter of luck, or the opportunity to fish choice waters, or things of that sort; others regard those who regularly catch big fish as having skill or knowledge far in excess of the average. They are all wrong. Catching big fish is a specialized branch of angling, and success in it is well within the powers of any ordinary man.

It would be idle to deny that I have caught a large number of big fish of many different kinds and in many waters. I am not very skilful, nor is my intelligence above the average, and there are thousands of anglers who could do very much better than I, if they would only believe in the possibility.

I am sure that you would like to catch some really big fish, and there is no reason why you shouldn't. My difficulty lies in convincing you that you can. If you and I could go fishing together half a dozen times, it would be easy. You would believe you could catch a big fish readily enough if you had one kicking on the bank, and I know what you would say, because I have heard it said several times by men whom I *have* convinced in that way. You'd say, 'Why, it's easy! I wouldn't have believed it! If I'd only known this years ago . . .' As it is, I can only tell you that there are very many more big fish about than most anglers think. It is true that some of them are in private waters, and it is true that there are waters in which there are none. But in most waters there are specimen fish in numbers, and there are very few anglers who have no chance to fish for really big specimens of one kind or another. The fact that on most waters very few are caught does not mean that few are there.

Big fish are not caught by luck. They are caught by

deliberately setting out to catch big fish, and by an unshake-able determination to be content with nothing less.

I know that now and then a big fish is caught by someone who is fishing for 'anything that comes along,' but very few anglers do catch specimens like that. The Notable Fish List in the *Angler's News* averages 200 fish each year. We are told that there are two million anglers in Britain, but if there was only a tenth of that number it would still mean that only one angler in a thousand catches a big fish once a year. Perhaps that is why such fish are often called 'The Fish of a Lifetime.' They need not be, for you can catch fish of that size several times in a season, if you go about it in the right way.

The right way is to be methodical and do everything in its right order of importance; and obviously the most important thing is to find the fish.

I shall have more to say in another chapter about ways of deciding how rapidly the fish grow in a given water, and whether it is likely to contain big ones or not. We will assume at present that you are going to fish a water which you are confident contains some big ones and you are deter-mined to catch some of them. Bearing in mind that the average angler does not catch big fish, we may learn some-thing by seeing what he does and then deciding how our methods must differ from his.

What he does is to choose his spot on three main grounds —a comfortable place to sit, a part of the water free from weeds and snags, and with the wind at his back; and having found such a spot, he starts fishing right away.

His chances of catching big fish are already slight, and if you think, you will see why. Big fish are not rare, but they are not so many that you will find them wherever you choose to sit. They do not care a bit whether you are comfortable or not; they do not care to be far from cover, and in still water they are much more likely to be in places where the wind is in the angler's face.

Before you start fishing you must locate your fish, and that takes time. Some species are easier to locate than others, but even with the easiest, you will be doing well if you find them in a day. Sometimes you can only guess where they will be, but there is a world of difference between a guess based on knowledge and a blind guess. You must take into account the way in which the fish feed, what they feed on, the effects of the weather on the water, the depth, and many other things, and all this takes time. It is not enough to know exactly where the fish are; you must try to find out where they will go from there, where they will be at any given hour of the day or night, and when they will be most likely to feed. Until you have come to a conclusion about all these things, you should not think about setting up your tackle. In any lake or river, there are far more places where big fish hardly ever go than where they go often, and if you fish at random, or simply because a place 'looks a good spot,' you may fish season after season and never show your bait to a single good fish, though there may be dozens in the water.

I do not know how often your decision on where you will fish, after you have done your best to study the circumstances, will be right, but if you are correct on every fourth attempt, you will be doing much better than I. You must expect to be wrong often, but you will be right often enough to catch some big fish, if you realize that you cannot catch them unless you fish where they are.

The second essential is to avoid frightening the fish. It is not a bit of use finding them if you frighten them away. Let us look at our average angler again. If you ask him whether fish can see an angler on the bank, or feel the vibration of his tread, he will tell you quite emphatically that they can, and while he is telling you he will as likely as not be stamping to warm his feet, or fanning his brow with a white handkerchief. You will notice that if there are marginal rushes, he will have cut or beaten them down in front of him, and he will probably be sitting on a basket or stool, or standing upright. His rod will be coated with shiny varnish. He may be wearing a white shirt, or hat, or doing many other fish-scaring things which I have not space to 'mention. You say he does not do *all* these things? Perhaps not; but how many of them can he afford to do, if he wants to catch big fish?

You cannot take too much trouble to avoid scaring fish. Whatever you do, you will scare too many—in fact you will scare far more than you ever know about. Sometimes a fish you have scared will return later; but the more care you take not to scare it at all, the more likely you are to catch it.

The third essential is to use the right tackle. Our average angler is inclined to use what he sees others using, or what tackle-shops advise him to use, and since he is copying unsuccessful people, he is unlikely to do much better. You must choose your tackle on two grounds: ability to put the bait where the fish can find it and also to hook and land the fish if it takes the bait. Here we come to an important point; each essential must be fulfilled without cancelling out the others. We have seen that the second essential is not to scare the fish, and our third, the choice of tackle, must be governed by that too. It is no use locating your fish, and concealing yourself or creeping stealthily to within casting range, and then dropping an ounce of lead on its head, or fishing with such coarse line that even the most stupid fish would be afraid. Equally, however, it is useless to use tackle so feeble that you are bound to be broken if you hook the fish, and you must use your judgment in striking a fair compromise. I shall have more to say about tackle later; here I will say that you will not lose by being careful with it to the point of fussiness and by being always anxious to improve its efficiency. If you spot the slightest weakness or falling-off in effectiveness, stop fishing and put it right. Lots of big fish are hooked and lost; some because the choice of tackle was wrong in the first place, some because the angler failed to keep it up to scratch. You will often find your tackle fails you, however careful you are; you may not be able to cast far enough, or you may find the fish is too much for your gear and breaks away; but if you do your utmost to make your tackle perfect, you will be repaid.

You will inevitably be told about the small boy who caught the big fish with a stick cut from the hedge; the great angler whose favourite rod was described as 'a dog's hind leg with more wrappings than Jack Hobbs' favourite bat,' and the famous Thames angler who caught big trout on a twopenny garden cane. Perhaps we can agree that they succeeded in spite of rather than because of their tackle. Tackle means *all* your tackle; not just rod, reel, line and hook, but all the sundry items, and the landing-net too.

The fourth essential is to choose the right time to fish. Fish are not always feeding, and the bigger they are, the less often they feed. They do not grow big by abstaining from food, however. Here, study will help you to choose your time, for you cannot fish continuously for a week. You must not fear early rising, nor even spending nights at the waterside if necessary. You will put in many hours fishing at wrong times; I do—but you will be right much more often if you try to decide what is likely to suit the fish, and don't consider yourself.

The fifth essential is to use the right bait. Our average angler is inclined to put this choice first, and to have a great deal of faith in special baits. Some people believe that there are secret ingredients which can be put into baits to make them irresistible to fish. It isn't true. The majority of big fish are caught on very simple, ordinary baits or lures, and if you carry out faithfully what I have laid down as the first four essentials you will be astonished to find how relatively unimportant your choice of bait is. That does not mean that it is of no importance at all; it means that you should not blame your bait until you are sure that you have carried out the first four essentials. If you have located your fish, and put your bait where the fish can find it at a time when they are feeding, using the right tackle and avoiding scaring them, and after an hour or two have not had a bite, then you may start wondering whether a different bait might be advisable. Give the bait you are using another three or four hours to confirm this, before you make a change.

In choosing baits, I would advise you to try first a bait which you know has often been found attractive to the kind of fish you are after, and if you find that it is not successful, then choose another for a definite reason, not just for the sake of making a change. For example, if you were tench-fishing and could not tempt a fish with worm, you might consider changing to bread flake, if the water was a heavily fished one in which the tench had had ample opportunity to discover that bread was good food. But if the water swarmed with small roach or rudd, you might choose instead a water-snail, which the little fish would not pull to pieces as they would flake. That is what I mean by choosing an alternative bait for a good reason.

One of the difficulties of catching big fish is that in every water there are a great many more little fish than big ones. A big fish cannot take a bait if a small one has taken it first, or if a horde of small fish have pulled it to pieces or off the hook. As a broad generalization, the adage 'a big bait for a big fish' is a good one, and mainly because a big bait is less liable to be first taken by small fish. The average angler uses baits which are generally much too small. He would be astonished at the size of bait which I usually use. Your choice is more likely to be too small than too big.

These are the five essentials, from what one might call a material point of view. I know that they do not cover the problem completely; what I want to stress is the importance of feeling your way to success, step by logical step. If you fish in this way, you are bound to succeed sooner or later. A blank day is only a failure when it has taught you nothing. If you treat your fishing as a lucky dip, you will learn little and catch few fish. It was said of Christopher Columbus that when he sailed, he didn't know where he was going; when he arrived, he didn't know where he was; and when he came home, he didn't know where he'd been. Something similar might be said of the way many men fish.

You will see that what I have advised takes no account of angling methods. An extensive repertoire of ready-made methods is most valuable, but they must be your slaves, not your masters, and if you aim to fulfil the essentials, you will often find that methods will choose themselves. A great many anglers are masters of more than one style of fishing, and yet fail because they lack flexibility of mind. They become like card players who can only play the cards they have been dealt. You are faced with a given set of circumstances: do not ask yourself 'Shall I float-fish, or ledger? Shall I use threadline technique or the Nottingham style?' Start from basic principles and build up a technique of which every part is germane to the task in front of you.

Down the years, fishermen faced with problems have attempted to develop cut-and-dried procedures, and millions of words have been written about how these should be carried out. When one of these methods is found to be successful, anglers suppose that they can follow it without thinking, and that is fatal, since fishing will always exceed in diversity all the ready-made angling formulae ever devised. The methods of which I shall speak later in this book will not be of much use unless you realize this.

In addition to the material approach to angling, there is the question of the angler's outlook. It is perhaps more important. I have already spoken of confidence. If you remain confident in the face of disappointment, you will succeed in the end, but this will not be easy if you have not yet caught a big fish. Like learning to swim or to ride a bicycle, it is making a start that is difficult. The more big fish you catch, the easier you will find it to catch the next one; but begin by facing the fact that when you have turned to fishing for big fish only, the whole tempo of your angling will be slowed down, for you cannot use methods which successfully combine the ability to catch little fish and big ones. Very often you will have to fish in a way deliberately designed to avoid catching little ones, and since, as I have said, there are many more small fish than large ones, you must be prepared to exchange quantity for quality. I am sure that you would not mind fishing for six days without a single bite, if you could be perfectly certain that on the seventh you would catch a monster fish —one which would be called a glass-case specimen by your friends.

Besides confidence, there is another element in your approach to big-fish catching which is not always there to begin with, but which I believe anyone can cultivate. It is a mixture of enthusiasm, determination and persistence. Maurice Ingham reminds me that once when we were discussing the catching of big carp, I summed this up by saying 'You've got to be *deadly*.' Kipling, writing of things other than fishing, speaks of 'the calculated craftsmanship that camps alone before the angry rifle-pit or shell-hole, and cleanly and methodically wipes out every soul in it.' That must be your attitude. If you think that no fish can matter that much, you will fail. It must matter tremendously that you should catch the fish you are after. An intense feud must exist between you and it—a feud that can only end with your success.

This kind of approach will help you to understand better the limited mental powers of fish. Nowadays, people are inclined to talk about 'conditioned reflexes' in fish, when they mean that the fish have learned something. Species of fish differ in their ability to learn, but all of them can learn to some extent and the older they are the more they are likely to have learned. The more exactly you are able to assess how much they know, the more easily you can predict what they will do and thus circumvent their knowledge. I find that anglers are apt to be extremists in their views about the intelligence of fish; some credit them with mental powers almost equal to those of humans, while others treat them as if they had no more sense than an earthworm. You will not greatly overestimate their intelligence if you think of it as nearly equal to that of a domestic fowl. Those fish which lead solitary lives seem more intelligent than those which swim in shoals. You will find that fish are greatly affected by the amount a water is fished.

On little-fished waters, the fish are relatively unsuspicious of tackle, but very easily alarmed at seeing the angler or by the vibrations of a heavy tread, while the more intelligent species are very suspicious of unfamiliar baits. Thus you will find that in a lonely private lake, such species as roach and rudd are very easy to catch if you do not alarm them, but carp are most difficult. Where a water is heavily fished, and many fish are caught and returned, or are hooked and break away, the more intelligent fish become highly suspicious of tackle, but their familiarity with ground-baits and lost hook-baits and with the presence of humans on the bank will often allow them to feed freely on anything except a bait to which they know a line is attached, even when they know anglers are there. Shoaling fish, on the other hand, seem unable to discriminate in this way to anything like the same extent; in well-fished waters, they become more suspicious of the baits offered, while their instinct to flee at the indications of the presence of humans is overcome very slowly indeed. All fish are inclined to take their cue from others and this is specially true of shoal fish, whose opportunity to observe the action of their fellows is greatest.

You will see, therefore, that the commonly-held idea that the less a water is fished, the easier the fish it contains will be to catch, is really only true of such fish as roach, rudd, bream and small perch; most other species may be easier to catch in a much-fished water by the exercise of a little thought, and the more you learn about the fish you are trying to catch, the more likely you are to hit upon a way of out-thinking them.

You will find that preoccupation with a particular kind of food is not confined to chalk-stream trout, but happens with many other kinds of fish. In cases of this kind, keen observation will repay you well. There is reason to suppose that preoccupation with a particular kind of food, displayed at times by most species of fish, depends on the number of particles of the food available and also upon the particle size. The greater the number of particles or food-units, and the smaller their size, the greater the preoccupation displayed by the fish. Additionally, large fish seem to show greater preoccupation than small fish. The bearing of all this on choice of ground-bait and hook-bait is obvious, though it runs counter to the accepted notions of ground-bait in small particles and a larger hook-bait.

Obviously the greater your total knowledge of angling, the better your chances will be. I do not think you can read too much about fishing, but you will often find opposite opinions expressed, while now and then you will find that the books are all agreed about something you are sure from your own experience is quite wrong. But you will find a great deal that throws more light upon your problems and that your own experience will tell you is sound, while you will pick up a lot of small but useful tips; the combined effect will much increase the efficiency of your angling. I advise you to accept with reserve the dictums of any angling writer who is for ever using the words 'always' and 'never.' Lord Grey was right when he said that those were the two words least appropriate to any angling matter.

Manual skill cannot fail to help, but I am sure that it is greatly overrated. Perhaps my own limited skill makes that statement suspect, but I cannot help noticing how many very skilful anglers there are and how very few big fish they catch. Provided you are not downright clumsy, you need not feel overawed at the sight of another angler casting twice as far or more accurately than you can. He may know less about *where* to cast than you do, but he is worth watching all the same. Practice will improve your skill, but it is very easy to become obsessed with it, so that the means become more important than the end. Some men even participate in casting competitions.

You must be careful, too, not to jump to conclusions. To some people, the best bait, or the best tackle, or the best time, are those which featured in the capture of the last large fish they heard about. You may begin to think a bait is a good one when it has accounted for a dozen or more big fish, in different waters, and you will do well to regard other details in a similar way.

All angling is a series of problems. The more you fish, the more problems you will be set, for the solution of one very often sets a number of fresh ones, and it is probably true to say that the greater your experience is, the more unsolved problems will confront you, and you can never solve them all. The best advice I can offer you here is that before you try to solve a problem, make sure you know what the problem is.

When you have done your best in every way you can think of, you must wait. Kipling's Gilbert de Aquila said 'We wait. I am old, but still I find that the most grievous work I know.' Waiting is, indeed, hard work. Catching big fish involves a great deal of hard work, of which waiting is only a part. Perhaps that is why you will feel so tremendous a sense of satisfaction when you succeed.

CHAPTER I

ABOUT STILL WATERS

THE history and theory of angling as we know it today has been based on river-fishing. As a result, the literature of the sport has neglected still-water fishing altogether, or has treated it as a branch of angling requiring no more than a modification of the methods used in running water. As long as this attitude persisted, the possibilities of still waters could never be fully realized; but in recent years there has been a growing understanding that though still waters vary widely—perhaps more widely even than running waters—they all have certain points in common which demand very different angling methods from rivers and streams.

For instance, it would be untrue to say that a lake or a pond has no current, but its currents are slight and mainly dependent on wind direction, and, even where surface-feeding fish are concerned, they will not bring food to the fish in such a way that the fish need only maintain their position and wait for food to come to them. Still-water fish must go in search of their food.

As the current is hardly ever so strong that the fish must lie head-on, still-water fish cannot be stalked from downstream as they can in rivers; they may be facing in all directions and are thus much more likely to observe the angler. They are also much more susceptible to vibration and take alarm at the lightest tread. In rivers, the angler usually makes use of the current, to some extent, to carry his bait to the fish. The technique of long-trotting is the ultimate expression of this use; but even where a ledger is employed and the bait anchored firmly, the current is still often used to carry particles of ground-bait, or the scent of the hook-bait, downstream and attract the fish to its source. None of this is possible in still waters; the possibilities of wind or drift to carry a bait to fish are very limited, while if it is desired to spread ground-bait over an area, or in a line, it must be done by the angler. Because fish may often be a great distance away from the bank, very long casting is frequently necessary.

Still-water fish travel extensively in search of food, while temperature influences their movement (or lack of movement) far more than it would in a river, where currents are constantly mixing the water and keeping all depths at more or less the same temperature. By contrast, in a deep lake in summer temperatures may vary as much as 40°F. between the surface and the bottom, and at the surface the temperature may be very much higher at one side of a lake than it is at the other. The amount of dissolved oxygen in the water, which has a great effect on fish, does not vary greatly in rivers where the current is constantly mixing the water, except that there will be more oxygen immediately below waterfalls and rapids. Otherwise the oxygen is fairly evenly distributed at all depths, and its amount is governed mainly by temperature. In a lake, the water is mixed almost entirely by wind, and in its absence the oxygen-content may be lowered considerably by rising temperature or by decaying vegetation, or both.

In some lakes the water below a certain depth may, in summer, become completely de-oxygenated and uninhabitable by fish. In small ponds, during drought conditions or hot weather, the oxygen content of the entire water may even fall so low as to kill some of the fish. Long before this state of affairs is reached they will have become disinclined to feed.

Various species of fish have decided preferences for one kind of bottom or another, and that preference may be for anything from thick black mud to hard rock. It is necessary to find out what the bottom consists of, as well as the depth, to determine where the fish are most likely to be. Often such study will show you that you must use special tactics to overcome silkweed or blanket weed, or to deal with a bottom of soft mud.

Great changes take place in a lake through the year.

Let us start with a lake in autumn and see what these changes are.

All the water is warmer than about 42°F., some, and perhaps all of it much warmer, as we shall see later. The autumn frosts and cold winds chill the surface water, which sinks, warm water rising to take its place and to be chilled in turn. Circulation continues until all the water is cooled to 39.2°F.

At 39.2°F. water is at its heaviest. Any water which is cooled below that temperature will no longer tend to sink; instead it forms a thin layer at the surface, whose depth is not great and only in the shallowest of lakes does it reach bottom, which otherwise is at 39.2°F. If the weather is cold enough, the surface freezes, freezing point being 32°F. As long as the temperature at the top is between 32°F. and 39.2°F., this layer of cold water stays at the top, and the bottom of the lake is the warmest place in it. Circulation has stopped.

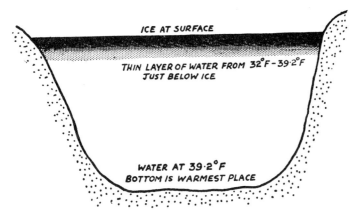

ICE AT SURFACE

THIN LAYER OF WATER FROM 32°F – 39·2°F
JUST BELOW ICE

WATER AT 39·2°F
BOTTOM IS WARMEST PLACE

LAKE IN WINTER WHILE AIR TEMPERATURE IS BELOW FREEZING

In early spring the sun warms the surface. As the cold surface is warmed up to 39.2°F. it sinks, the layer circulates and is eventually all warmed to 39.2°F., and is eliminated. Once the temperature at the surface rises above 39.2°F. the circulation again stops and a layer of warm water forms, which increases in depth and temperature as the season progresses.

The water will only be warmed as far as the sun's rays penetrate, and, except during transitory weather conditions described later, the warmest water will always be at the top.

Between the warm upper layer and the cold one below, there will be a region through which the fall in temperature is very rapid for a small increase in depth. This region of rapid change of temperature with depth is called the *Thermocline*.

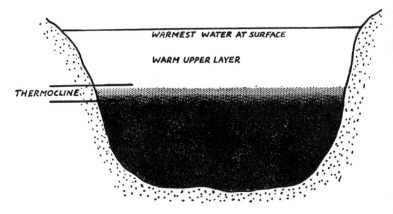

WARMEST WATER AT SURFACE

WARM UPPER LAYER

THERMOCLINE.

LAKE IN SUMMER.   THE WATER BELOW THE THERMOCLINE IS NOT ONLY COLD BUT MAY BE DEOXYGENATED

One of the effects of wind is to lower water temperature; you can prove this by wetting your finger and blowing on it. If there is wind, not only will the water at the very top be cooled but it will be blown along with the wind. As it is blown along it tends to sink, and a current is therefore caused which travels along the surface in the direction of the wind, and then, falling to the top of the thermocline, goes back along it to where it came from. The wind thus has several effects. It mixes up the water of the warm upper layer, so that its temperature, and the oxygen dissolved in it, is fairly constant, and it pushes the whole of the warm upper layer towards one side of the lake to a greater or lesser extent, depending on its force and duration. If these are great, the thermocline will be in effect tilted towards the side of the lake against which the wind is blowing, and the cold bottom layer may even rise to the surface on the other side.

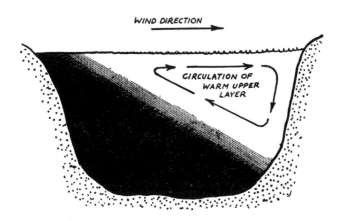

SHOWING THE EFFECT OF WIND IN CIRCULATING THE WARM UPPER
LAYER AND TILTING THE THERMOCLINE

If the wind drops at all quickly, the thermocline swings back to level *and beyond*; in fact, it overshoots; and it continues to swing back and forth for some time before it settles down. The bigger the lake is, the longer the time occupied by the cycle of the swing.

In comparatively shallow lakes, the upper warm layer reaches the bottom in spring, and the cold layer and the thermocline are both eliminated. The deeper the lake is, and the more coloured its water, the longer this will take, and in the deeper lakes and reservoirs the thermocline and the cold bottom layer remain all through the summer, only increasing in temperature by a degree or two, through conduction. The actual depth of the thermocline varies widely in different lakes and can only be found by experiment.

Plants of all kinds are continually dying, and as they sink down into the cold bottom water their decay, and that of other organic substances, will use up oxygen. This cold water never comes to the top except in strong sustained wind, and it gets very little oxygen. If it is fairly small in volume and much decay takes place, its oxygen may be partly or wholly used up, but in very deep lakes where its volume is many times that of the layer above it, or where plant growth is poor and little decay takes place, it will retain most of its oxygen right through the summer, but even then it will remain cold. Fish will avoid it and plants will not grow in it.

In autumn, the effects of wind, rain, and radiation loss continue to cool the warm upper layer until eventually its temperature falls below that of the cold water beneath it. This then rises to the surface, and a circulation, with re-oxygenation, takes place until the conditions are reached at which this discussion began.

A particular case must be mentioned in considering the tilting of the thermocline by wind. In reservoirs which are made by damming a watercourse in a valley, and in other waters with similar bottom contour, a wind of sufficient strength and duration blowing towards the deep end will cause the lower layer of cold and perhaps deoxygenated water to spread over a very wide area at the shallow end, and the more gradual the slope of the bottom, the greater this effect will be. An opposite wind will have much less effect, causing the cold water to rise at the deep end over only a small area; but if the wind drops rapidly, the swing back will produce temporarily the effect of an opposite wind.

You will realize that the effect of these changes on fish will be enormous. In later chapters I shall deal with this in greater detail, at this stage merely pointing out that we can conveniently divide lakes and ponds into two categories; the shallow ones in which the thermocline and the cold bottom layer are eliminated early in the year, and the deep ones in which these layers remain all summer. In the shallow lakes, water temperature fluctuates greatly, since the volume of water is smaller, and such waters are much more 'temperamental' than those with a deep-water reserve. In these, fish can always find some part of the lake where the temperature lets them feed, whereas in a shallow lake all the water may be too warm or too cold.

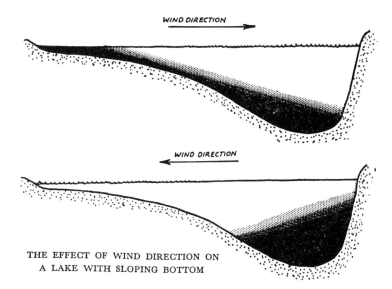

THE EFFECT OF WIND DIRECTION ON
A LAKE WITH SLOPING BOTTOM

When fish have stopped feeding for reasons like this you have
to calculate when and where they will begin again, but in
these shallow lakes it is easier to see the fish or signs of their
whereabouts, while a bigger proportion of the bottom
receives light and grows plants well, so that the fish grow
well too. You will see that while fish may be harder to
tempt in these smaller or shallower waters, they are likely
to be well worth catching, so that extra investigation and
thought will be repaid.

The effect of wind on the fish will be great in all lakes, but
greater in the deep ones. If it tilts the thermocline, fish
will be driven right out of parts of the lake and may be
concentrated in others. Wind and rain increase the amount
of oxygen dissolved in the water as well as lowering its
temperature except sometimes when it is already very cold,
when rain or a warm breeze may have the opposite effect.

I mentioned earlier certain transient conditions when
surface water may be cooler than that at greater depths.
Where there are wide areas of very shallow water with
adjoining deeps, radiation losses at night or the cooling

effect of wind may reduce the temperature in the shallows faster than the circulation caused can carry the chilled water to the depths and replace it by warmer water from them. As this cooling takes place, the surface water over the deeps may be temporarily warmer than that over the shallows. There will be a current along the bottom travelling from shallow to deep and a return current from deep to shallow along the surface. The effect upon fish will be great and must be considered if their movements are to be understood and predicted.

In calm, still weather, a further temporary stratification by temperature occurs, in which the upper two or three feet of a lake, irrespective of depth, becomes very warm, as swimmers have often found in such conditions. Under such circumstances, this temporary layer above will circulate when wind or radiation losses cause cooling, until it is eliminated. Circulation of the water below will only then commence, and meanwhile there may be quite a considerable loss of oxygen due to decay. In such conditions in the smaller, shallow lakes, fish will be found very near the surface, or in shallow water, and will tend to move towards, and feed in, that part of a lake which is first re-oxygenated by any breeze that may spring up.

As temperature rises, fish need more and more oxygen, but at higher temperatures less is available. Very hot weather therefore has different effects on fish in different lakes. In shallow ones they are driven to the surface; in deep ones they go down to the thermocline where it is cooler and their oxygen requirements are less.

Many fishermen have a great fund of proverbs and maxims about the effect of weather on their chances of catching fish. I think it is much better, although it often involves thought, to treat the problem in a logical and scientific way, and to make the best of weather conditions as you find them by calculating how they will affect the water and the fish in it. If I believed all the wise saws about weather and fish I should hardly ever go fishing at all.

Note.—'*Life in Lakes and Rivers,*' *by Macan & Worthington (Collins) is a book every angler should read.*

Following the first publication of this book, a great deal of conversation and corres-
pondence with readers has made me realize that the question of the thermocline
needs some clarification ; it has been assumed by some that this phenomenon is a
factor with which anglers have to contend in every sort of pond and lake. This
is not, of course, the case ; it is only in quite large lakes and reservoirs having
depths in excess of fifteen feet or twenty feet where a cold lower layer of
water exists as late in the year as June. In shallower and smaller waters it has
disappeared well before this time and there will be no marked point where the
temperature falls considerably.

FURTHER NOTES

It is well known that many species of fish feed more freely at
dawn and dusk, and in the dark.   It used to be thought that
this was because a cooling of the water took place in the
evening, but we have since found that some species of fish
commence feeding in the evening, even in the depths of
winter with ice forming at the water's edge.

We also found that the perch at Arlesey Lake fed best on
bright sunny days in winter, from about 10 a.m. to 3 p.m.,
in water from 35 to 40 feet deep.

I have now come to a tentative conclusion that the angle
of the sun is what causes these effects.

Because of refraction, the light from any source that makes
an angle of less than about 10° to the surface of the water,
will fail to penetrate.   As the sun on a clear day sinks through
this angle, there will be a comparatively sudden and sharp
reduction in the amount of light that penetrates the surface,
and a correspondingly sharp reduction in underwater
lighting.

Once this has happened, it will be much more difficult for
predatory birds to see what goes on under the water, whereas
the fish will be much better able to spot them above the
surface or on it.   Fish will feel far safer once the sun sinks
below the critical angle of 10°.

In the morning, they will continue to feel safe until the
angle of the sun increases beyond 10°.   This may account
for fish commencing to feed in the evening, and ceasing at
that point in the morning which anglers describe as 'the sun

fully on the water'.

This effect is clearly much less marked on a dull day, when light reflected from cloud cover strikes the surface at all angles, and it is very noticeable that the combined effects of dull sky and a wind that ripples the surface often leads to fish feeding at all hours of daylight, even such species as tench, roach and bream whose preference for early morning and evening feeding is, in sunny weather, very obvious indeed. In these conditions, also, the underwater scene is less brightly illuminated, while the ripple makes it difficult to see through the surface.

Although fish nowadays have relatively little to fear from ospreys, fish-eating eagles and the like, it seems certain that they inherit deep-rooted instincts to protect them from avian predators and this may lead them to feed most freely in conditions of light that are safest.

The case of the perch in deep water is an allied one. No fish in water as deep as 35 feet feels at risk from ospreys, but at that depth the light penetration is small. Perch hunt mainly by sight and will therefore, provided they feel safe, seek food in deep water when the lighting is at its brightest. This occurs in those hours when the sun is high and light penetration is greatest.

Despite expressed views to the contrary by many capable anglers, I continue to regard barometric pressure as having no direct bearing on fish behaviour. A fish has only to change the depth at which it swims by a foot or two to undergo a change of pressure far exceeding any atmospheric pressure change that could possibly occur.

Changes in barometric pressure often precede, and predict, considerable weather changes, and wild creatures of all kinds, including fish, seem to know in advance when the weather is due for a change. By what means they know this is not clear; but it is a mistake to think that consulting a barometer can tell you anything about whether fish will feed or not.

I also reject utterly the so-called solunar theory, whereby the feeding of fish is alleged to be linked to moon phases and tide states. American tackle firms even publish calendars that purport to tell you which days through the year are most favourable and least favourable to the angler; these are totally unreliable.

Anglers who fish very large lakes from boats will find a simple echo-sounder of great value. Such devices are now available at prices that most anglers can afford. Mine is a 'Seafarer'. It is not often that an echo-sounder can locate fish directly in freshwater lakes, but it tells you the depth and something about the nature of the bottom, and thus helps you to locate places where fish are most likely to be. In the U.S.A., not only echo-sounders but also electronic temperature recorders are used, and again, anglers who fish large sheets of water from boats will do well to investigate the uses of such devices. What I have explained about stratification of lakes by temperature will indicate the value of temperature-measuring equipment, which can also locate underwater springs, pockets of cold or warm water, and levels at which fish are most likely to be found.

Even a slow-registering ordinary thermometer can be of great value, used on a line with a short rod and a reel.

Algal growth in some waters may have a very considerable effect. The water may be any colour between deep green and dark brown.

CHAPTER II

TACKLE

THE importance of using good tackle which is right for the job is very great. It is no good knowing where the fish are and what bait they will take if you cannot reach them with your tackle; it is useless to hook a fish if you have no hope of landing it. A great many of the big fish I have seen caught would not have been taken without the right tackle—in some cases specially made.

Rods

For many years the emphasis on the design of rods for what people are pleased to call 'coarse' fishing (perhaps because it demands more finesse than any other branch of angling) has been on rapid striking. This has given rise to a rod stiff in all parts except the top thirty inches, or thereabouts. Match-fishing is so organized that the waters best fitted for it are canals and rivers of moderate flow, and the fish mostly caught are small roach. In spite of exceptions it is true to say that no match-fisher can do without a rod capable of catching small roach as rapidly as possible, and for that purpose the one I have described fills the bill. It is a type which has now reached perfection, but for all purposes other than that for which it was intended it is thoroughly bad. Its rapid striking powers are lost at long range and for playing big fish it is ineffective. The fact that many of our skilled match-fishers often succeed in overcoming the handicaps such rods impose is a tribute to their skill, but no justification for the enormous popularity this type of rod now enjoys.

The only fish that require rapid striking are roach and dace, and I am becoming more and more convinced that even in heavily-fished waters where roach have a reputation for being 'hard to hit,' and dace for lightning-like bites, only the smaller specimens need a particularly fast-striking rod to connect with them. In still-water fishing we are not concerned with dace, but I have yet to find still-water roach of a size worth catching that needed a faster strike than can be got with a rod such as the Wallis design. When it is a matter of striking at ranges greater than fifteen yards, these more flexible rods are actually faster than the match-rods, while for casting, and playing good fish, they are so infinitely superior that one wonders they are so little used.

A well-made Wallis Avon rod is a very good thing to possess, and at the time of writing I do not know where to get a better one for catching in the ordinary way such fish as tench, bream, perch, roach and rudd, except by having one made specially.*

In considering how to design a better rod, we run into a good deal of prejudice. All my friends in the tackle trade, not only in Britain but in the U.S.A. and on the Continent, agree that anglers will not buy rods that pack up into a length of much more than four feet, except when the total length exceeds twelve feet. Anglers are apparently willing to put up with a longer joint length for rods from twelve feet upwards, probably because experience has shown just how horrid a thing a long rod with *three* sets of ferrules can be. But while anglers are prepared to accept longer rod-joints in order to have a longer rod, they are not prepared to accept them to obtain better action. A rod, especially a flexible rod, is so much better in two joints than in three, and the additional inconvenience of carrying a rod whose joints are five, or five and a half feet in length instead of three and a half or four feet, is so slight, that I have long given up designing rods of lengths up to eleven feet in more than two pieces.

For most angling purposes the best rod is one whose action

* Since this was written, a lighter version of the Mark IV rod has been designed, built, and tested. It is known as the Mark IV *Avon* and has a test-curve loading of 1 lb. compared to 1½ lb. for the Mark IV, so that it will take the same range of line-strengths, 3–7 lb., as an Avon rod, which I think it will with advantage replace. Subsequent references in this book to the Wallis Avon rod should be taken to include the Mark IV *Avon*.

is described as mildly progressive. The simplest type would bend to a quarter circle. That is, when loaded to such an extent that the tangent to its tip is at right angles to its butt, the radius of curvature is constant in all parts of the rod. It has its limitations; it feels weak in the butt if the load is further increased and will therefore be unsatisfactory for controlling big fish and for casting the heavier weights. To counteract this, we can increase the rate of taper in the lower half of the rod, so that with the condition of loading described, the radius of curvature at the butt is about double that above the middle of the rod. That will make the rod capable of dealing with heavier weights and bigger fish without making it feel much heavier, because the increase in diameter is for the most part near the grip. The rod can be further improved by increasing the rate of taper at the tip for about twenty per cent of the total length of the rod, i.e. for about two feet in a ten-footer. This will enable lighter baits to be cast, and will increase casting accuracy. Such a rod can handle a wide range of casting weights and take a wide range of line-strengths. It will absorb shocks that would otherwise break light lines and at the same time allow considerable pressure to be applied where it is necessary to use a strong line, and still have a reserve of resilience in hand. Finally, it should take up the curve which brings the tangent to the tip at right angles to the tangent to the butt when the load is about one-fifth of the breaking strain of the line that will usually be used, the pull required to do this being known as the test-curve loading. A latitude of about thirty per cent either way in line-strength, and more in skilful hands, can be allowed.

My Mark IV carp-rod is designed on these principles, and it will take lines from 6 lb. b.s. to 12 lb. b.s. (dry strengths), since its test-curve loading is 1½ pounds.

The maximum weight which such rods will throw satisfactorily is about one-sixteenth of the load required to bend the rod as described earlier; for the Mark IV rod it is in the region of 1½ ounces. These rods will really *throw* a bait; it is they and not the angler that do the work. The ease with which they cast to great distances is a revelation to those accustomed to the usual type.

We must consider what rods will cover most of the needs

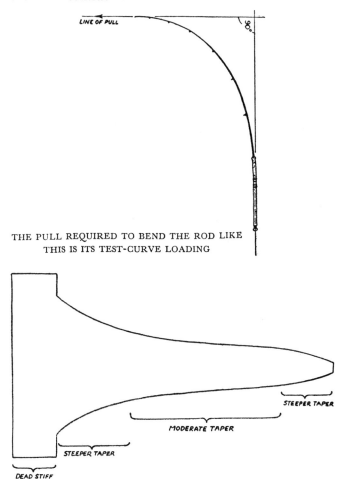

THE PULL REQUIRED TO BEND THE ROD LIKE
THIS IS ITS TEST-CURVE LOADING

THE KIND OF ROD TAPER RECOMMENDED FOR CASTING RODS SHOWN
GREATLY EXAGGERATED

of still-water angling; and I believe that for about seventy-five per cent of them, two rods will suffice: a carp-rod and a lighter rod for general purposes. Their length and weight are largely a matter of choice, but for my own part, I have decided views on the length of a general purpose rod. Now-adays, the majority of rods which make at least a pretence of being suitable for casting are short. They are usually described as light spinning rods, or threadline rods and are based largely on the late Alexander Wanless's ideas on what is suitable for salmon-spinning with fixed-spool reels. Whether or not he was right about that, I am not qualified to say—certainly these rods are not suitable for the sort of fishing that I do—though the value of his work in showing the importance of a correct relationship between the curve of the rod, the weight to be cast, and the strength of the line is beyond doubt.

These so-called threadline rods are too short for fishing from the bank in a great many waters. No doubt the dainty single-handed flick is pleasing, but since I am interested in the kind of casting needed to catch a given fish rather than what fish I can catch with a given form of casting, and since, after hooking my fish, I like to have the best chance of landing it, my vote will continue to go to the longer rod, even if I am forced to use two hands to cast an ounce to its maximum distance. It is possible, with correctly designed rods, to use two hands quite effortlessly and without any necessity to perform pirouettes or to begin one's cast facing in the opposite direction.

In playing a big fish, the advantages of a rod ten or eleven feet long over one of six or seven feet are considerable. The fish is played much more on the rod and less on the reel; shocks are much better absorbed, and for keeping a fish out from under the bank or from marginal vegetation the longer rod is the only one which has a chance. Though the heavier carp-rod should not be more than ten feet long, the lighter rod can measure from ten to eleven feet, and I think that with such a rod, having a curve suitable for lines from about 3 lb. b.s. to 7 lb. b.s. and also the Mark IV, giving together two rods which will handle a total range of line-strength of from 3 lb. to 12 lb., most of the needs of still-water fishing in Britain can be met.

Obviously, unless the material and workmanship in a rod are sound, the action must fail. Various materials are used; nowadays tubular steel and fibreglass, either solid or hollow, are much discussed. Apart from any other consideration, they are only economically possible when manufactured on a large scale, and since the demand for rods of the right kind is at present very small, it will be a long time before we shall see them made in glass or tubular steel. We shall not lose by that, for in first-class solid single-built baked split-bamboo, cemented with modern adhesives, we have a material which surpasses any steel or glass rod which I have ever handled. It has been explained to me that you can run into brick walls with glass rods, drop them on a hard floor, or beat down nettles with them, without their suffering damage. For such uses they may be excellent, but I use fishing-rods for fishing, and for fishing I prefer split-cane. I have yet to see good split-cane broken through any fault in the material, but there is much split-cane which falls far short of the best; and some of the best I have seen has come from James, of West Ealing, and Walker, of Hythe in Kent.

Rod Fittings

About the fittings of rods, there is little to say. The heavier of the two rods I have described, the Mark IV, should have a cork handle about thirty inches long; that on the lighter rod can be six inches shorter. I have not yet seen a completely satisfactory fixed screw reel fitting, other than on fly-rods, and until I do I shall continue to use the light duralumin knurled sliding fittings, or the light sliding screw-grip type made by Hardy Bros. The advantage of a shoulder collar on modern rods lies in appearance only, and the butt cap, into which the rubber knob screws, might just as well be cylindrical as tapered; duralumin is the stuff from which it should be made. If they are well designed and well made in the first place, ferrules are not improved by various devices intended to prevent them coming apart, and the fitting should be parallel and not tapered. As for rings, the butt and tip rings should be lined with agate or some other very hard, smooth material. Intermediate rings of the full-open bridge type are satisfactory, and would be better still if the larger sizes available on the Continent could be got here, so that the change of diameter between the big butt ring, which is necessary when fixed-spool reels are used, and the next ring, could be less abrupt.

In Britain, my friends who run tackle-shops all tell me that closely-spaced intermediate whippings are necessary to sell split-cane rods. These whippings do very little harm, and it is the buyer of the rod that pays for them; if he likes them, who shall say him nay? I prefer to do without them, and without paying for them.

Specialized Rods

I spoke earlier of specialized work for which different rods are needed. There are times when a very long rod is useful, and the only practical way is to make them on match-rod lines and to put up with match-rod disadvantages. When float-fishing in deep water for roach, bream, tench, and perch, a rod of fourteen or fifteen feet is sometimes a good thing to have; its tip need not be quite so fragile as would be used for match-fishing, and a little 'give' in its middle sections is a decided advantage. It remains for someone to design a really effective long rod; much could be done with bored-out tonkin cane or hollow-built split-bamboo, if the importance of obtaining flexibility without 'sloppiness' were kept in mind.

Another kind of fishing that needs a special rod is live-baiting for pike. Where baits up to half a pound or so are to be cast, a powerful rod will have to be used, but its design must always be a compromise, because a rod designed to cast such a weight would be too stiff for lines under about 30 lb. b.s., which is twice the strength we should need to use for playing the fish. The compromise lies in using one with a half-circle load of about 3 lb. (allowing us to use a 12-lb. line), and in *swinging* the bait out rather than using the spring of the rod to throw it; in live-baiting this gives us another advantage in that the bait is then less likely to be thrown off. I can again see no benefit in making the rod short, and would suggest something between nine and ten feet, which need not weigh much more than 1 lb. in split-cane.

For trout- and rudd-fishing, we shall need a fly-rod, and here I come into a field where my experience is small, for the greater part of my fly-fishing has been done on little rivers. On lakes, the ability to throw a long line is important, and I *think* that the right kind of fly-rod is the longest and most powerful with which the user can continue to cast for hours without getting over-tired. Tom Ivens, author of *Still-Water Fly-Fishing*, recommends a ten-foot two-piece split-bamboo fly-rod with a decided butt-action. There are occasions, however, even on still waters, when accuracy is more important than range, and then a more conventional dry-fly rod nine to nine and a half feet in length is useful.

All rods should have the flash removed from their varnish by rubbing-down with a paste made of linseed oil and fine silica powder, about 120 screen.

Reels

The question of reels is obscured by prejudice and it would be useless to repeat here arguments which have appeared time and again in the angling Press. The fixed-spool reel has come to stay. Most of the objections that have been raised to it are due to an error I have already mentioned—i.e. wondering what fish a tackle will catch, instead of what tackle will catch the fish.

Because the first fixed-spool reels were designed for use with very fine lines, they were called threadline reels, a term which is now quite meaningless and would be better dropped. Nowadays fixed-spool reels can take lines of any strength one is likely to need in freshwater fishing. The slipping clutch, designed as a mechanical device needing neither skill nor judgment on the part of the angler, has been found to be no such thing. We now know that the right way to play a fish on a fixed-spool reel, or any other reel, is by finger-control of the drum. In a subsequent chapter I shall enlarge on this; for the present, it is the advantages and disadvantages of the fixed-spool reel that we must consider. It enables a wide range of weights of bait to be cast accurately for considerable distances and is therefore specially suitable for still-water angling, which should always be done, if at all possible, from the bank. Apart from fly-fishing, for which it is useless, it can cope successfully with every kind of fishing. To cover all contingencies, two are needed; a small one, which need weigh no more than 6 oz., to carry lines from 3 to 6 lb. b.s., and a larger one which will take at least 150 yards of 12-lb. b.s. line. This latter need weigh no more than 12 oz. at most. I use an 'Altex' and a 'Mitchell.' A couple of spare spools for each, carrying different lines, are advisable.

I am not suggesting that an angler who has a decided preference for centre-pin reels, or multipliers, should change to a fixed-spool. As far as I and many of my friends are concerned, fixed-spool reels have our confidence, but I know some good anglers who use centre-pins and multipliers very successfully. The best example of a centre-pin I ever saw was the old Coxon Aerial, and it is a tragedy that it is no longer obtainable. I might like multipliers more if they were not all made for left-handed anglers, i.e. with right-hand wind; I want my best hand, which is my right hand, to hold the rod. My second-best hand can perform the simple operation of winding and there is no need to change the rod from one hand to the other.

For fly-fishing, a satisfactory reel has yet to be made. There has been no progress in their design for at least fifty years, and those available now fall into two categories. Those that allow for finger control when a fish is hooked are so heavy that they interfere with the action of all but the stoutest fly-rods; those light enough not to do so have no provision for finger control. All have too slow a winding speed and nearly all are made for left-handed anglers as regards the graduation of their checks and the position of their line-guards if any. Whatever kind you buy, you may be sure it will be unsatisfactory unless you are easily pleased. One famous firm sells a reel that incorporates a heliograph, consisting of a highly polished metal back which reflects the sun into the eyes of the fish as you cast, thereby warning them of their danger. I prefer to assume that this is unintentional and that fly-fishers are normally satisfied with the handicaps already imposed by fly-reels! There also seems to be a tendency to paint more and more reels in flamboyant colours, which makes them appear more suitable for a Christmas Bazaar than for a tackle-shop.

Line

Tackle-strength, within the meaning of the words 'fair angling with rod and line,' is a matter for each individual angler. A great variety of lines is available, and the detailed merits of each are best considered in the chapters dealing with the fish we mean to catch. In discussing the strength of your line with other anglers, you will be told variously that it is unsporting to use so strong a line because the fish stand no chance and that it is unsporting to use so weak a line because too many fish will be left with hooks in their mouths. My own choice is a line that will give a fish no chance at all unless I make a mistake. I find that I make quite enough mistakes to give fish all the chance they need. But under certain circumstances it may be necessary to cast a heavy weight a long distance, which means a line strong enough to stand the force of casting; and this line may be of a strength which gives fish of some species, such as roach and bream, a poor chance of escape. Because thicker lines are usually more easily seen by the fish, the price is usually paid in fewer bites; to avoid this, a reduction of the diameter of the link next to the hook, where this does not have to stand the shock of casting, may be made.

There are also circumstances where weeds and snags are so bad that the only way to catch a fish is to use very strong tackle so that you can hold it hard from the moment it is struck, or even drag it forcibly from a dangerous place. If a fish goes round a sunken log, no tackle on earth will help, and the angler must have sufficient presence of mind and resolution to prevent it. In the case of large pike and carp, not only presence of mind, but powerful wrists are needed to catch them in circumstances where they have only a yard or two to travel to reach certain safety. In its first rush, a big carp can easily apply a steady pull of 15 lb. to

the rod-top for a second or two, and if you don't know what
that feels like, tie a 15-lb. weight to the end of your rod and
try lifting it. The fact is that the use of stout tackle is
neither pretty nor pleasing, and any angler would choose the
finest tackle which circumstances allow; but when strong
gear is needed, it will be found that its use is no substitute
for skill.

It is important to stress that in fishing for really large
specimens the tackle used does not often allow small fish
to put up much of a fight. It so happens that the flexible
type of rod best for dealing with large fish does allow smaller
specimens to fight better than the stiffer and usually shorter
kind of rod often used with lines of breaking strains upwards
of 4 lb. or 5 lb.; but although a small fish hooked on the
flexible rod may fight better, its chances of escape are less.

Many anglers prefer the sport provided by smaller fish
caught on tackle which gives them a better chance of
escape, and are willing to take the greater risk of being
broken if a really big fish should be hooked—a perfectly
understandable attitude. A man may greatly prefer the
enjoyment of half a dozen really good scraps with 4-lb.
tench, and being broken by a 6-pounder, to a tremendous
battle resulting in the capture of the 6-pounder, and six
very much poorer fights with the smaller fish. My own
preference is for the occasional *really* big fish, and I choose
my tackle accordingly, which does not mean that it is coarse.
A match-fisher does not consider that he is using coarse
tackle if he employs a line with a breaking strain of 1 lb.
to catch a 1-lb. roach, but a good many match-fishers have
called the 11 lb. b.s. line I use for carp, where they run up
to 40 lb. or more, 'cart-rope'—an illogical attitude, especially when the line is used on a rod lighter than the majority
of roach-rods.

In the following chapters I can only indicate in a very
general sense the line-strengths I think appropriate for fish
of various species and sizes in the circumstances in which
they are found. The final choice must rest with the angler
on the spot, and he should depend on his own judgment
and common sense rather than on custom and the advice

of the unsuccessful. Old sayings are often true ones; in 1846, Edward FitzGibbon ('Ephemera') wrote: 'Touching the practice of angling, there are many moot points. One maintains this, another that, and a third differs from both. In doing anything there is but a right way and a wrong; but common sense has not enough following to give the right a majority.'

There has been much debate about the best colour for a line, especially the part of it, or of the gut or nylon, nearest the hook. We have been told lately that the eye of a fish does not respond to violet light. That may be true, but it is no reason for using a violet-coloured line. If the eye of the fish cannot see the colour violet, then any violet object will appear to the fish not *invisible*, but *black*. If it is desired that a line shall appear black to the fish, the line can be dyed black, which is in practice a good all-round colour for it. Other colours such as brown, olive and green, which harmonize with the underwater environment, are equally effective.

Hooks

The same preoccupation with match-fishing that has given rise to the use of rods unsuitable for catching big fish is also responsible for the use of unsuitable hooks. A recent 'All-England' match-winner said that it was the first time he had used hooks as large as 14's for a very long time. It is a very long time since I have used hooks as small. The late J. H. R. Bazley, twice winner of the annual 'All-England' match, said: 'The wide popularity of match-fishing seems to have cramped anglers' ideas, and begotten an era of light shotting and tiny hooks and baits quite out of proportion to the needs of ordinary angling: and the habit thus contracted is difficult to shake off.' The range 12 to 2, Redditch scale, will do all that is needed in catching big fish; but there are considerations other than size. Probably the type of hook requiring least force to effect penetration is a fine-wire crystal bend, with a fairly long shank; but all hooks having a sharp bend at any one point are weak hooks, and my use of crystals is limited to such

fish as roach, rudd, and bream. Perhaps I can cut the
long and involved story of what constitutes a good hook
short by saying at once that to my mind the best hooks
for all-round big-fish catching are the Model Perfects, made
by Messrs. S. Allcock & Co., and they do equally well for all
kinds of fish. Like all hooks, they could be improved in
the larger sizes, from 6 to 2, by having slightly shorter
points and smaller barbs, when the fish that it is intended
to catch is what Walton calls one of the 'leather-mouthed
fishes.' Bickerdyke pointed this out in the last century, but
hook-makers have never taken any notice of him. I agree
with him, and suggest that it is well worth using a suitable
tiny file or fine oilstone to sharpen, and reduce the barbs of
these larger sizes of hook; indeed all hooks should be kept
as sharp as possible.

The attachment of hooks has always been a difficulty.
One can choose from the following: turned-down eye;
turned-up eye; ringed; spade-end; whipped-on.

I would recommend the avoidance of hooks which are
bought whipped to nylon or gut. I do not trust the pro-
fessional whippings and the gut or nylon is seldom the
diameter you need. Hooks with serrated taper-shanks are
excellent if you whip them on yourself and make a sound job
of it. Ringed hooks are excellent; the smaller and neater
the ring, the better. I should perhaps explain that a
'ring' is the trade name for an eye which is straight and not
turned up or down. These hooks can be attached by the
ring, or as is a spade-end hook. After some unfortunate
experiences, I would not again use a hook with a turned-
down eye, except for fly-fishing; hooks with upturned eyes
are, I think satisfactory, but all eyed hooks larger than
No. 8 have eyes which are much too clumsy and large. An
eye large enough to pass 0·018 in. monofil is big enough
for the largest of freshwater hooks. Spade-end hooks have
never let me down, and still I do not like them. Without
the least evidence in support of the idea, I am afraid that
the spade may cut the nylon or gut. I confess, however,
that this is sheer prejudice. Need I stress, as so many have
done, the importance of testing every hook before use to

make sure the temper is right, and that the hook will not open or break? Not only hooks, but every part of the tackle, should be tested before fishing.

Floats

Floats are such pleasing things to possess that most anglers use them when they could do very much better without. I find myself using floats less and less, and the number of big fish I catch is not decreasing as a result. There are times when a float is needed; its design depends upon whether visibility, sensitivity, or buoyancy is most important. Invisibility, from the point of view of the fish, is probably unattainable, but camouflage is not, and it is worth going to the trouble of staining or dyeing the underwater part of floats so that they look like what the fish might expect to see in the water. Bird quills, which make excellent floats, can be dyed quite easily in the dyes sold for colouring nylon fabrics. Floats made of balsa wood, with a central spine of bamboo, and well painted, are excellent too, and can be made in any shape desired.

Landing-Nets

Smaller items, such as leads, shot, swivels, and the like, are best dealt with in later chapters; it remains only to discuss landing-nets. Plenty of landing-nets are so small that it looks as though their owners' hopes of ever catching a good fish must be as small as their nets. The smallest net for which I have any use has a circular ring whose diameter is fifteen inches; the depth of the mesh is rather more than two feet. This does for roach, rudd and perch, and at a pinch for tench, where they do not exceed about 4 lb. For bigger tench, and big bream, the diameter of the net ought to be at least eighteen inches, and the depth of the mesh at least thirty inches. And for carp and pike, the biggest net you can wield with one hand will not be too big. Mine is more or less triangular, with thirty-inch 'arms' made of laminated bamboo and a mesh four feet deep. Others as well as myself have had cause to bless its size, and sometimes the length of its handle, which is five feet. Smaller nets may also benefit from having long handles with a blunt spike at the end so they can be stuck into the ground, which avoids the annoyance of finding, when they are needed in a hurry, that their mesh has become entangled with a thorn-bush.

Painting the net-ring white is helpful for night-fishing, but such nets, or those having plated or polished rings, or even a light-coloured mesh, are a handicap in daylight. Many a fish has broken away in its last frantic dash on seeing a conspicuous landing-net.

Many will prefer a gaff to a large net for pike-fishing. I think the pike is the only fish which can be landed with a gaff without injury; a gaff should not be used on any other species, except eels.

Tackle Make-up

Before concluding this chapter it may be well to speak of general principles in tackle make-up. Simplicity is their keynote. With modern monofilament lines, the day of the running line, cast, and hook-length is over. Every 'junction,' whether by knot or loop, is a source of weakness. Naturally, one attempts to place the weakest spot where, if it fails, it will prove least expensive; and that may easily be done by letting it be the half-blood knot by which an eyed hook is tied to the end of the monofil. Where hooks are whipped-on, the hook-length may be two feet long, of the same strength as the running-line, and tied thereto by a four-turn blood-knot; but in carp-fishing I often whip a hook direct to the end of the running-line, be it monofil or plaited. There is then no loss of strength whatever.

I try to avoid laying down rules or maxims which may be followed blindly, but if I were to recommend a rule at all, it would be never to have anything on your line which, after weighing the pros and cons, seems unnecessary.

Do not ask yourself 'Do I need the float, or lead, which I have on my tackle?' but 'What is the simplest tackle with which I can catch this fish?'

Two Hooks?

I cannot condemn too strongly the common practice of

(*above*) Richard Walker prepares to make a long cast at Wilstone Reservoir, Tring; (*below*) a pond in Epping Forest

Woldale Lake: (*above*) the author extracted a carp of 15½lb from this mass of weed; (*below*) Maurice Ingham playing a big carp

fishing with two hooks—not on grounds of sportsmanship, but efficiency. If your tackle is strong enough to land two large fish together, in the unlikely event of your 'hooking them, it is unnecessarily coarse. If it is not strong enough, it will fail if one of the hooks is in a fish and the other is in a snag. If a fish bites, the other hook may catch a weed or snag before you strike, either impeding your strike or warning the fish. The advantages of offering simultaneously two baits, or a bait at two depths, or both, are outweighed by the risks and disadvantages.

I do not advocate the use of treble hooks in fishing for Walton's 'leather-mouthed fishes.' It requires twice as large a bait to cover a No. 4 treble as it does a No. 4 single, and a bait twice as large weighs eight times as much. Three times as much force is needed to pull the treble out of the bait, and three times as much to stick it in the fish, if all points penetrate. Usually, two do. If the bait comes off, the chances of being hung up on the retrieve are trebled, and there is always a possibility that a hooked fish may use any spare points to attach the hook to a snag and thus free itself. Finally, a fish hooked on a treble may very likely have its mouth sealed and as a result die if it escapes. Any sporting angler would willingly handicap himself to avoid this, but he need not do so, for to catch big fish the single hook is superior. The sole advantage of the treble is that the bait remains more firmly on the hook during the cast, a doubtful benefit, since it implies greater difficulty in striking the hook out of the bait and into the fish.

Two Rods

I have seen much written against the use of two rods at once, and there is, indeed, much to be said against it. Nevertheless, I do use two rods at once quite often, to gain the advantages of using two hooks without their being attached to one line.

The usual trouble with using two rods is that anglers *will* fix up two entirely different outfits, and even attempt two styles of fishing. Apart from the fact that one outfit is

often a wretched affair which, if it were their only one, they
would refuse to use at all, they usually, in fact, fish with one
rod and leave the other to fish for itself. I think it is unwise
to use two rods unless both can be placed in rests and when
frequent bites are not expected; and then only in cases
where both rods are used to try to catch the same fish or
kind of fish. Where two rods are used, they, their reels,
and tackle strengths should be as nearly alike as possible,
and each should be placed within easy reach. There remains the danger that a fish hooked on one tackle may foul
the other. This danger is minimized if the reels are fixed-
spool, with pick-ups left 'open,' and the lines are both sunken.
My way of using two rods, when I do, is to treat one as the
'fish-catcher' and the other as the 'experimenter.' The
first is tackled and baited in a manner which has been
found reasonably successful before. This tackle is cast into
the most likely spot. The other tackle is used either to test
a different bait, or a different way of presenting a bait, or
a different spot within casting distance of the same pitch;
for it does not do to have to walk—or run—continually
from one rod to the other.

Obtaining Tackle

Many may with reason decide that tackle is sufficiently
expensive without duplication. Good tackle is expensive;
but it pays to consider something besides the initial cost. A
rod at £10 which will last twenty years is no dearer than one
at £5 which will only last ten; and the trustworthiness and
efficiency of the more expensive weapon ought to weigh the
balance in its favour. It is no use pretending that cheap
tackle is as good as expensive gear. Some tackle is expensive
because you pay for the name, money that is not wasted,
since it is spent on what the Americans call 'know-how' and
on an unwritten guarantee of quality. But all tackle-makers
do not charge for their name, because they have spent little
or nothing in making it known. They rely on recommendation, and because their sales are direct and their advertising
costs small, they can often turn out splendid tackle, especially rods, at very reasonable prices. If you are fortunate

enough to find a small firm, or an individual craftsman, of this kind, and know yourself what a good rod should be, you can get the very best and save yourself pounds.

Good tackle can be made at home although it is seldom worth while making reels, hooks, and rod-fittings. But the angler can make his own rods, nets, floats, leads, plugs and many other items of equipment, and to a very high standard. Home tackle-making has come to stay, and many an angler has been able to provide himself with a wide range of good rods and other gear which he would never otherwise have been able to afford.

Making your own tackle has another advantage. You can have exactly what you consider best for the job.

Good tackle will soon be spoiled if you neglect it. Every item should be checked when you arrive home after a fishing expedition, and again before you start off on another. Rods should be cleaned with a damp rag, given ample time to dry, then rubbed down with a rag soaked in linseed oil and finally polished with a soft cloth. The rings should be examined, especially agates. Any chips or cracks in the varnish should be made good, and the ferrules cleaned. They should, of course, be very lightly greased before the rod is reassembled. Meanwhile, the rod should preferably be stored vertically in a rack, like a billiard cue, with the thicker end of each joint downwards and the ferrule plugs in place. Failing that, the joints may be laid flat.

Reels should be carefully cleaned and oiled sparingly. Everything else should be carefully dried if necessary, sorted out and put in order so that it is ready next time it is needed. Only by constant care can an angler be certain that his tackle will never let him down.

FURTHER NOTES

Very great changes have taken place in tackle design and manufacture in the last twenty years. The advent of fibreglass as a rod material has, with the aid of mathematic-ally-calculated compound tapers, enabled rod weights to be greatly reduced for given lengths and test-curve ratings.

Anyone now buying a new rod will do well to choose fibreglass; but anglers who still have split-cane carp rods that are in good order and substantially straight are advised to keep them; changing to glass will not catch more carp, and for kinds of fishing where the rod spends most of its time in a rest, a few ounces of weight matter little.

For float-fishing, especially where the rod is hand held, fibreglass has given us longer, lighter rods that are very good indeed, and I now use 12-, 13- and 14-foot, 3-piece rods by Hardy Bros., with spigot ferrules, for all my fishing of this kind. The 12-footer is also excellent for light legering for everything except large carp and pike.

I have now become convinced that outsize butt rings offer no advantages whatever. My conviction stems from extensive trials with a number of different rods, reels, lines and casting weights. If anything, butt rings of about 8–10 millimetres diameter did a little better than 20–26 millimetre ones. Since the smaller butt rings are less susceptible to accidental damage, I regard them as preferable.

Fixed-spool reels have not improved as much as I had hoped and expected. The introduction of rotating rollers or bollards in their pick-ups, and the universal adoption of the bail-arm principle, are important advantages and I would not now choose a reel in which either of these features was absent. The provision of a rotating roller or bollard is more important than is generally supposed, for it allows much heavier pressure to be kept on a hooked fish while the angler recovers line, and it also allows a more positive response by the slipping clutch to a sudden jerk.

Closed-face or semi-closed-face reels have become very popular among match anglers, but they are quite unsuitable for handling heavy fish, owing to the friction of all the combined angles over which the line has to pass. This friction makes it necessary to reduce the pressure on a hooked fish to a few ounces before any line can be recovered.

I gave closed-face reels a very extensive trial, hoping that I could learn to compensate for this grave disadvantage, but concluded it was inherent. After playing a 15 lb. carp for forty minutes on a closed-face reel, I eventually brought the fish to net by pulling line through the butt ring by hand. I then unhooked the carp, cut off the hook, wound in the line, detached the reel from the rod and threw it as far as I could into the deepest part of the lake, where it now rests unmourned.

I also think it is important that the pick-up of a fixed-spool reel should rotate in the correct direction. For a right-handed angler winding with his left hand, the correct direction of rotation of the pick-up, when viewed from the front, of the spool is clockwise. That allows the line to be picked up with the forefinger, after which the pick-up will take it off the finger nicely. Opposite rotation simply presses the line against the finger, making the transfer from finger to pick-up difficult. The bail pick-up should trip at a point that prevents it from slamming one's finger like a breakback mousetrap.

Multipliers are good for pike-fishing. On large lochs where there are islands, granite boulders, fallen trees, weed-beds, reed-beds and huge pike, I use small sea-multipliers carrying upwards of 200 yards of 25 lb. b.s. line. With a rod having a test-curve of from $3\frac{1}{2}$ to 5 lb. you can throw a dead-bait a long way with such reels and they are ideal for coping with big fish, with their optional checks and star-drags.

For pike-fishing in Southern and Midlands lakes and reservoirs, the same tackle is quite satisfactory for big dead-baits, but for sprats, plugs, spoons and the like, a carp rod and a salmon-size multiplier capable of holding about 150 yards of 12–15 lb. line is more suitable. I think such an outfit is in many ways preferable to a fixed-spool reel on the same rod, although there is reason in the advocacy by many of a big fixed-spool reel for pike-fishing; if when dead-baiting the pick-up is left open, there is no danger of an overrun and a tangle.

Monofil lines are now used universally, and the choice nowadays is between an ultra-strong and a normal grade. The ultra-strong appears to be pre-stretched so as to raise its static tensile strength at the expense of elongation. Such lines stand up to greater steady pulls, but fail more easily to sudden jerks, whereas the normal grade is more forgiving. If the ultra-strong grade is used, care must be taken to combine it with a rod of sufficient flexibility to cushion sudden shocks.   In the first edition et. seq., I suggested that a line whose wet strength was five times the test-curve of the rod, plus or minus 30 per cent was about right.   With the ultra-strong nylons, I would suggest that the same figure without the minus 30 per cent, applies.   In other words, with such nylon don't go below 5 lb. wet b.s. per 1 lb. of test-curve.

The 4-turn water knot has been shown to be more reliable and stronger than the 4-turn blood knot, while the safest way of attaching eyed or spade-end hooks is by the means illustrated.

WATER KNOT
To clarify this knot, I have shown only 3 turns.
Add an extra turn to obtain greatest strength.

The quality of hooks still leaves much to be desired. Hooks that are over-tempered and soft, or under-tempered and brittle, are all too common and I have yet to see any hook whose barb is not too deeply cut and turned up far too much. A very small barb suffices to prevent a hook from falling out, whereas an oversized barb often prevents the hook from penetrating properly.   A big barb involves deep cutting into the hook-wire, with consequent weakening.

There are few fishing situations in which a round-bend hook is not the best choice.   A very slight offset of the point ('reverse' or 'sneck' in trade terms) of perhaps 3–5° has a small advantage in theory, but I doubt if it makes much difference in practice.

There is at present a vogue for short-shank hooks.   Shank length in relation to gape must always be a compromise. The longer the shank is in relation to the gape, the smaller will be the angle of penetration, so the hook will go in more easily, but to a lesser depth, while the long shank will exert more leverage on the hook-hold and may lead to the hook opening out or breaking its hold.   Very short shanks have the opposite effect.   It takes more force to effect penetration, but the hook goes in deeper and is more lightly stressed after it has penetrated.   To my mind, the most useful compromise is found in a hook whose length from bend to eye or spade, is about two and a half times the gape.

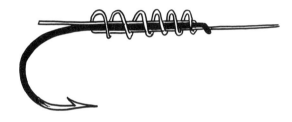

Knot for attaching eyed and spade-end hooks.

CHAPTER III

FIXED-SPOOL REEL TECHNIQUE

UNTIL recently, I thought that fixed-spool reels had been available to the angling public for so long that they were fully understood by those using them. Lately, however, I have had reason to wonder if this is so. The first thing that made me wonder was a passage from a recently-published angling book which ran, 'I wound, and wound, and wound, and still the fish took line. I thought he was never going to stop.'

Not long after reading this, I had sent me a copy of the catalogue of a fishing-tackle firm which is one of the most up-to-date and progressive in England today. In the section dealing with their fixed-spool reels I found this: 'When playing a fish all that is necessary is to keep the rod well up and to keep winding.'

And soon after came a letter from a very efficient angler who has just begun using a fixed-spool reel. He says, 'With the reel I find I can throw a crust forty yards, and this I did right to the middle of the pool. A big unseen carp took it and I found on the reel I could make no impression. He just rushed off sixty yards against my frantic winding and then the reel fell off.'

All this has made me think, and it also made me remember the number of times I have seen anglers who for one reason or another were failing to make use of the advantages of fixed-spool reels.

First, the fixed-spool reel chosen must be suitable for the kind of fishing you are going to use it for. These reels are made in various sizes; in the early days they were usually referred to as 'trout-size' and 'salmon-size' reels. Now-adays there are too many sizes to classify so easily, but you will not go far wrong in choosing a reel which will take *at least* one hundred yards of whatever line you intend

using on it. If a small-size fixed-spool reel is used with
a too-thick line, casting range will be shortened a lot, and
winding-in speed will decrease to a great extent when a lot
of line is out. On the other hand, there is no point in choosing a reel too big. The larger sizes cost more and weigh
more and to use a big reel with a fine line and light rod
means an ill-balanced outfit.

Most anglers think that because a fixed-spool reel has a
slipping clutch, finer lines can be used than would be satisfactory on rotating-drum reels. Indeed, this has been
laid down in print on more occasions than it would be
possible to count. The truth is that a line should be chosen
to suit conditions—weight and fighting capabilities of the
fish, presence of snags, weeds, or heavy water, weight of
bait, or tackle, size of hooks, etc.; and if the line-strength is
correctly chosen it will be satisfactory whether the reel is
fixed-spool or rotating-drum. If, for example, a 10-lb. fish
has to be stopped or turned in twenty yards, the fact that
the reel has a slipping clutch will not mean that a finer line
can be used than if it had not. If there is all the room in
the world in which to play a fish, a fine line can be used
equally as well for the job on a rotating-drum reel as on
a fixed-spool reel with a slipping clutch.

A great many people have bought fixed-spool reels, used
them with lines too fine for the fishing they are doing, suffered
breakage after breakage, and then condemned the reel out
of hand. Others have been at pains to explain that while
fixed-spool reels are good on open waters, they are useless
where there are many snags or much weed.

Unless the way in which a fish should be played on a fixed-
spool reel is properly understood, trouble is certain to arise.
Perhaps I can best explain the right way of going about it
by describing the playing and landing of a 15¼-lb. carp
from a water in Lincolnshire. The man who caught it
really knows how to deal with a big fish on a fixed-spool
reel, and the battle was a pleasure to watch.

Before beginning to fish the angler had set his slipping
clutch to a light tension—one allowing it to slip when the
rod was bent in such an arc that the tip was about at

right-angles to the butt. When the fish was struck, the rod was held with the right hand close up to the reel-seat and the reel-handle held in the left hand. On feeling the hook, the fish made a long, fast run of about sixty yards straight out into the middle of the lake. While it did so the angler made no attempt to wind, but knowing that it takes a greater pull to *start* a clutch slipping than to *keep* it slipping, he applied a very light pressure to the drum with a finger, and eventually the fish slowed down and rolled.

It then jerked savagely, causing the rod-top to nod and the clutch to yield line in a series of spasmodic buzzes. Still no attempt was made to wind or to increase pressure above that needed to keep the rod well bent. Next, the fish made off towards a sunken tree that lay in the water on the right-hand of the big bay in which the angler was fishing. This tree was nearer to the angler than the point the fish had reached during its first run, and as the fish made towards it, the rod was swung over to the right, parallel with the ground, and the line retrieved, by winding, until the fish was within twenty yards of the danger-point. It was then evident that pressure would have to be increased in order to turn it, and the angler's index finger was pressed more firmly on to the spool, while he backed and increased the bend in the rod. This manoeuvre was successful; the fish was swung off his line of run and found himself running into the bank five yards to the angler's side of the sunken tree. So he turned and dashed out into the middle again. Directly he turned, the finger on the spool was relaxed and the rod swung up to vertical again. Many and powerful were the runs that followed, those that would have taken the fish into danger being nicely checked by the ever-ready finger applied to the reel spool, which was always relaxed a little if the strain on the line approached the danger-point, the rod being held so that the applied pressure was used to turn the fish rather than to stop it.

The angler's strategy was obviously to encourage the fish to run as much as possible against a relatively light pressure (except when it appeared to be running for a dangerous place) and thus tire itself out. Presently the fish began to tire, and as big carp so often do under the circumstances, sulked on the bottom. Now the angler changed his tactics. Easing pressure a little, he wound the rod-point towards the fish, then, with finger pressed against the spool, he bent the rod so as to apply quite a heavy pressure that told on the fish and moved it a little nearer.

Again the rod-point was wound towards the fish and the process of applying pressure repeated. Now and again the fish 'jagged' heavily; each time it did so the finger on the drum was relaxed enough to allow a few inches of line to be taken and the shock on the tackle eased. Eventually, by repetition of the 'pumping' process, during which the line was never allowed actually to slacken, the fish was brought to within five or six yards of the bank. The wind-down and the pull were always long, smooth and steady. Then the carp saw the angler and at once dashed out again; but the strain of the fight had weakened it. Though all pressure except that supplied by the clutch tension was at once relaxed, the fish went no more than twenty yards, and was soon brought back again. Three times more did he try to run, each time stopping in a shorter distance, and at last rolled on the surface under the rod-point, a beaten fish.

Now the angler again changed his tactics. Instead of his fore-finger being applied to the spool, it was now pressed on the 'flyer'—the part of the reel carrying the pick-up—and used to prevent it from turning backwards. This allowed the reel handle to be released and the left hand was free to use the landing-net. Keeping the rod bent, the angler knelt down and pushed the net out, just under the surface.

The fish was towed towards the net but, just before reaching it, made a final effort which took no more than a yard of line against the clutch. Once more he rolled; then over the net he was drawn. Simultaneously the rod-point was dropped and the net raised with the fish inside. The angler then laid down his rod, and, taking both hands to the net, soon had the fish ashore. At no time had he attempted to 'wind the fish in' or to wind at all, except when there was line to be gained. At no time did he rely on the clutch-tension to turn the fish from a place where it might become entangled. And always he was alert for the sudden jerk or rush which, had he not relaxed pressure, might have resulted in breakage. Although my account may have given the impression that the battle lasted a long time, it actually took fourteen minutes by my watch, and I do not think that, on the 8 lb. breaking-strain line used, the fish could have been landed quicker with any other kind of reel.

Anglers seem to pass through three stages in learning to play big fish. At first, they are inclined to hang on, refusing to yield an inch of line. After being broken repeatedly they suddenly go to the other extreme and allow a fish to go where it likes; then they lose many in weeds or snags. With experience, however, they learn to control a fish and to apply the right counter-measure to its attempts to escape. A very few, however, pass to a stage where they seem able to divine the intentions of the fish and play it in such a way that it is persuaded not to do anything that will endanger the tackle. Such anticipatory genius is uncommon, but not beyond the powers of most people to learn.

Many users of fixed-spool reels fail to obtain maximum casting range for one reason or another. It is seldom necessary, of course, to throw one's bait to the limit, but it still pays to ensure that the tackle is at the peak of efficiency, for you will be able to cast with less effort and therefore more accuracy, and to load your tackle more lightly.

An important point in achieving maximum range is the filling of the spool. It should always be filled right up to the lip when plaited line is in use. With nylon or perlon monofil lines, it need not be quite so full, but even with monofil there should not be more than a sixteenth of an inch or so between the pile of line and the lip of the spool, which should always be kept polished and free from mud or adhering particles of paste or ground-bait.

If it is necessary to grease the line, use a grease which is not too soft and sticky, and afterwards rub the line well until the coils on the reel show no tendency to stick to one another. A line smothered with sticky grease will not only fail to cast smoothly, but will pick up minute particles of grit that will wear the pick-up of the reel, the rings of the rod, and the line itself.

The thicker and heavier the line, the more important it is to have a large-diameter butt-ring fitted to the rod. Even with the finest lines, a big butt-ring is a help; with lines of 10-lb. breaking-strain and over, a butt-ring specially made for use with fixed-spool reels can double the casting-range. Indeed, with the heavier lines it pays to graduate the rings from butt to tip so that not only the butt-ring but the next two or three above it are larger than usual. Monofil lines will always give greater casting-range than plaited lines, but their springiness is a disadvantage. The possibility of their becoming caught round the reel-handle or getting behind the spool, or twice round the pick-up where this is of the 'claw' type, is much greater than in the case of plaited lines. These dangers can be largely avoided by always taking care to keep the line reasonably taut. The rod should be raised to take up slack or the line caught with a finger before bringing the pick-up into action; if there is a great deal of slack it is best to run the line between the fingers when winding-in, and the same applies if the tackle is very light. In short, the use of monofil means additional vigilance, and for that reason many anglers will be happier with a plaited line.

Last season I was talking to a keen pike-fisher who had been trying a big fixed-spool reel for the first time, after many years of successful fishing with a high-quality American multiplier. He said he liked the fixed-spool job; it gave him greater accuracy, enabled him to use lighter baits when necessary, and did away completely with overruns and 'bird's-nests.' But there was one thing he did not like. If he put a little too much force into the cast, he said, he could only prevent the bait from going too far by dropping-in the pick-up, bringing the bait up with a sudden jerk that usually lost him his live-bait, and, with sinking plug and spinner, caused slack which had to be taken up quickly to avoid the bait fouling the bottom.

A few seconds' explanation solved his difficulty. All that is necessary is to drop a finger towards the lip of the spool as the bait flies out.　Each turn of the line then has to brush past the finger, and the nearer this is to the spool-lip, the more it slows down the flight of the bait, which can with a little practice be slowed down gradually and made to fall exactly where it is wanted.　Exactly the same method can be used when swimming a float in running water, the finger being used to check the rate at which the line is taken out just sufficiently to cause the baited hook to travel ahead of the float and to ensure the minimum of slack in the event of a strike.

The fixed-spool reel has a number of advantages and if correctly used it can help you catch more fish, but it is not, and can never be, a substitute for intelligence and skill.

CHAPTER IV

CARP

SEVERAL species of carp exist, some of which are sub-divided into varieties. Of these species, the largest and most important is the *Common Carp*, and its varieties. In its natural or 'wild' form, it is covered with regular scales, except on the head; but there are types with different forms of scaling, in most cases the scales being enlarged and covering only part of the fish's body. There appear to be two definite basic variations: the Leather Carp, which has very few scales indeed, confined to a small row next the dorsal fin; and the Mirror Carp with two rows of large scales along the lateral line, and smaller ones near the tail, on the belly and along the root of the dorsal.

Since these varieties are all of the same species, they interbreed freely, and various additional types of scaling are produced. The varieties which do not have Common Carp scaling are usually known as 'King' Carp.

The issue is further complicated by the fact that in Europe the King Carp has been bred selectively for many genera-tions to provide a quick-growing fish for eating, and various strains have been developed with body-shapes which differ considerably from the wild fish. The strain that has been imported into this country is the Galician carp-race, a type chosen for quick growth, but which has a body-shape not too greatly differing from the wild form. This strain pro-duces a proportion of fish that have the common carp or wild form of scaling, and are indistinguishable, scientifically, from the true wild carp; they are biologically identical, except that they inherit a greater capacity for growth. I have come to the conclusion, as a result of observation, that these scaled fish, whether they be true wild carp, or bred from imported domesticated stock, are appreciably less affected by extremes of temperature when feeding and breeding. The tendency of the semi-scaled type, or 'King Carp,' to revert to this type in a few generations of breeding has been frequently noticed and I believe this is due to the wild form's greater chance of survival in our climate. Several of the semi-scaled types will breed a proportion of common or fully-scaled carp, and the offspring of two common carp will all be common, a process leading, eventually, to an overwhelming preponderance of common carp. The eventual death through old age of the original King Carp and of their few partially scaled descendants will complete the process of reversion to the wild form of scaling.

There is, however, a considerable difference between the imported Continental carp, whether semi-scaled or scaled all over, and the wild carp that have bred in Britain for hundreds of years. These wild fish are longer and slimmer, and much faster swimmers. They will feed at slightly lower temperatures and are less inclined to feed at the surface.

Another variety is the Golden Carp or Higoi, a xantho-chroistic form; in colour it is similar to the common goldfish, but rather more yellow. It is seldom found in a wild state, its colour being against its survival. One often hears anglers speaking of 'golden carp' but they seldom mean the Higoi. Any carp having brassy scales is liable to be called a 'golden carp.' I have even known a tench to be so described.

Before considering angling methods, it is perhaps desirable to deal with the smaller varieties of carp. The commonest of these is the *Crucian Carp*, a much smaller species. The colour is similar to the Common Carp, but the fish has no barbules, the dorsal fin is convex (that of the Common Carp and the goldfish being concave), and the tail is only very slightly forked. The Crucian is much deeper in body than the Common Carp and flatter, i.e. not so thick from side to side. It seldom exceeds a weight of $4\frac{1}{2}$ lb. There are variations in shape, and one variety, the Prussian Carp (usually much smaller), differs by being less deep in body and in other very minor characteristics. Both the Prussian and Crucian Carp are powerful and determined fighters,

(*above*) One of the lakes at Exton, Rutland. It holds big bream, tench
and pike; (*below*) dawn at Redmire Pool

(*above*) The author's record 44lb carp, taken at Redmire Pool in September 1952. Its supporter is Peter Thomas; (*below*) the author lands a 31¼lb carp from Redmire Pool

but they lack the speed and acceleration of Common Carp of similar weight. They do not appear to compete seriously with other species and a head of Crucians in a large water is an asset. In small waters they are liable to become over-crowded and stunted.

The Goldfish is well known. It is not a golden variety of the Crucian Carp, but a separate species. It is really a variety itself, its parent species being an olive-backed, brassy scaled fish intermediate in appearance between the Common Carp and the Crucian. These 'uncoloured' gold-fish are much more common than is generally supposed. When caught, they are seldom recognized for what they are, being usually described as Crucians, Prussians or by the all-embracing term 'Golden Carp.'

They may be distinguished from the Common Carp and its varieties by the absence of barbules, and from the Crucian by their broader back and concave dorsal fin; the tail, too, is forked like that of the Common Carp. The scales are larger and fewer than those of the Crucian, and the fish is less deep in body. It sometimes grows to a fair size; speci-mens of 4 lb. or more in weight have been taken, but much larger fish undoubtedly exist. Too little is known about this species for me to say whether it is an asset to a fishery.

The Bitterling Carp, a small fish, is very rare indeed in open waters in Britain. Aquarium specimens are about three inches long; I understand that these fish seldom exceed a length of six inches. From the angler's point of view the Bitterling is of little interest. The female is unique in that her eggs are shot into the open shell of the fresh-water mussel, the fish being provided with a kind of pea-shooter for the purpose.

Hybrids

Common and Crucian Carp are said to produce hybrids which resemble 'uncoloured' goldfish in most respects, except that, unlike the goldfish, they have small barbules, and their barbule equipment may consist of one or two pairs; where two are carried the upper or forward pair will be very small indeed. Small Common Carp, under 1 lb. in weight, are very much like what one would expect a Common X Crucian hybrid to look like, and I wonder how many alleged hybrids were small Common Carp. I never saw a fish I could definitely identify as a Common X Crucian hybrid, even in waters where both species are numerous.

Hybrids of Crucian Carp and Goldfish may be very common, and they would be difficult to distinguish except by someone thoroughly familiar with the characteristics of the parent varieties, including the fin-ray formulæ, the scale-counts, and the pharyngeal teeth. (I shall deal with methods of catching these smaller, barbule-less species of carp at the end of this Chapter.)

The Common Carp and its various varieties can be distinguished by their four barbules and a long dorsal fin with about twenty-two rays.

On the Continent, the Common Carp grows to enormous weights; Travis Jenkins mentions a figure of 60 lb., but much larger fish than this exist, 80 lb. being the largest to be recorded, as far as I am aware. In Britain, it used to be supposed that a weight of about 25 lb. would be the maximum; this was the view held by Tate Regan. However, there is now no doubt that carp of at least double that weight exist, and a weight of 60 lb. is by no means impossible. By ordinary angling standards, a carp of 10 lb. is big and a 20-pounder is a monster. Above 20 lb. carp tend to lose their speed, and from my own experience I think that, as far as the fish's fighting ability is concerned, one is as likely to land a 40-pounder as a 20-pounder, always provided that suitable tackle is used. I do not mean that playing carp upwards of 20 or 30 lb. in weight is *easier* than dealing with 15-pounders, but what these great fish gain in power from their additional weight, they lose in speed.

Carp are the fastest and most powerful of our freshwater fish. I am tempted to draw comparisons with salmon, but it is really impossible to do so, since individual variations are so wide, and the habitat is so different. Of all British freshwater fish, the carp is certainly by far the most difficult to catch; so much so that most people think its pursuit is not worth while. Recent developments in technique, however, have resulted in a quickening of interest among anglers generally, and there is no reason why anyone who has access to waters containing really big fish should not be able to catch them.

There is no fish which is more suitable for stocking still waters. Carp will thrive and grow big in lakes of every size and type, except very cold and barren waters; and it has been said that a lake will sustain four times as many pounds of carp as of trout. In such waters as flooded gravel and clay pits, and those reservoirs which have no feeder-streams, or whose feeder-streams are unsuitable for the breeding of trout, carp are by far the best fish to introduce. Under favourable circumstances they will grow at a rate of well over 2 lb. per year; a fish of 44 lb. was found to be only fifteen years old.

Although I would rather fish for carp than trout myself, I would not advocate putting carp into waters in which trout will breed and thrive, since more anglers are attracted to trout-fishing than to carp-fishing, just as more shooting men like partridges and fewer prefer grey geese.

The breeding of carp is uncertain in Britain. Spawning usually takes place in late May but in some seasons may be as late as early July. For some reason, carp, when first introduced into a water, usually succeed in breeding as soon as they are old enough, but after the first season they may breed only at irregular intervals, and a number of years may elapse between seasons in which successful breeding takes place. The presence of fish of other species, particularly perch and trout, is bad for the breeding of carp and the carp themselves consume much of their own spawn; yet they seldom fail to make good their numbers. Nor do they often over-breed, though a few cases of waters becoming overcrowded are known.

The existence of large beds of reeds, reed-mace, or other cover, helps breeding; and the more sun a lake receives, and the more shelter there is from cold winds, the greater the likelihood of success. A good supply of microscopic organisms, on which the carp-fry feed, is also necessary.

From the angler's point of view breeding is not necessary in the ponds and lakes he intends to fish. Carp live four or five times as long as trout, and since the majority of anglers return all the fish they catch, a modest restocking every five or ten years is sufficient to maintain stocks in waters where the carp breed little or not at all.

Habits

Angling methods and the habits of the fish (especially feeding habits) must be discussed together. Let us consider first the barbuled carps, their way of life and how we may catch them.

These great fish feed almost entirely on things which cannot be used as bait—microscopic organisms, both animal and vegetable, and quantities of algae, especially when it grows on or adheres to weeds and water plants. Soft shoots of weeds, and silkweed, are eaten; the eggs, larvae and nymphs of insects, bloodworms and other mud-burrowing larvae; daphnia and other small crustaceans, freshwater shrimps and, in brackish pools, sea-shrimps, form the natural diet of the fish. Molluscs are eaten; a fish of 33 lb. was found to contain two matchbox-sized mussels in their shells. They will, however, eat practically anything that they realize is both edible and safe; but they are usually either indifferent to, or suspicious of, anything unusual, so that it is often necessary to teach them to eat what you want them to by means of ground-baiting.

Effect of Weather on Feeding

Carp are very much creatures of habit. They learn quickly, form a habit, and provided nothing occurs to break it, will follow it for a long time. They are highly susceptible to temperature changes. I do not know the upper limit of temperature at which enjoyment changes to distress, but they appear to enjoy warm water, even though it is far too warm for them to feed. They seldom feed if water temperature exceeds 68°F. or falls below 58°F., though those with the wild type of scaling are less affected; it takes a higher temperature to stop them feeding and to persuade them to bask, and they will feed at lower temperatures than the semi-scaled King Carp. There are rare occasions when all varieties of carp will feed in water temperatures much below 60°F.; carp have been caught in the winter when the lakes they lived in were fringed with ice; but for practical purposes, the first frosts of October mark the end of the carp season, and in general they cannot be expected to feed in water much below 58°F. The frequently debated effect of weather on the fish is mainly, if not entirely, due to changes in temperature and in the oxygen-content of the water. Other things being equal, an increase in oxygen-content seems to increase their appetite. The amount of dissolved oxygen is influenced by the temperature and depth of the water and the degree of agitation, as for example by wind or rain. Other factors which affect the amount of oxygen in the water are weeds, which give off oxygen in the daytime and carbon dioxide after dark, and decaying matter, which absorbs it. There is less oxygen in deep water than in shallow.

If we consider a typical period of twenty-four hours in summer and what will happen to the carp during that time in a small lake containing both shallow and deep water, i.e. over seven or eight feet, we shall see what the general pattern of their movement is and how different conditions may modify that pattern.

We will begin by observing the carp at mid-afternoon. Nearly all of them will be at or near the surface, where there is most oxygen, and most of them in the shallows, for on this day there is very little wind, the sun is shining, and the water temperature at the surface is well over 70°. Many of the carp will be gliding slowly back and forth, some raising a glistening back or dorsal fin above the surface. Others will be almost motionless among the weeds. Few of the fish will show any sign of willingness to feed.

When evening arrives, and the temperature begins to fall, the carp will show more activity. Some may begin to feed at the surface; others at the bottom. As temperature falls, there may be some leaping, and a general movement towards the east side of the lake will begin, as this side gets the last of the sun. If the sky is cloudless, temperature will fall rapidly after sunset, and the majority of the fish will make their way into deeper water. If there are trees which prevent radiation losses, or a high bank which radiates heat stored during the day, some will be found near them.

If the weather has been generally warm, and the lake contains a reserve of warm water in the deeps sufficient to maintain some areas at a temperature above 60°F. or thereabouts, carp may feed there all night. Otherwise, they will cease feeding, but will spend the night in deep water in the warmest places they can find. If, instead of a clear sky, a warm day is followed by a clouded sky, radiation losses are less severe, and the carp may remain in shallow water all night, usually feeding there. If, during the day, wind or rain keep the temperature on the shallows between 60°F. and 70°F. approximately, and by agitation increase the oxygen-content of the water, carp are likely to feed there during the daytime; if the temperature on the shallows is reduced below 60°F. or thereabouts, the carp will tend to move into deeper water which cools more slowly. Most commonly, midnight finds most of the fish in the deeps, unless the night is exceptionally warm. Just before dawn, the fish usually begin to move to the edge of the deep water nearest the west side of the lake, which first receives the morning sunshine, and with first light a few will venture into shallower water on this side. This they often do from habit, even when the temperature fails to rise. With rising temperature, activity among the fish increases and some leaping may again be seen. No one knows exactly why carp leap, but I have noticed that it often accompanies changes of temperature, and that the more rapidly such changes take place, the more the fish seem inclined to leap. Though I am not certain, experience makes me think that leaping may often be a preliminary to feeding; it may be done to shake off excreta. A further increase in temperature attracts the fish towards shallower water, especially on the western side, until by midday they will again be nearly all on the shallows and, if temperature has risen too high, no longer feeding. Usually, rain or wind in the early morning will delay the emergence of fish from the deeps, and if there is no rise in temperature, the fish will remain there until there is. Whether they feed there will depend on the temperature, and in a shallow lake, i.e. one which has no depths greater than six feet or so, feeding is unlikely. Deeper waters, however, may take longer to cool, especially after a spell of warm weather, and since carp do tend to be creatures of habit, a trial at the western edge of the deep water may prove successful.

On very rare occasions, the fish seem to lose most of their customary caution and take the angler's bait one after another. A few of these memorable catches are recorded in angling literature, and on other unrecorded occasions anglers hooked several big carp in the course of a day, and, fishing as they were for smaller fish, were broken again and again. Such instances are rare, but there has been much speculation about the reason for this extraordinary behaviour. It may be temperature. Perhaps for days on end the carp are prevented from feeding by the water being too cold, and yet not so cold that they are in the state of suspended animation that is normal in the winter months. In such conditions, the fish will usually be in the deepest and most barren water. Then comes a rise in temperature, and the now very hungry carp begin to feed with abandon; if you are lucky enough to be on the spot at such a time you may add another chapter to angling history; or, if not properly equipped, end the day without fish or hooks.

It will be seen, then, that *weather affects the fish only in so far as it affects the water;* and that the direction of the wind, the state of the moon, the height of the sun or the type of cloud have no bearing on the matter except in that way. No particular wind-direction is in itself good or bad, though winds from the east and north are usually colder, and will lower water temperature more rapidly. *And the lowering of temperature, whether by wind or rain, may start or stop the feeding of carp, depending on what the conditions were previously.*

Similarly, the value of fishing at night is much more due

to water conditions than to darkness. It is often good to fish at night in summer, because frequently the temperature only then falls sufficiently to induce the fish to feed, especially in small shallow lakes, and such conditions may persist for a week or more. There are numerous occasions, however, when fishing at night is useless and the daytime is much better. Other factors, such as the presence in the daytime of anglers or other people who scare the carp, all have their effect. If throughout the day the carp are kept continuously alarmed, they may commence feeding only at night after the disturbances have ceased, though water conditions may be less favourable then.

As a fish that has eaten as much as it needs will obviously not be inclined for more, carp may often prove difficult or impossible to catch under apparently ideal conditions. Having eaten their fill, carp digest their meal, so that favourable conditions extending over a long period will result in fish feeding at intervals: the larger the fish, the more it will eat and the longer it will take to digest its meal. Therefore, the angler's best chance is often at the beginning of favourable conditions.

Low temperatures probably slow down the fish's rate of digestion. Consequently, carp may sometimes resume feeding in conditions which would normally be too cold, if these conditions have lasted for long and all food eaten by the fish is digested. It may be correct to say that the lower the temperature the longer the interval between spells of feeding, and the shorter the time spent feeding, will be; this is only one instance of how very limited an angler's knowledge really is.

Rising mist during the evening and morning, except in so far as it indicates a change of temperature, has no effect on the fish. As described earlier, in lakes with large areas of water more than fifteen feet or so in depth, a surface layer of comparatively warm water begins to form in spring and increases in temperature and depth through the early summer. Below this layer, the temperature of the water varies only slightly throughout the year and is always, I think, too cold for carp, which seldom enter it except to hibernate. The effect of strong wind, if it lasts long enough, is to push this layer of warm water to one side of the lake. On the side *towards which* the wind is blowing, the warm surface water will then extend to much greater depths, while on the side *from which* the wind blows, the colder water from the depths will rise to replace it. This will naturally tend to drive the carp from that side of the lake; at the same time, not only will the dissolved oxygen increase, especially on the side *towards which* the wind blows, but, since warm water will extend much deeper on that side, feeding grounds will be accessible to the fish which would normally be too cold for them. They will not necessarily have been too cold for various organisms such as blood-worms, however, and these may have existed and mul-tiplied undisturbed until the effect of wind on the upper layer of warm water allowed the carp and other fish to get at them. Wave action, too, may wash edible material from the banks.

As explained in an earlier chapter, the cold lower layer of water will not only return to its former position when the wind drops, but will over-swing, becoming deeper against the opposite shore for a time. In these large deep lakes or reservoirs, if there is much wind, it is usually best to fish with the wind in one's face, and at a depth of fifteen feet or more. This applies to many species of fish besides carp. Mr. W. Penney, whose knowledge of big reservoir roach is unequalled, advises fishing directly into the wind, at depths of about twenty feet; and it is perhaps significant that the late Albert Buckley found that his only opportunity to catch carp at Mapperley, a twenty-nine-acre, thirty-foot-deep reservoir, was to fish when there was a high wind blowing towards the deeper end of the lake. He fished at a depth of fifteen feet or more.

Not only does the wind, in big deep lakes, push the warm upper layer to one side; it also sets up a current which travels along the surface in the direction of the wind. As it travels, this moving surface-water, which has been cooled to some extent by evaporation, tends to sink, carrying down with it material washed from the banks, or blown across the lake. Then it travels back, decreasing in speed, along the lower level of the upper surface layer—not along the bottom, unless the upper surface layer is as deep as that. In intermediate-sized lakes, the upper surface layer of warm water in summer may, after warm spells, or longer spells of equable weather, eventually extend to the bottom at all depths, until the autumn, especially if the water is clear, while in the shallower lakes, it will have done so before coarse-fishing begins in mid-June. This is a point to remember.

Large deep lakes with extensive shallow areas should be treated as if the lower limit of the warm layer were the bottom, except, as previously mentioned, when there is high or protracted wind.

It must not be supposed that carp are driven about a lake in a shoal like a flock of sheep. There will be wide variations in individual behaviour, and often fish will be found in unexpected places. The effects of ground-baiting, or frightening of the fish; decaying matter at the bottom; shelter provided by reeds or weeds—all these, and other factors, may influence the whereabouts of the carp.

Feeder streams, too, may affect them. The temperature of the water these streams bring into a lake may be either warm or cool and thus attract or drive fish away, while food may be carried into the lake by their current. The same will apply, though it is hard to detect, if a lake is fed by springs.

Anything like an accurate sizing-up of carp movements and feeding is as difficult as it is valuable. Because he often fails to take one of the many factors into account, the angler is more often wrong than right. All the same, he will not waste his time if he studies prevailing conditions and does his best to calculate their effect on the fish.

Tackle and Methods

Having considered the effect of circumstances on the feeding and movements of the fish, we now have to consider in a more detailed way their habits and our methods of angling.

Albert Buckley caught carp up to 26 lb. on 4x gut and No. 10 hook; lack of strength in his tackle was compensated for by quantity of line; he used from 250 to 300 yards and, fishing in open water, was thus able to allow his fish to travel more or less where they liked. But such conditions are seldom found in waters containing big carp, and gear of stouter calibre is necessary.

Rods

In most of the waters I fish, in hopes of landing a 20-pounder, I have to use lines with breaking-strains of from 6 lb. to 12 lb.; in exceptional circumstances even stronger lines may be needed. For this to be used to advantage, one must couple it with a rod with plenty of backbone. As I could not get one that combined strength with sufficient whip to cast comparatively light baits, like a single large lobworm without lead, I designed and built a number of rods myself, and finally, with the help of other anglers, arrived at the design known as the Mark IV carp-rod, which I mentioned earlier.

This rod is of split-cane, with non-fouling agate tip-ring, large full-open bridge intermediate rings, and agate stand-off butt-ring with a diameter of twenty-six millimetres. The length is ten feet in two joints, the handle of cork, thirty inches long. The action is designed to cast a wide range of weights and still be suitable for dealing with powerful fish. The design has done well, and many successful carp-fishers are very pleased with its performance. Details of the taper are included in my book *Rod-building for Amateurs*.*

The design was, of course, intended for dealing with heavy carp of 10 lb. upwards; for smaller fish in waters which are not too badly weeded, the Avon rod, designed by Mr. F. W. K. Wallis, is excellent; the line can be from 3 to 6 lb. breaking-strain according to circumstances.

Hooks

Hooks, of course, must be of a size to suit the bait and of a strength to suit the rest of the tackle. I have yet to find

* Published by Belfield & Bushell, Folkestone.

a hook to beat the forged 'Model Perfect,' and I use these almost exclusively for carp-fishing; sizes 2, 3 and 4 on the stout outfit, and sizes 6 and 7 on the lighter gear. It is of no use having a line which will lift 10 lb. if the hook is going to straighten on a 5-lb. pull; the ordinary gilt crystal hooks, excellent though they are for some kinds of coarse fishing, are too fine in wire and wrong in shape for heavy duties, and should be avoided, not only for carp, but for big tench, barbel and chub, where any of these fish require really firm handling. All hooks should be very carefully sharpened before use. Treble hooks are advocated by some authorities but, as explained in the first chapter, I, personally, am against their use.

Reels

It is a matter of opinion as to what constitutes the ideal carp-reel. It should have the following features:

1. It must be capable of holding at least 100 yards of 12-lb. breaking-strain line; preferably 150 yards, for while a hooked carp seldom travels 100 yards, you may on occasions cast sixty, which leaves only forty on your reel if the total is 100 yards.

2. It must be capable of recovering line rapidly: a fish may come quickly towards the angler.

3. It must offer easy and comfortable means of varying the pressure applied to a fish, preferably by finger control.

4. It must minimize the likelihood of the line being caught where it shouldn't; for example, round the handles or the reel-seat.

The ordinary Nottingham reels are hardly satisfactory. Their diameter, even in the four-inch size, is not always sufficient to enable an angler to keep in touch with so fast-moving a fish, while even when line-guards are fitted, the line is liable to become caught up round the reel-seat, especially in the dark. The only kind of non-geared reel which I would consider is the 'Flick-em' type; the 'Eureka' (Hardy), and 'Rapidex' (Young) are similar.

These reels have a drum and cage construction which greatly reduces the chance of fouling the line, and at the same time have an overhanging flange for finger-breaking. Their main drawbacks for carp-fishing are lack of line capacity and winding speed, and the fact that one must be careful to see that the line does not pile up on one side of the drum and eventually foul the crossbars of the frame. I made scaled-up versions of this type for myself and 'B. B.' in 1947, with diameters of $5\frac{3}{4}$ inches. They proved very effective and 'B. B.' still uses his, and swears by it. For playing big carp it would be hard to beat.

This leaves us with two other types from which to choose; the American type multipliers, and the large (salmon) size fixed-spool reels. The level-wind multipliers are excellent for playing a fish; they have rapid line recovery and good finger-control. Like the ungeared reels, they will not work as casting reels with light baits, but they will enable a biggish potato or paste ball to be cast from the reel; most of them have sufficient line capacity. The main objection I have to them, is that they seem to be without exception right-hand-wind jobs; being a right-handed angler, I prefer to control my rod with my best hand and wind with the other, my left. Multipliers are not satisfactory when used with monofil lines, owing to their small spool diameter.

Big fixed-spool reels are excellent, and to my mind the best proposition for large carp. There is a choice of several which will take 100 yards of 12 lb. line. At present I am using the 'Mitchell.' These reels make casting very easy, but that is not their chief recommendation; for long casting, as will be shown later, is not often either necessary or desirable in carp-fishing; in any event one does not cast frequently, and when a long throw *is* called for, it can be made from coils on a newspaper or mackintosh sheet, with any kind of reel on the rod. No, the advantages of the fixed-spool reel lie elsewhere. When a carp bites, he will frequently rush off at high speed, even before the angler has made any move to strike. With all reels except the fixed-spool, it is therefore desirable to place coils of line on a mackintosh sheet or something similar, between the butt-ring of the rod and the reel, otherwise a rapid run will cause the reel to spin violently and overrun. Even with a slow run, the carp will feel a check which may alarm him and cause him to eject the bait.

A serious overrun brought about by a fast-running fish may cause a tangle and jam, and if the fish at the same time hooks himself, the least that can happen is a smash; and at the worst, if the angler fails to grab his rod in time, he may see it fly into the water and disappear for ever. I have actually seen this happen, when after an overrun the line has caught round the handle or under the frame of someone's Nottingham-type reel. Some rotating-drum reels have centrifugal governors which may get over this difficulty. I mean to try Hardy's 'Elarex' next season.

With the fixed-spool reel these dangers and difficulties are absent. It is only necessary to leave the pick-up in the 'open,' or 'off' position to allow a fish to run without check as far as the total line capacity of the reel will permit, a distance which not even the biggest carp is likely to go unless actually hooked. There is some danger of the line fouling or being caught twice round the pick-up, but this can be avoided if care is taken to check that the line is properly picked-up whenever the rod is lifted. With me, the habit of picking up the rod and catching the line with a finger, so that it is drawn taut to the reel, has become automatic, in daylight or in the dark. If this is done, the pick-up cannot fail to catch the line correctly when the reel-handle is rotated. With fixed-spool reels having claw-type pick-ups, the pick-up should be opened towards the rod, that is, *upwards*, and kept there while awaiting a bite.

Fixed-spool reels have a high speed of line recovery and in addition to the action of the slipping clutch, they allow any desired degree of finger-braking to be applied.

My personal preference is for a big fixed-spool reel, then; but some people find these more complicated types of reel difficult to work with, and they are advised to use whatever suits them best, bearing in mind its drawbacks.

Line

Then there is the line. Its strength must be suited to the conditions and the size of fish, and I prefer to have the entire

length in one piece. H. T. Sheringham said, 'The carp
themselves prefer fine gut, but where you are likely to get
hold of a big one, I should advise you to disregard their
preference'; a wise pronouncement indeed. The reason
why carp prefer fine tackle needs examination. There is no
tackle so fine that carp cannot see it. I do not find that
carp are much alarmed by the sight of it, unless they have
previously felt its effects. If they have, they are likely to
be scared by any conspicuous tackle; and fine tackle may
be conspicuous, and coarse tackle unnoticed, if the one is
unnatural in appearance and the other natural, by being
dyed or disposed so that it does not alarm the fish. While
the sight of the line may alarm carp, the effect of it on a
bait is much more important. A stiff terminal tackle is
likely to be felt by the fish even when they cannot see it,
especially in bottom-fishing.

Where long casting is necessary, it is desirable to use
nylon or perlon monofilament line; otherwise, a sound
undressed plaited nylon is preferable. For bottom-fishing,
the terminal tackle can be either monofil or plaited nylon;
but recent experience shows that there may be a definite
advantage in using the softer plaited material, especially
where lines upwards of 8 lb. b.s. are needed. Plaited flax
may also be used. For surface-fishing, the less obvious
monofilament is probably better, especially as one can see
the bait taken and strike before the fish can reject it. Whatever the material, it should be dyed as far as possible to
suit the conditions under which it is to be used.

Some carp-fishers advocate the use of wire traces. Provided a good wire is used, wire traces can be of great help
where weeds are very bad. They will cut through quite
thick growths and are invaluable where there are big beds
of water-lilies. Twisted or plaited wires are not of much use
for this; single wire is much better. Some kinds of wire are
very poor, and it is always a source of wonder to me to hear
them so highly praised. A wire for weed-cutting purposes
ought to be of high-tensile steel; the best I know is that used
for the strings of musical instruments. A banjo 2nd (B)
string is strong enough to hold any fish in British waters and

is much thinner than 10 lb. b.s. nylon. Its shine can be removed by immersing it in a ten per cent silver nitrate bath for one second, after which it must be rinsed, dried and oiled.   Banjo 1st (D) strings are even thinner and still have tremendous strength, but owing to their extreme thinness they must be kept very carefully, as the least speck of rust spells their doom.   These thin wires should always be attached to a small metal ring or swivel to which the reel line is knotted, otherwise the wire will cut the line.

I would not recommend the use of wire traces except in very weedy conditions, and it is a long time since I used one; but where wire is considered necessary, let it be the best possible quality.

Baits

Baits for carp are numerous.   Beside the various forms in which bread can be used (with or without honey), lobworms, boiled potatoes, redworms, gentles, slugs, snails, freshwater mussels, small fish, wasp grubs, boiled beans, peas and chestnuts, cheese, banana, macaroni, shrimps, prawns, cake, caterpillars, dock and other grubs, congealed blood, and many other baits have all tempted carp at one time or another; but the first three have probably accounted for more carp than all the rest together.   Carp in different waters show decided preferences.   For example, in 'B. B.'s' book *Confessions of a Carp Fisher*, a water called the Old Copper Mine—Beechmere—is described.   In this water no carp has ever been known to take lobworms; what the Beechmere Carp like is bread paste or bread crust.   In the Temple Pool, described in Michael Traherne's *Be Quiet and Go a-Angling*, the carp prefer a fat lobworm to any other bait. They will sometimes take paste and crust, but they much prefer the lob.   At Croxby Pond in Lincolnshire, numerous carp are taken on potato; I have never had a bite at Temple Pool or at Beechmere on this bait.   Fish have local preferences.

Then there is the question of fish other than carp.

Even where carp like paste and take it readily, roach, rudd and bream often prove such a nuisance that it is impossible to keep the paste on the hook long enough to attract a carp. Small roach and rudd can be circumvented to some extent by using a very large ball of paste, one the size of a golf-ball; but where bream exist in any numbers, even this is of little avail; I have known a bream of 3 lb. take a piece of paste fully golf-ball size. Lobworms, too, are subject to the attentions of undesired fish. Eels and perch attack them at every opportunity, and roach, rudd, tench and bream take them sufficiently often to be a nuisance. The only bait which is more or less immune to the attacks of fish other than carp is a boiled potato of a size which is too large for the smaller fish to eat. It is generally supposed that only carp like potatoes, but I don't think this is correct. You can catch roach, rudd, bream, and tench on potato if you use a comparatively small piece, but potato is not easily nibbled away by these fish, which have no teeth in their mouths; they have to take it whole or not at all, and if a potato is large, only a large fish, like a carp, can take it. In the U.S.A., 'dough-balls,' which are balls of flour paste which have been boiled, like dumplings in a stew, are popular, and they resist the attacks of small fish better than bread paste, but not so well as potato.

Carp view any new bait with suspicion, and a strange bait is inspected warily; a carp will look at it, go away, return, taste, eject, retreat, and so on, for a long time, usually finishing by taking the bait very gingerly and bolting in alarm at its own temerity. This sort of thing goes on even when the bait is a free offering, but after the carp have consumed a number of pieces of bait without ill effect, they gain confidence and will take the baited hook without suspicion. This is one of the purposes of ground-baiting, and applies whether the bait be paste, potato, worm, or other bait. But if the ground-bait is never allowed to remain long enough for the carp to sample it, their suspicions will remain. That is why methodical ground-baiting with pieces of potato of sufficient size to defeat the unwanted fish, will often result in potato being taken as a hook-bait while paste and worm are refused. In relatively unfished and unbaited waters, potato usually has less attraction than paste or breadcrust.

Any bait begins to lose it effectiveness after a certain number of fish have been caught with it and returned to the water; and the education of the fish to a new bait while they are still taking the old one is well worth while when you intend to fish a water season after season.

Another consideration when deciding on a bait is the weather. After a spell of rainy weather, or heavy night dew, large quantities of lobworms will probably have found their way into the lake, specially if it is fed by a stream. Under such circumstances the carp will have tried enough worms to allay their suspicions and *ought* to take the angler's lob with reasonable confidence. Black slugs favour the same weather conditions.

As previously explained, sustained warm weather has the effect of bringing the carp on to the shallows. It also brings them to the surface and often close to the banks. Under such conditions a floating crust is a useful bait, especially on waters which are well fished and where the carp are accustomed to find crusts, either deliberately thrown in to attract them or the remains of ground-bait or sandwiches, drifted against the bank or the edges of the weeds. When, however, colder weather, or the effects of rain or wind, have driven the carp to the bottom, and perhaps into deeper water, obviously a bait fished on the bottom will be the thing to use.

I have never been able to determine whether the use of honey in pastes has any attraction for carp. They certainly have no objection to it, but I seldom use honey-paste myself, though many expert carp-fishers have great faith in it. We are often told that the smell of tobacco is a great deterrent to carp, but I have never found it so. Likewise, carp are said to be able to detect the scent of the human hand on a bait. I would not deny the possibility and from time to time, when carp are proving difficult to catch, I become convinced that this is the reason, and take elaborate precautions to avoid the scent of my hands, or tobacco, from contaminating the bait. But I have never been certain that it made any difference, and I have caught plenty of carp without taking these precautions. However, there is not the least doubt that carp can smell, or rather, detect a flavour in the water in much the same way that we can detect a smell in the air. In fact, I believe that nearly all their feeding is done by scent and touch, their barbules being used in the latter case. Certainly some scents or flavours are disliked, among them petrol, paraffin and formalin.

The question of what size of bait to use is often answered by saying that it should, if paste, potato or other similar bait, cover the hook completely. With many species of fish this matters little, but with carp I am convinced of its importance. Where roach and rudd are present, a ball of paste large enough to take them some time to whittle away may be necessary. I usually use very large baits, pasteballs the size of pheasant eggs, and two-inch cubes of crust, without having very much evidence that they are preferred by the fish to something smaller. I feel that a carp is at any rate unlikely to overlook them!

From time to time we see reports of carp having been taken on live bait or on a spinner of some kind. A carp of 16 lb. 8 oz. was caught on a spinner in 1927, and another fish of $8\frac{1}{2}$ lb. in 1908, and, more recently, a 21-pounder caught in June, 1951, took live baits. One often sees small fish making off with all possible speed when a big carp approaches, and there has been much discussion as to whether a small fish might prove a useful bait for carp. I am told that small dead fish have been used in the U.S.A. with success.

I have never given this bait an exhaustive trial, the presence of eels in most carp waters making it virtually impossible, but on one occasion, while fishing in Lincolnshire in June, Maurice Ingham and I, using small dead fish as baits for big eels, had several runs which were very different from what we normally expect from eels. Following our usual procedure, we did not strike until the initial run stopped (see chapter on eel-fishing), only to find that the bait had been discarded unmarked, again unusual for eels. I have the strongest suspicion that carp were responsible for those runs, and had we struck sooner, we might have confirmed it.   Subsequent attempts to do so have produced only normal runs from eels.

Another interesting suggestion is that, since carp feed on minute crustacea, such as daphnia, it might be possible to excite their appetite by means of a bait consisting of, or strongly flavoured with, some more easily-handled crustacean, such as crayfish or shrimp, which could be used as it was, or minced and mixed with bread paste.   Cholmondely Pennell mentions a paste of bread and herring-roe.

How Carp Feed

Carp do not shoal, like roach and bream, and one can often observe them feeding in several different ways even in the same lake and in the same conditions of weather. 'B.B.,' well-known author and sportsman, has invented a number of words to describe these different kinds of feeding, to which others have been added from time to time by other members of the Carpcatchers' Club.

A *Bubbler* is a carp which is routing about in the mud and sending up large quantities of bubbles.   You can trace the course of the fish along the bottom by watching the bubbles. Carp bubbles are quite unmistakable; they come up in a wide patch, usually two bursts in one place, then two more in another, perhaps a foot, perhaps a yard away, and so on. Generally speaking, the bigger the carp, the more impressive the bubbling.   A really big fish may send up a patch of bubbles a yard wide.

Of all the problems encountered by the carp-fisher, I think that presented by the Bubbler is the most intriguing. On nearly every carp water, during summer mornings and to a lesser extent, evenings, the activities of Bubblers can be observed, unless the temperature is too low or the surface too ruffled.   We can see where the fish are, and we know they are feeding.   If an acceptable bait could be found for even one in ten of these fish, carp-fishing would be revolutionized.   Unfortunately they have never been found to take any kind of bait, except on a few occasions, and these are usually in the first few weeks of the seasons, or in early autumn.

We do not know what these fish are eating nor how they are finding it, but I believe that it is mainly chironomid larvae that they are feeding on and that they use their barbules to probe the soft surface mud and feel their movements. Chironomid larvae are those of various gnats and midges, for instance the plumed gnat, whose larva is the well-known bloodworm. It has been suggested that carp use their sense of smell to locate their food, and no doubt this is so, but I think, bearing in mind the stench of disturbed pond-mud, that the Bubblers depend more on touch. I have been able to observe Bubblers at close range; the bubbles come mainly from under the gill-covers. Sometimes the head of the fish is buried deep in the mud, well beyond the eyes.

Sometimes 'colonies' of red worms, or larvae, can be seen on the bottom of ponds, and if they are disturbed they disperse, burying themselves in the mud. One can readily imagine the carp probing in the mud for them.

Whatever it is the carp are eating, they seem completely preoccupied by it and only a bait which seems similar is likely to attract them to bite*.

The surface mud has numerous inhabitants beside chironomid larvae, and I think leeches, alder-fly larvae, and pieces of freshwater mussel might be tried as baits. It may be that some or all of the Bubblers are eating algae, and if this is suspected a fish might be tempted with a bunch of silkweed or some other variety of this numerous family.

Alternatively, it might be worth trying a small bag, with a drawstring to close the mouth, just big enough to hold a small walnut, and dyed the colour of the bottom, or black. It would be made of muslin or something similar so that bloodworms could just squeeze through the weave, the hook and numerous bloodworms would be put in and the drawstring pulled tight, above the end of the hook-shank.

Tubifex worms, which can be got from aquarists' suppliers, or by washing shovelfuls of mud from the river-bed below a sewage outfall, may also prove effective as a bait for bubbling carp; certainly tench eat them greedily. A bunch of these red worms will twine together to form a

* See note at end of chapter.

living ball, into which a hook could be introduced. By enclosing worms and hook in a piece of hair-net, the ball would be hindered from breaking up when cast out. Yet another idea is to enclose a lot of bloodworms, and the hook, in a ball of mud or clay. The hook might well be a bright-metal one, painted with the appropriate shade of red nail-varnish. The brown rust-proof finish can be removed by boiling in soda and water.

A friend has described these suggestions as untried and 'far-fetched.' Untried they certainly are, as yet, but they can hardly be called 'far-fetched.' One bait known to be very effective for a variety of fishes *is* 'far-fetched.' The seeds of a special kind of grass are collected and ground up by machinery to a powder which is passed through a series of sieves to remove the husks. This powder is then mixed with salt and water, and a living plant is allowed to grow in it; the mass is then heated until the plant is killed and, later, a reddish-brown hard skin forms on the outside. After cooling for a day or so, the outside is removed and the white sponge-like inside wetted and kneaded-up to form a soft white putty-like material, lumps of which are moulded round the hook and used as bait. It is called bread paste. If this complicated use of a food completely alien to fish is not 'far-fetched,' surely bloodworms and tubifex worms can hardly be so described! These methods are suggested for the fish whose bubbling is confined to a comparatively small area. Sometimes, however, successive patches of bubbles will show that a carp is moving from one part of the lake to another and feeding as it goes. Such fish can often be tempted with conventional baits, as can fish sending up bubbles very near the bank.

Of course you must distinguish the natural bubbler—the fish which is searching the mud for its natural food—from a fish raising bubbles in a ground-baited pitch, eating the ground-bait provided by the angler. In such a case, of course, the hook-bait will be a superior sample of what the fish is already eating. It is worth remembering that where a ground-bait consisting of bread and meal or bran, has been used, some of the meal should be mixed in the paste used on the hook; when meal and boiled potato are used it is a good plan to enclose the potato on the hook in a ball of the ground-bait mixture, an old but very effective carp-fishing dodge.

A *Clooper* is a fish which is making loud sucking noises, usually in the weeds, rushes or water-lilies. 'Clooping' describes the way a carp take a floating crust. Carp fishers who stay out all night are sure to be familiar with the sounds of clooping.

Tenting is the action produced by a carp which is surface-feeding in thick weed, or, sometimes, among lily pads. The vegetation is lifted up in the shape of a little tent, hence the origin of the term.

Smokescreening describes a fish that works along the bottom and leaves a long trail of disturbed mud. This is not the same as bubbling; it can be done without raising any bubbles at all. Sometimes just a few fine bubbles come up. Smokescreening fish will often take a bait placed carefully in their path.

Lastly, there is the *Margin-patrol*; those fish which, during warm nights and in the early morning, patrol up and down close to or even right under the bank, eating any tit-bits which have fallen in or drifted to the side.

Cloopers will often take a floating crust if you can put it near enough without disturbing them. Getting them out of their thicket is your problem. The same applies to Tenters, for which water-snail eggs and the snails themselves are also attractive. The eggs are those little jelly sausages which you find on weeds or under lily-leaves, full of little brown dots. A piece of lily-leaf with several close together on it is the bait; just stick the hook through the leaf. Don't waste time offering Cloopers or Tenters paste, potato or worm, though Smokescreeners and Margin-patrollers may take them. Margin-patrollers are on the look-out for anything edible; they're not fussy. This being the case, it is probably best to use floating breadcrust. There is a special way of fishing this, known as margin-fishing. A rod rest is placed so that the top ring of a rod put in it just overhangs the edge of the water. It is as well to choose a spot towards which the wind, if any, is blowing, and if possible one with some grass or other herbage at the edge of the bank to help screen the angler.   Failing this, a screen can be made from willow-shoots.   The rod is put in the rest, a strong sharp hook is attached direct to the line, and a piece of crust about the size of a matchbox is impaled on the hook so that it hangs *crumb* side down and both the point and shank of the hook project on the crust side.   This is now lowered into the water.   A coil of line is placed on a sheet of paper or mackintosh between the reel and the bottom ring of the rod.   No line is allowed to touch the water, only the crust.   The angler then sits back and waits for the crust to be 'clooped.'   If small roach and rudd attack the crust too energetically, it can be pulled up just clear of the surface, by pulling on the line, without lifting the rod, and a loose crust thrown in instead, this being replaced as often as the small fish finish it off.   Bread, soaked in water and mashed up to a sort of thin gruel, poured into the water, is a good attractor for this fishing.

When a carp appears, the crust on the hook is lowered. There must be enough slack line in readiness to allow the bread to be sucked *in*; if the line is taut the crust is often sucked *off* the hook.   Apart from the loose crust, thrown in for the roach, being actually taken by a carp, there are other signs by which the angler may deduce the presence of a big carp in the vicinity.   One is by the sudden cessation of activity on the part of the small fish.   Another is a small but sustained eddying of the water near the bread.   But specialist carp-fishers develop what almost seems to be a sixth sense, which tells them when a carp is near the bait.   It probably sounds incredible to the layman, but I am always aware of a sort of deathly hush just at the moment before a big carp sucks in the bread; many other carp-fishers have had the same experience.

There is no doubt that, given suitable conditions, this margin-fishing with floating crust is a most deadly method of fishing for big carp.   The fact that there is no tackle in the water is a tremendous advantage; as it is unseen the tackle can be as strong as desired, provided the line runs smoothly through the rings and the hook is not so large and heavy as to sink the crust. It is not, however, quite as easy as the foregoing description may have made it seem. If there is sufficient wind to make the surface choppy, the crust will wash off the hook very quickly, and, as in cold weather, the fish may be driven into deeper water. Perfect quiet is essential; one is hoping for the fish to approach closer than in any other mode of angling, and a time must be chosen when the water is in no way disturbed by other people; one must be immobile and inconspicuous, and, at night, take great care to show no lights, not even a glowing cigarette-end. It is also a way of fishing that has a great effect on the mind, raising one to a fever-pitch of excitement that often results in a premature or violent strike, or in clumsiness or neglect of an important detail, all of which are likely to cause failure.

Other baits can, of course, be fished close to the bank, but baits fished on the bottom should not be under the rod-point, or the line leading straight up and down will be sure to alarm the fish. To avoid this, it is best to make a cast of ten yards or so parallel to the bank, so as to give the line a chance of lying along the bottom; and a small split shot a yard from the hook will help to ensure that it does so.

Ground-baiting

Ground-baiting is very important, for reasons already given. Not only does it attract fish, but it introduces them to the food the angler proposes to offer them on a hook. I have mentioned several ways of tackling carp that are eating or searching for either their natural food or what might be described as unintentional ground-bait.

They are best where continuous ground-baiting is not possible; in addition they are perhaps more active methods than the usual technique of casting out and waiting until a carp comes along. But where ground-baiting can be carried out over a period of three or four days, or more, fishing over a baited pitch is likely to prove more profitable than pursuing the fish.

The first step is to decide on a pitch. Observation of the

lake and the weather conditions ought to show where the
carp are to be expected; failing any obvious indications, a
pitch should be chosen where the shallows drop off into
deeper water. Having decided on the spot, it should be
vigorously cleared by means of a double-sided rake on a
rope, so as to remove all weed growth from the bottom and
to clear any snags or obstructions. Then a landmark on
the opposite bank should be noted, and the ground-bait
thrown in a line with it and the spot from where the fishing
is to be done.

This fixing of a 'mark' is very important indeed. By its
help one can ensure that not only is the ground-bait lying
more or less in a line, but that the hook-bait is lying in that
line too. Handfuls of ground-bait seldom all go the same
distance, but they ought to go in the same *direction*, and the
result will be a trail of ground-bait along the bottom which
will lead the carp to the baited hook. The hook-bait *must*
be cast out accurately; if it is not in the right place, the
ground-bait will attract the fish away from it instead of
towards it.

Although small fish are a nuisance in many ways, their
interest in ground-bait probably helps to attract carp. For
this reason, ground-bait should always include material to
attract the small fish, except in waters where only carp are
found.

In most waters a mixture of boiled potato and meal, with
some mashed soaked bread, will be found as good as anything; where only carp are found, either soaked bread and
bran or handfuls of lobworms, according to local preference,
will serve. Otherwise, potatoes should be chopped, not
mashed, and there should be plenty of pieces too large to be
taken by fish other than carp.

An account of a long-term policy of ground-baiting on
these lines, and its result, will be found in *Drop me a Line*,
by Ingham & Walker.

In some waters, carp eat large quantities of weed and
algae. Where suitable varieties grow the carp become very
fat, and sometimes clear or grub up the weed completely,
often by the middle of June. In such waters they are in

their best condition at the opening of the coarse fishing season, but being so well fed, are not as easy to catch as one might suppose they would be after a long spell of rest from the attacks of anglers.

In such waters a course of ground-baiting on the 'little and often' principle, extending over a period of several weeks before the fishing season begins, will wean the carp away from the idea of weed as their only food.

I have known private waters where keepers have been in the habit, when they were paunching rabbits, of throwing the unsavoury refuse into the lake. The carp have soon learned to feed greedily on it; they became confirmed margin-feeders and succumbed readily to a piece of rabbit's guts as a hook-bait.

Margin-fishing can of course be tried whether the fish are seen to be feeding at the edge of the water or not, and the fish can be encouraged to seek floating crust at the edge. An alternative is to lay trails of ground-bait along the bottom close to the bank; fish following these trails usually spot a crust floating, or a piece of paste or potato fished on the bottom.

When carp are well on the feed, a cloud ground-bait similar to that used for roach can be employed to attract them; it should be used in large quantities and cover an area of three or four yards. It should be thrown in loose and not in large balls, so as to avoid disturbance of the water.

As autumn approaches, one's chance of a fish at midday increases and it is not so necessary to remain out all night or to rise at dawn, as it is when the weather is hot. There are, however, exceptions to the latter rule; I hooked one of the largest carp I have ever connected with at 2 p.m. on a blazing hot day, when every carp in the lake appeared to be basking and utterly indifferent to food.

Much has been said about the best month for carp-fishing. From June 16th to mid-October and sometimes even later in the year, there is always a chance, and obviously the smaller the amount of natural food available the better it will be, provided the conditions are otherwise favourable.

Therefore, the first two weeks of the season, and from the beginning of September until the first cold weather are often the best periods.

After the first autumn frosts it is seldom worth fishing for carp until the following June. There are plenty of instances of carp being caught in winter, but, as with tench, most of them have come from rivers or fenland drains. A long spell of fine weather early in the year may bring carp on feed before the coarse fishing season ends, but my own experience has been that they are careful not to commence their spring feeding until March 15th!

Terminal Tackle

We must now consider the arrangement of the tackle which is actually in the water—the 'business end' of the equipment. That for margin-fishing has already been dealt with; it remains to choose terminal tackle for the other methods.

Opinions differ as to whether lead should be used for bottom-fishing, and, if so, how it should be disposed. Some people use a coffin-lead, others a pierced bullet. I seldom use either, contenting myself with, at most, one shot at least four feet from the hook, to ensure that *all* the cast or line between the hook and shot lies on the bottom. Heavy leads cause considerable splash when cast, and however freely the line may run through the lead (no one, I hope, would ever consider a *fixed* lead larger than a single shot) it can never run as freely as it would without. If the bottom is soft, the lead may sink into the mud and impede the running of the line. I am sure, too, that the disturbance caused by the heavy lead, whose weight is *concentrated*, is much more likely to scare the fish than a big ball of ground-bait, though the disturbance caused by the latter may seem greater to the angler.

It has been suggested that the weight of the lead helps casting. This is quite true, but the difficulty, if it exists, can be overcome in other ways. One is to squeeze a ball of ground-bait round the bait or the shot; another is to use mud which can be jerked off after the cast has been made. A third is to use a wooden ledger weight consisting of a tor-pedo-shaped piece of wood drilled from end to end and held in position on the cast, which has been threaded through it, by a shot on each side of it, the buoyancy of the wood being such that one shot on each side, or two, as desired, will sink it. Its weight in air helps the cast, but its weight in the water is negligible, and it thus offers little resistance to a biting fish. Wooden ledgers should be painted a neutral colour. A small bubble-float, completely filled with water, answers much the same purpose, but the tor-pedo-shaped wooden ledger offers less resistance when drawn through the water.

It is, however, seldom necessary to cast to such a distance that any weight over and above that of the bait itself is necessary. Carp normally prefer to feed fairly near the bank, and it is not often that a cast of more than twenty yards is needed to reach them. This is well within the range of any angler, even when the bait is a single large lobworm. A ball of paste or a potato can be thrown to a much greater distance, if necessary.

The use of a float is debatable. It provides a more sensitive indication of a bite, but the usual carp bite is strong enough to pull under not only the float, but the rod as well. The float does give prior warning, however, and it helps the line to be kept floating and thus not only reduces the resistance against a running fish but permits a sharper and cleaner strike. As against this, there are times when the line is better sunk; when the wind and drift are sufficient to take it round in a bag and even to pull line off the reel, it is better to sink the line and arrange the rod-rest so that the rod-point is as near to the surface as possible. There is no necessity to use a cocked float; one lying flat provides just as good an indication, except in a bad light, when a black feather stuck on an upright float remains visible longer than anything else. I have yet to find a luminous float which worked satisfactorily. But under ordinary condi-tions, the flat float is best, and it should be attached to the line by two one-inch lengths of valve rubber, one at each end, so that if it goes into a weed-bed it will not catch up;

alternatively, it can be attached by the bottom ring only, which has the same effect. Floats can be made of balsa wood, with a central stiffener of bamboo, and painted a conspicuous colour; alternate broad sections of black and orange are good, the orange appearing bright red in the water. Red itself looks black at a distance, except in sunshine. A small goose-quill is probably as good and much easier to make. Bubble-floats are sometimes useful; I very seldom find a float of any kind necessary.

To fish floating crust, other than directly under the rod-point, the line should be well greased, and in conditions when grease is insufficient to keep the line properly afloat, a small ball of cork or balsa wood can be attached four feet or so from the hook; its diameter should not exceed three-eighths of an inch at most. Floating bread in open water is not always effective; the fish often appear to be suspicious of the gut or nylon, especially where one or two have been caught by this method, and it is best, if possible, to fish the bread in such a way that the line and cast can lie over surface weed or lily-pads, which also help by preventing the bait from drifting.

Even then the carp will sometimes behave in an exasperating way, approaching the crust and then turning away with a great swirl, or just nibbling at the edge of the bait. In either event the bait is soon broken up or washed off the hook. Under such circumstances one can try using a large and a small crust, the cast being threaded through the large one twice, and the small one impaled on the hook so that it is separated from the large one by three or four inches. Suspicious carp, having 'come short' at the large crust two or three times, and perhaps nibbled a bit off it or broken it up, will often take the small crust and be soundly hooked. A small crust may be cast a considerable distance with the aid of a bubble-float half-filled with water; instead of the large piece of bread.

Where the bottom is very soft indeed, or covered with silk-weed, it is possible to fish a crust sunk, with a running lead (which should be as small as possible) on the cast, stopped by a shot an inch or more from the hook, according to the

depth of the silkweed or mud. The buoyancy of the crust
keeps it just above the level of the mud or weed. Or a
composite bait consisting of crust and paste, can be used.
If the right proportions of crust and paste are chosen, it
can be made to sink very slowly, and will rest on the surface
of the mud, or on silkweed, without sinking into it. The
bait, if properly balanced, takes a minute or two before
beginning to sink. The crust should be put on the bend
of the hook, and the paste moulded round the shank. The
bait then comes to rest with the line emerging from underneath, where it is not encountered by the lips of a fish investi-
gating it.

If potato is used over soft mud or silkweed, a large flat
slice should be used, which will sink with a slow swinging
motion.

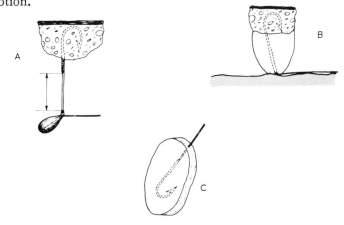

THREE WAYS OF OVERCOMING SILKWEED OR SOFT MUD

The length arrowed should be chosen to suit the length
of the silkweed

I believe in as few gadgets as possible on the tackle in
carp-fishing. One often sees contraptions of corks, leads,
swivels, etc., advocated, but my view is the less complica-
tion the better, and I am always happiest when using a
tackle consisting of line and hook with, at most, one small
shot, though it does not do to become pigheaded about such

things; one must try to choose one's tackle and tactics to suit the circumstances.

Striking

As stated earlier, the bite from a carp is often powerful, and, unless a fixed-spool reel is used, it is necessary to coil a couple of yards of line between butt-ring and reel so that the carp can run a little way without check, before the angler strikes. Sometimes, however, the bite indication is a slackening of the line between rod-point and water, showing that the fish is moving towards the rod. It is impossible to indicate the right moment for striking. It is up to the angler to strike directly he thinks the fish has the bait well in its mouth. With such baits as bread-flake or crust, a quicker strike is necessary than with paste, potato or worm, for the former baits are much more likely to be removed from the hook. The easiest bite to strike is the slow, steady run of a fish which has taken the bait with complete confidence.

A carp running away fast probably finds it difficult to eject a bait until he slows down or stops, and all that is needed with that kind of bite is a firm tightening-up. If, on the other hand, the line from the rod-point suddenly falls slack, it is probably best to wait till it runs out steadily. The same applies to sudden quick pulls or a succession of twitches. If you are in doubt it is better to miss a chance of striking than to miss and alarm the fish.

Where large hooks are in use, a firm strike is necessary, as a carp's mouth is not as soft as is commonly supposed, and it takes a fair amount of force to embed a No. 2 hook firmly into it, especially if the strike is made with a sunken line, and still more if the fish is any distance away. With the correct tackle and a flexible rod, breakage at the strike need not be greatly feared. Floating bread is usually absorbed with a loud suck and swirl, but sometimes a fish will quietly close its mouth over the crust and sink backwards in a most unobtrusive and stealthy way. I remember catching two common carp in a Lincolnshire lake, one of which took the bread without any visible disturbance of the water—the crust appeared to sink suddenly of its own

(*above*) Early morning action for a BBC broadcast. The author is attached to a 16¼lb carp; (*below*) Peter Thomas nets a 25lb carp caught by D. A. (Pat) Russell

(*above*) Jack Hilton with a Redmire carp weighing over 40lb; (*below*) a 27lb carp rolls at the surface. The angler's shadow indicates its size

volition, and the other must have done the same thing, except that I never even saw it go and my first warning was seeing the rod-point curve slowly down to the surface of the water.

When trying mud-ball or similar tactics on Bubblers one must strike at the first twitch of the line, otherwise the bait will probably be blown out pretty quickly.

Playing Carp

Having hooked your carp, you must bring all your skill and determination to bear on the task of playing him. You are up against a powerful and cunning antagonist and you cannot afford to give him any chances. It is impossible to hold a really big carp, and line he must be allowed to take, but he should be made to work hard for every inch he gains, except, of course, when you *want* him to run, perhaps towards more open water. Usually, a hooked carp goes off in a long fast run, and, to anglers who have never hooked a carp before, the speed and power of the fish is almost frightening. Side strain is the counter-measure; if the fish is running straight out—as they usually do—it pays to run along the bank, if possible, so as to put a side strain on the fish and swing him round. If this can be done, the battle becomes a matter of runs and checks, borings and tuggings, which in the case of a big carp may continue for hours, especially when it 'lies doggo' on the bottom and the tackle lacks the strength to move it. A friend of mine, who hooked a 17-lb. carp on light tackle took six hours and twenty minutes to bring it to the net.

A hooked fish must be kept out of the weeds if possible, but often a carp will succeed in getting into the weeds in spite of all that can be done to prevent it. When a carp enters a weed-bed, not only is he slowed down a great deal, but he forces the weeds aside and makes quite a tunnel. The pressure applied by the line and weed will bring him to a stop, and if he can then be dragged out before he can start off in another direction and wind the line round the weeds, the angler has a much better chance. Failing that, hand-lining may free him. There is no necessity to get hold of the line at the rod-point in order to hand-line a fish; all one has to do is to point the rod at him and, grasping the line between butt-ring and reel, pull and slacken with a jerking or sawing motion. There is nothing magical about hand-lining; it is effective because far greater pressure can be applied than with a bent rod, which 'irons-out' any jerks applied, as indeed it is meant to do. Have a yard or so of slack, between your reel and hand, which will allow the rod to come up in time if a fish bolts suddenly. Of course, if a fish has got well into a bed of soft weeds, and is still travelling at a fair pace, it may pay to do no more than keep the line taut until the fish emerges on the other side, which he will often do.

Anglers are often advised to keep the rod well up when playing a fish. Illustrations have been published showing anglers holding their rods well back over their shoulders. This is a stupid way of using a rod and a certain way of ruining the top joint. A rod designed for playing heavy fish is made with action right down to the butt; the top is tapered down fairly sharply to make the casting of light baits easier, and although it can do its share in applying pressure to a fish, to ask it to do all the work is unfair to the rod and the man who designed it.

The proper angle at which to hold a rod, if it is correct for the tackle in use, is with the butt at right angles to the line running from tip-ring to fish, and if the rod is then bent until there is no angle at all between the line and the first few inches of the tip of the rod, it is being used to the best advantage, each part doing its job. If greater pressure is needed to hold a fish out of lilies or snags, the rod must be inclined towards the fish to throw more of the strain on to the lower part of the rod. This, however, lessens the friction of the line in the rings, so that when it is done, more finger-pressure must be applied to the drum of the reel.

Never attempt to land a big carp until you have him well beaten, and then be careful, for an apparently beaten fish will often make a mighty rush directly he sees or feels the net, or if, in the dark, a light is switched on; and tackle worn and weakened by the strain of a long battle may not

prove equal to it.   I always slacken off the tension on my
fixed-spool reel before netting a fish, so as to avoid accidents
of this kind.

The fight put up by a carp varies in its tactics according
to the situation.   In shallow water the fish will usually
make a series of long, fast runs; if there are deeps adjoining
the shallow, the fish will nearly always make for them, and
unless the deeper water is known to be snag-infested, it
is much better to allow the fish to get there, as there will be
less likelihood of his running into dangerous situations there
than in the shallows.

In the deeps the fish can be allowed to stay well down
until thoroughly tired, and will probably settle down to
circling and tugging tactics which though they may result
in a prolonged battle, are far less likely to endanger the tackle
than long powerful runs all over the lake.   It is a great
mistake to try to bring the fish to bank or to the surface too
soon.   If this is done, the fish will often roll on to its side,
on the surface, lashing with its tail and slapping the water,
and it is a very dangerous trick; the line should be slackened
to avoid its being struck while taut.   Sometimes, in shallow
lakes, a carp will lash at the surface whatever the angler
does.

Sometimes a carp will resort to a tactic known as 'kiting.'
He travels at such an angle to the line that the resultant
force of the angler's pull and his own swimming power
brings him headlong into the bank on which the angler
stands, but some distance away.   If the bank is snaggy or
reeded this is a dangerous tactic to which I know no counter
save a friend with stones, or something with which to splash
and frighten the fish out again.   'Kiting' is probably
involuntary from the point of view of the fish, but it is most
dangerous, nevertheless.

I have heard much of the danger of the line or cast being
cut 'against the sharp edge of the dorsal fin' of the fish.
Having on several occasions tried to cut line on every part
of the dorsal fin of a landed carp without success, I do not
believe this can happen.   Indeed, I once played for over
an hour a carp which had somehow got the line firmly

half-hitched round the big front spine of its dorsal fin. After the most exciting struggle I have ever had with a carp—over a hundred yards of line were taken at the first rush and subsequent runs of seventy and eighty yards were frequent—the fish was landed. If dorsal fins could cut line, this one had an excellent chance. The only conceivable way in which line might be *cut* on the fish itself is by its becoming caught under a scale, but this is unlikely. However, the line will often be caught across the dorsal fin, from which it slips, producing a sensation at the rod-end like the plucking of a giant harp-string. The sudden removal and reapplication of strain often proves too much for fine tackle.

Beware of the mighty rush, with tremendous acceleration, of the carp hooked when margin-fishing. Directly he realizes he is in trouble, his reaction is to put as much distance as possible between himself and the bank.

The body-shape of carp causes a great difference in their speed. In some waters they are long and slim, especially the wild common carp, and when hooked make the line fairly hiss through the water. They can travel at forty feet per second, and it often requires quick action and a cool head to turn them clear of awkward places.

Sometimes these fast fish will double back like lightning and unless one is quick, gain yards of slack which they will use to full advantage.

The very big and usually fat carp are quite different. Their speed is less, but their strength is greater. They are to the wild type as a carthorse is to a racehorse, and they take much longer to reach full speed, but having done so, take a great deal of stopping. They will try again and again for the same snag or weed-bed, unlike the fast fish who, turned from one refuge, seeks another. Even in waters free from weeds and snags, carp will often burrow deep into mud and unless the tackle is strong enough to move them they are likely to escape; so that really the only opportunity for using fine tackle, that is, roach-tackle, is in weed-free and snag-free waters with hard bottoms.

Playing a big carp takes experience, and a novice must expect to be broken often; even anglers of many years' experience and with dozens of big carp to their credit lose their tackle now and then. Perhaps the most valuable possessions for playing carp are a cool head and what horsemen call good hands. For a long fight, you need strong wrists; if you're sensible enough to be an all-round angler, and have been fly-fishing for trout often enough between April and June, you need have few worries on this score! It is the casting, of course, that improves your muscles, not the playing of the relatively insignificant trout. If, before you hook your fish, you have examined the place you are fishing and decided what a hooked fish will most likely do, and what counter-measures you will have to apply, it will help you a great deal, especially if you eventually hook your fish after dark.

Landing

Your landing-net for carp should be big and deep, with a mesh made of stout material which is all the better for a double dressing in linseed oil. Mine is triangular with thirty-inch arms and a mesh four feet deep. I like a handle not less than five feet long, made of stout bamboo about seven-eighths of an inch in diameter. Landing-nets sold for salmon-fishing are all much too heavy for single-handed use. One well-known type weighs 8 lb.; my own home-made carp net, which is quite as large, weighs 2 lb. only and has landed many big carp, including a 44-pounder. Never attempt to lift a big carp; get him in the net, drop the rod and reach down and get a grip on the rim of the net, or the mesh itself, if at all possible. Then you can drag net and fish up the bank. A stout cord attached to the net-ring can be a help, and I have recently been shown a net with a thin sash-cord threaded through the meshes about twelve inches below the ring; a pull on it closes up the net above a netted fish and spoils his chances of escaping; the angler can then take his time about getting his catch out of the water

Some carp-fishers use a gaff. I hate the idea of sticking a gaff in any kind of fish, except pike, and even a pike can be landed with a gaff under the chin without injuring him;

but the gills and chin of a carp are quite different, and the fish usually have to be gaffed in the belly or shoulder, which means killing them. I can see no reason why anyone should want to kill a fish, unless it is to be set up, and in that case a gaff-mark is not going to improve its appearance. So let it be a big net, and unless your carp tops 20 lb. and you want to put him in a glass case, let him go when you have weighed him, and perhaps photographed him with a ruler or your reel alongside. An excellent instrument for removing hooks is a pair of artery forceps, or failing these, long-nosed pliers.

I always carry a ½-cwt. sack, which makes an effective keep-net for a big fish; a cord is attached to draw up the mouth of the sack and to attach to a peg in the bank. A big carp lies quiet in a sack, he cannot see, so he does not try to get away. A modification suggested by Peter Thomas is to have a sack open at top and bottom with draw strings so that either end can be closed. A fish can be put in at one end and let out at the other, which avoids its fins being caught and perhaps broken or split. A carp can be transported a long distance in a sack with plenty of wet weeds round his head, and if you want to take your fish home and keep him in the bath overnight, it is easy enough. You can have him officially weighed and photographed, and still return him alive. If your carp fishing is as successful as I hope it will be, a photographic record of the notable fish you catch will be preferable to their stuffed skins, as it will allow room in your house for you to live.

Clothes and Camouflage

The angler's clothes are important in all kinds of fishing, and especially in fishing for carp, which have keen eyesight, and can detect the presence of a fisherman at a distance. According to some authorities, a fish cannot alter the focus of its eye, and is thus short-sighted. It may be true that fish cannot see *clearly* for a very long distance, but they can see enough to alarm them at distances up to fifty yards or more. It is therefore desirable to wear drab clothes; army battle-dress is an excellent outfit. Even so, the carp-fisher should take advantage of every bit of cover available, and if none exists, an artificial screen made of twigs and small branches stuck into the bank is an advantage. Obviously it is important to avoid being silhouetted against the sky or any light background.

Anyone who has had army training must know how conspicuous a man's face is, even a long way off, both by day and night, and particularly in moonlight. Commandos used to blacken their faces to overcome this: snipers used camouflaged veils. I think something of this kind would be an advantage to carp-fishers, and I suggest a bee-keeper's veil, which is very light and may also keep mosquitoes at bay. I suppose most fishermen would think it undignified to use the obvious camouflage—mud. I suffer a great deal of leg-pulling from fellow-anglers over some of my antics and devices, but I catch quite a lot of carp.

Footwear is important, too. Unless the banks are exceptionally difficult, crêpe-soled shoes are best, though for early morning walks through wet grass, gumboots are perhaps advisable. Whatever the boot, a pair of old socks worn outside them will help to soften the tread and avoid one causing vibrations of the bank. Carp are incredibly sensitive to people walking about: even the lightest tread can alarm fish a hundred yards away. If fish are to be stalked —and they *can* be—the pace should be that of a snail, and preferably done on all fours. Obviously all unnecessary movement should be avoided, and the length of one's shadow, especially when the sun is low, remembered.

It is generally believed nowadays that, while fish can feel vibrations, they are unable to hear noises. I am not sure that this is correct. Not long ago, I was fishing in a Bedfordshire lake. Sixty yards out from the bank there was a large shoal of basking rudd. Ten yards behind me a car was parked, and the owner slammed the door. Almost simultaneously there was a great splash as every rudd bolted. There are many other instances, which indicate that it is unwise to talk loudly or make other noises while fishing, especially for carp.

I always do better with carp and with chub when fishing

alone; even when my companion is a skilful angler, the
catch is hardly ever as great as when I am unaccompanied.
Whether this is due to extra vibrations, to a double chance
of being seen, or to their having overheard our conversation,
I cannot say. I think that it is best to play safe and make
as little noise as possible.

Carp Make You Think

The carp, being the most difficult of all freshwater fish
to catch, is not a favourite with the majority of anglers. In
recent years, however, the number of carp-fishers has begun
to grow, and with it, the increase of knowledge, while one
hears of more and more waters being stocked with carp.
Its difficulty of capture is a spur to greater efforts and study,
and carp-fishers will feel well rewarded by the capture of
one or two big ones in a season; while the passing of a
whole season, or even several, without such reward will
cause no dismay.

Arthur Ransome says 'A man who fishes habitually for
carp has a strange look in his eyes. I have known several
and have even shaken hands respectfully with the man who
caught the biggest carp ever landed in England. He
looked as if he had been in heaven and in hell and had
nothing more to hope for from life. . . .'

I cannot detect any particularly strange look in the eyes
of my carp-fishing friends, but I do know that of all specialist
anglers, those who pursue carp are the most fanatical.
Carp-fishing has another effect, too. It makes a man think;
and in my experience a man who can catch carp will find
no difficulty in catching any other sort of fish.

Crucian Carp

Crucian Carp are in their habits representative of all the
carps which lack barbules, i.e. Crucians, Prussians and
Goldfish, uncoloured or otherwise. They seldom exceed
4½ lb. in weight and consequently there is no need to employ
stout tackle. None of these fish have the speed of the barbuled carp, but they are strong and dogged fighters, and
where they run to weights of 2 lb. and over, it is unwise to

use the very finest tackle, unless the water is completely free from weeds and snags. A line of 3 lb. or 4 lb. breaking-strain will be suitable, and hooks from size 14 to 10, sharp and fine in the wire, meet most cases.

Nothing stouter than the Avon-type roach-rod is necessary and an even lighter weapon can be used. Almost any reel will be found satisfactory, as these fish seldom make runs exceeding ten yards, and, though they are not slow, they lack the breath-taking speed of their larger relatives. The smaller sizes of fixed-spool reel are excellent, and so are the large diameter 'Flick-em' patterns.

Crucians seldom, if ever, feed on the surface and must be sought on the bottom, though sometimes a bait fished dangling a foot or so off the bottom will catch these fish. Generally speaking, however, bottom-fishing is the most effective method. And here we have to consider a peculiarity of these fish. They have a habit of picking up bait and remaining perfectly still with it in their mouths. Sometimes, they will suck in and blow out a bait a dozen times before deciding to take it or leave it alone, and without causing even the lightest float to as much as tremble.

Many are the times I have attempted to withdraw my tackle after a long spell during which I never saw the float move, only to find a Crucian attached. For this reason the tackle should be as light and sensitive as conditions of wind and drift will permit. On a still, breathless morning or evening, a tiny antenna float made from balsa and bamboo, with a single small shot to cock it, will be the best thing to use. The depth should be most carefully plumbed (with as little disturbance as possible) and the float adjusted so that the bait and six inches of gut (or nylon) but *not* the shot, are on the bottom. This tackle is very sensitive but subject to drift; if drift becomes a nuisance, either a heavier lead and float will have to be chosen, or an anchoring device used. This consists of a forked stick with a bit of old line and a stone tied to the end, arranged so that the forked stick, when thrown into the water, cocks like a float with the fork above water, and the stone on the bottom. This device is put in an appropriate place so that one can cast over it, then when one's float has cocked, the line above the float can be lifted into the fork. This avoids the effect of drift, but of course one must take the risk of a fish going round the 'anchor.'

The movements of the float, if any, are usually no more than a series of trembles, and it is very difficult to know when to strike. I seldom do so at the first movement, but it is no use waiting for the float to go right under or run away. Sometimes, one observes a sort of 'settling down' movement and a strike then usually connects. Sometimes the float rises a fraction, and this is also a good opportunity to strike. But often there are just one or two tremors repeated at intervals; when this occurs, I usually strike at the third, a completely arbitrary measure which succeeds often enough for me to continue to practise it. I always strike gently when withdrawing my tackle whether I have observed a bite or not.

Of course, there are many occasions when Crucians bite quite definitely, after a few preliminary quivers the float goes decisively down and away. But very often one gets only the 'niggling' type of bite, and has to make the best of it. Ground-baiting for Crucians can follow the same lines as for small roach; cloud, with plenty of feed in it, is as effective as anything. All the baits which are good for still-water roach will tempt Crucians, paste, gentles and small redworms being the chief ones; perhaps of the three, the small redworm found in compost heaps is the most deadly, fished on a No. 12 or No. 10 Crystal hook. Flake is an excellent bait in some waters. Baits should not be large; a ball of paste the size of a pea, or two gentles, are satisfactory. I have never caught a Crucian carp on potato, and I suspect it is less useful for Crucians than it is for their big brothers. My best 'carp' of the 'barbule-less' category was an uncoloured goldfish weighing exactly three pounds, and it took a small redworm.

Crucians are found in all kinds of waters from large lakes to tiny farm ponds, though in the latter they seldom grow big. Weather conditions affect them in much the same way as their larger cousins; in summer, morning, evening, and night are therefore the best times to fish in normal weather. They hibernate in winter and are seldom caught then.

Sometimes it is possible to catch fish after fish, and where they run to a good size, they provide splendid sport on fine tackle. But perhaps the most enjoyable sport with Crucians is when on a still summer evening they bite at intervals of half an hour or so, and you can sit with a couple of friends, all fishing in the same pitch and restfully discussing angling matters, and giving attention only to your tackle when someone says 'You've got a knock!' For it never really *matters* whether you catch Crucians or not, somehow. A 2½ lb. roach looks a big fish, but a 2½ lb. Crucian is only a jolly, chubby little carp on which you've played a practical joke by catching him; and when you put him back, he scampers off full of beans. Like the Water Vole and the Little Owl, he attempts, but can never achieve, dignity.

Even when I first wrote the foregoing chapter I was careful not to recommend 'parboiled' potatoes, as the majority of angling textbooks do, as a bait for carp. I said boiled potatoes and I meant boiled potatoes; potatoes boiled to the stage where they would be considered well enough cooked for human consumption. I hate to think of how many good carp have been missed on the strike because the parboiled potato bait was altogether too hard to allow the hook to penetrate. When a boiled potato has lain in cold water for some time it becomes much harder than it would have been had it remained out of water, and it is hardly possible to boil potatoes to be used as bait for carp, too much, unless they are actually falling apart. Admittedly soft potatoes are very easily cast off the hook, but it is not necessary to use a treble hook to avoid this. Instead, having drawn the end of the line through the potato with a baiting needle, and tied the hook to it, stick a good sized flat piece of breadcrust on the bend of the hook. Then slide the potato down so that it rests against the breadcrust. If you are very meticulous you will cut the bottom of the potato off flat with a knife so that it rests snugly against the crust which, in case I have not explained it clearly, goes on the hook just as does the piece of crust in the illustration showing how to bait with crust and paste. A hook so baited with boiled potato will not only allow longer and stronger casting without risk of losing the bait, but will come to rest just like the crust and paste bait with the line coming away underneath with attendant advantages. In the event of small fish nibbling away the crust, nothing is lost; the potato will still be there and the sight of the hook projecting from it does not seem to worry the carp. Remember, however, that if there are small fish that worry the bait, you are likely to have a few pulls and little runs until the crust has been whittled away. You will have sense enough not to strike at these.

FURTHER NOTES

Developments in carp-fishing since 1953 have been less extensive than many present-day carp-fishers claim. We read nowadays of the novelty of long-range carp-fishing; a perusal of the following chapter will reveal that in 1952 I caught two carp, of 22¾ and 17½ lb., in one day at Dagenham, at a range of 60 yards or more, and many more were taken subsequently by that method from the same lake in the years following.

Even in the late 1930s we caught carp from various waters at considerable ranges, though we never cast farther than was necessary, and don't now.

We also read about the use of fine tackle as being of recent innovation. Way back in 1930, Albert Buckley used 3 lb. tackle to set a new record at Mapperley and until about 1950 the general opinion held by anglers was that nothing much stouter could be used, or there would be no bites.

Members of the Becontree and District Angling Club have a splendid record of 20 lb. carp taken on line between 3–6 lb. b.s., and 'BB.', Pete Thomas and I have always used 5–8 lb. lines where conditions allowed. So there is nothing new about relatively fine tackle for carp-fishing.

The real advances that have been made in carp-fishing since this book first appeared, are in new baits and in winter-fishing. The vast increase in the numbers of anglers fishing for carp nowadays has resulted in the fish being taught much more rapidly which baits are best to avoid, and this has led to many different things being tried. It has been found that in many waters, baits high in protein are favoured by carp. I must therefore add to the list of baits I gave in the first edition, the following: pastes made of breadpaste mixed with fishpaste, bloater paste, herring roe (soft and hard), tinned pet foods of various kinds, sausage-meat, minced meat, minced liver, dried daphnia, tinned luncheon meat, boiled sausages or pieces of sausage; bunches of maggots, bunches of caddis grubs with or without cases; lobworms and slugs inflated to float by injecting air with a hypodermic syringe; marshmallows; trout pellets, as used by fish farmers; crabmeat worked into breadpaste, and minced chicken or rabbit guts, also made into paste.

High protein trout pellets have proved very effective. The sinking variety is used as received for ground-bait; the hook bait is made by soaking pellets, pounding them up and mixing the result with equal parts of brown bread paste. A balanced bait can be made up with this paste, plus brown bread crust.

Tinned sweet corn, used for pre-baiting, groundbait and hook bait, with 3 to 6 grains on a suitable hook, is another deadly carp bait.

None of these baits has any magic properties. What is important is that carp can learn. They learn what is good to eat and they learn what is not. If you owned a carp lake where you allowed no one to fish, and if you fed the carp every day with any of the things I have mentioned, you would find that within a few months the carp were willing to take food from your hands, a point which those who argue that there is no advantage in ground-baiting would do well to consider.

If then you allowed carp-fishing, numbers of carp would be caught, but I doubt if more than a few weeks would pass before the fish became as difficult to catch as they are in any other carp water.

Experiments in Holland have shown that a carp caught on rod and line and returned to the water, becomes about eight times less likely to be caught again, than one that has never been caught. Remember, this is an overall average; we all know that there are individual fish, probably exceptionally stupid ones, that are caught several times in a season.

The value of a wide range of baits lies in the power it gives to the angler to offer the carp something they have not learned to avoid.

Not only in carp-fishing but in every field of angling, we find anglers following bait and fly fashions like sheep. They hear that good catches are being made on a particular bait, so that becomes the one they feel they must use. The truth is that any bait that has had considerable success, especially with carp, often is the very one to be avoided. If you can't bring yourself to eschew, say, potato, on a carp water where already in the season thirty or forty carp have been taken on that bait, then at least put out two baits, on two outfits, one potato and one something different.

When this book was first written, I said that for practical purposes the first frosts of October mark the end of the carp

season.   As far as my own fishing is concerned, that remains
true, because I go fishing for pleasure.   I am not willing to sit
freezing by a carp lake in winter, with much poorer chances
of catching fish than I would have in summer and autumn,
when I could be catching chub, dace, roach, perch, grayling
or pike, all species that are at their best from the end of
October until the end of January, and continue to provide
good sport till the end of the coarse-fishing season.   I am
not one of those who think that carp are the only fish worth
catching.   Those who are, may wish to continue carp-fishing
into the winter months, and this they can do with sufficient
hope of success to sustain them against the weather.

A good deal of winter carp-fishing by these dedicated
people has shown that there is a very wide variation between
one water and another in respect of winter carp-fishing
results.   The factors governing this are unknown, but I
would rate the best chances as being in lakes where carp do
not grow to the largest size, and where not only they but
other species of fish such as roach, rudd and bream are
numerous.   In other words, fish where there are plenty of
carp of medium size, plenty of other fish, and not too much
natural food in summer.

I am also inclined to think that the prospects are better in
hard-bottomed rather than muddy-bottomed lakes; and if
there are natural springs, so much the better.

Some hours taking temperatures with a thermometer on
the end of a line should yield information about whether a
lake has a few warmer-than-average spots; failing any such,
fish where, in summer, there were dense weed-beds or beds
of lilies that have now died off.   Use smallish baits, made
up very soft in the case of pastes, and fish sensitively.   It may
be desirable to use a float, because carp don't dash off with
a bait in winter so readily as they do in summer.

Talking of floats reminds me that in modern conditions,
with very heavy fishing pressure, the case for float-fishing for
carp is much stronger than it was when this book was first
written.   Mike Oyez, who runs his own carp lakes near
Hayes, is a strong advocate of float-fishing and uses float
tackle with considerable success.   As he rightly points out, a

float will always tell you when you have a bite, whatever the direction in which the carp is moving. A float can also tell you, more often than not, when a carp has taken your bait but is not going anywhere. For night-fishing, a float having a beta-light top can be both effective and fascinating to watch—this is described in the notes following chapter VI.

Much has been written about so-called 'twitch' bites. It is quite common when legering, or fishing floatless, leadless tackle, to see tiny pulls, tweaks and twitches on the line, and by striking at such indications, carp may sometimes be hooked. Whether to strike at these movements or to wait for a definite run, is a difficult decision to take.

In the first place, if the water you are fishing holds numbers of bream, roach, rudd or small tench and crucians, the probability is that twitches and tweaks are produced by small fish nibbling at your bait. If you strike at every twitch, you'll lose a lot of baits, you'll reduce the time your baited hook is where a carp can find it, and you may scare the carp as well.

Even if a carp is producing the twitches, you're never sure when the bait is in his mouth. He may be routing about near the bait and in so doing, moving the line; or he may be taking the bait into his mouth and immediately ejecting it. If you strike prematurely, you'll scare the fish.

You don't even learn much by striking successfully at twitches. So you hooked a carp; how do you know whether, had you waited, you would have got a positive run or not?

I don't pretend to know the complete answer, but I'll tell you what I do myself. If my line starts to twitch, I engage the reel pick-up and raise the rod slowly. If I feel positive resistance, I tighten very firmly. If I feel no resistance, I lower the rod again, into its rest, wind in the slack and wait to see if the twitches recommence. Quite often, the effect of raising the rod is to trigger off a positive run, or at any rate the start of one, and when that happens it is almost impossible to fail to hook the fish. It works equally well with bream, tench and other species.

Carp often take a bait into their mouths and then eject it immediately, and the angler seldom knows anything about

Chris Yates with his great 43lb 12oz carp, taken at Redmire Pool

(*above*) Fred J. Taylor lands a 5lb tench—with Joe Taylor watching and Ken Taylor officiating with the net; (*below*) a brace of big tench taken from a gravel pit

what has happened.

Although the use of fine line increases the risk of breakage, there is clear evidence that it also increases the number of positive bites from carp. Why?

I think carp feel the line, and the stiffer it is, the more likely they are to eject the bait before the angler can strike.

Now for a little arithmetic!

The *strength* of a line increases as the square of the diameter; that is, a line twice as thick is *four* times as strong, for a given material.

The *stiffness* of a line increases as the fourth power of the diameter; that is, a line twice as thick is *sixteen* times as stiff.

Therefore, the *stiffness* of a line increases with the square of its *strength*; a line twice as strong is four times as stiff.

So, you see, a small increase in strength means a much greater increase in stiffness and, consequently, in the likelihood of a carp feeling the line and ejecting the bait because of it.

I am well convinced that fish can always see your line, however fine it may be. They aren't scared or put off by seeing it. It is the feel of it that they don't like—its stiffness is most unnatural. Natural filamentous things in the water are soft, not stiff.

There is, therefore, a good case for using soft, braided nylon or terylene line next to the hook, if not throughout. I often do so. My 44 lb. carp was taken on a braided nylon line, soft in texture, dyed green and whipped direct to the hook, and I have caught many other carp on braided lines, with no monofil involved whatever. Monofil is, however, better for long-casting and one's reel holds much more of it, for a given strength, than of braided line. It therefore seems to me sensible, for bottom-fishing for carp, and for tench when a strong line is needed, to use a braided hook-length 4–6 feet long. This can be attached to the hook by a spade-end knot and to the monofil running line by a 4-turn water knot. It facilitates pulling such a knot up snugly if the part of the monofil that is to form the knot is dipped in liquid PVC ('Vycoat') which is allowed to dry before the knot is tied. I find the most convenient method is to attach the braided line permanently to the running line as stated above, and then coat the knot with 'Vycoat' for additional security. The hook can be spade-end-knotted to the braided end at the waterside.

It is advisable to carry a few spare lengths of braided stuff, with their ends treated with 'Vycoat', in case you are snagged and have to break out.

CHAPTER V

BIG CARP

O N Monday, 23rd June, 1952, the second largest carp then ever caught in Britain was successfully landed. It weighed 28 lb. 10 oz., and the manner of its capture was as follows.

Peter Thomas and I had arrived at Redmire pool two days before. Three carp had been caught, of no great account, during these decidedly wet and windy days; but during the afternoon the wind veered from S.W. to N.W. and the sky cleared, the late afternoon and evening being sunny and warm. As the light failed the wind dropped, and we commenced fishing with the last light.

In spite of the warmth of the afternoon, the clear sky and wind direction warned us to expect a cold night. For this reason, not only did we don extra sweaters, but decided to fish the deep water from the dam at the foot of the lake. Here there was a strip of clear water about forty yards wide, flanked each side with dense weed-beds.

Our outfits were identical. Lines were 11 lb. b.s. perlon, to which No. 3 forged eyed hooks were tied. The reels were fixed-spool, each carrying 200 yards of line, and the rods were designed specially for carp.* As one cannot buy such rods I have to make them, and the rod Peter was using was one I had finished just in time for him to fish with on this occasion. It weighs 10 oz., lighter than the majority of roach-rods; but its 10 oz. are distributed where they will do most good, in ten feet of good sound split-bamboo. As usual, no floats or leads of any kind were used. The bait was plain bread paste.

Now I must introduce Peter Thomas. He is, among other things, one of the best carp-fishers in England. When he was fourteen years old, he caught a carp of 14 lb., and

* Mark IV, of course, now made professionally and available to anyone.

he has been catching big ones ever since. His knowledge of carp is considerable, his casting a pleasure to watch, and his handling of a hooked fish is skilful past belief. If you look at his hands, you can, if you understand hands, see why. In my angling career I have met one or two men who by sheer skill can *master* a fish—can counter its every move with such speed and precision and exact appreciation of the strength of their tackle that it is brought to bank subdued, beaten, bewildered, but hardly *exhausted* at all. Peter can do this. If you have never caught a big carp, you may be inclined to say 'so could anyone, with an 11 lb. b.s. line and a No. 3 hook.'

Just consider. The gape of a No. 3 hook is about three-eighths of an inch. The gape of a No. 16 is about one-eighth. Would a No. 16 be a big hook on which to catch a 7 lb. fish? Would a line with a breaking-strain of 1 lb. be overstrong for a 2½ lb. fish, in weedy water?

At dusk, then, we cast out our lines. At midnight, Peter had a bite. His rod nearly leapt from the rest; he struck, but the fish had evidently felt the check and ejected the bait. From then on, until dawn, the baits lay undisturbed. Occasionally a great carp would roll on the surface, far out. Once or twice we heard slobberings and sucking noises from the weeds. Eventually the sun rose, and, shining through the gaps in the trees, sent golden-orange beams across the lake, from which misty vapour began to rise. Moorhens called to one another across the lake, and away in the distance we heard a curlew call—a perfect carp-fisher's dawn; but still the lines hung limp and lifeless from the rod-points.

At a little before 4 a.m., Peter wound up his line, re-baited with a piece of paste of pheasant-egg size, and made a long cast of some 40 yards to the edge of the weed-bed on his left. The ripples spread and died away. Said Peter, who had had some four hours' sleep during the last forty-eight hours, 'I'll give it five minutes more, and then I'm going to get my head down.'

At exactly 4 a.m., his line moved, and began to run out, very slowly and steadily. He engaged the pick-up of his reel, looked to see that the line was in no way fouled, waited until it drew taut and then struck with a long, sweeping stroke well back over his shoulder. His rod took on its battle-curve and, as the line began to swing to the right, I knew he was on to a fish. As yet its pull was moderate and its speed dead slow; but as it moved diagonally to the right and out into the lake, the curve in the rod increased. Then, suddenly, the fish surfaced with a tremendous lashing of tail; and as Peter reduced pressure, made three short but irresistible rushes which made the reel scream. The rod was now swung well over to the right to turn the fish, which, however, turned in its tracks and made for the weed-bed at the edge of which it had first felt the hook. Now came the testing-time for the angler, for once the fish had reached its goal it must have won free. But it was not to be. Every possible ounce of pressure was applied; the fish was swung off course and turned into the open water, and in the process twenty precious yards of line were gained.

Foiled in its first attempt to gain sanctuary, the fish tried again. It was on the bottom now; clouds of bubbles came to the surface, but try as it would, the pressure defeated it; and suddenly it gave up the attempt, surfaced, rolled, and set off across the strip of open water for the weeds on the opposite side. It was then that I knew that, save for the unforeseen, the battle was as good as won.

Until then I had been a passive spectator. Now I picked up the big, deep landing-net and put it in the water, for though the fish was still twenty yards away, I judged it safer to have the net ready and still rather than allow the fish to see it enter the water.

Before the fish had won to within ten yards of its new objective, it was turned again. A dorsal fin broke surface, coming straight in. While it was yet ten yards from the bank, Peter stopped recovering line and backed. I kept low and still. Straight over the net came the fish; as I lifted, Peter dropped his rod-point and the fish dived into the mesh, head-first, as neatly as one could wish. Then the commotion began. A lashing of water rose almost to a roar; the net was almost dragged from my hands; but I hung on, and

Peter, having carefully leaned his rod against a bush, came to my aid, and by grasping the mesh below the frame with both hands, with Peter holding the handle, I was able to heave the fish ashore. We carried it fifty yards from the water before putting it down; eventually it was slid into a sack, the neck secured by a stout cord, and—after careful testing of the knots—lowered into the lake. We had guessed the weight at over 20 lb.; but it was not until much later in the day that we were able to borrow a spring balance which showed us that the fish was over $27\frac{1}{2}$ lb.

When properly weighed, it was found to tip the scale at 28 lb. 10 oz., as I have said.

A month later, I was fishing the same water again with Maurice Ingham. This is what happened.

During the evening of July 30th, Maurice prepared a new position with all the care of a general expecting an enemy assault. On his right was a big willow tree, some of its branches in the water, and beyond that, in shallow water, was a big bed of exceedingly tough pond-weed. A willow branch, which might impede the playing of a fish or casting in the dark, was lassoed and tied back out of the way. A landing-stage was made with a piece of corrugated iron left by providence of the farmer at the lakeside. And finally, Maurice put on thigh-boots for a reason which I was to learn later.

I was still at the same spot where I had hooked a monster that morning, some forty or fifty yards away on Maurice's left. In front of us both, fifty yards out, was a mass of growing weed against which the wind and drift had piled floating algae, flannel-weed and accumulated scum. Five yards short of this lay our baits in about seven feet of water.

These baits consisted of crust on the bend of the No. 3 hooks, with enough paste on the shank to cause the crust just to sink, the whole being about bantam's-egg size. Such a bait, carefully balanced by trial and adjustment, can be made to sink slowly and settle on a soft bottom or on thin flannel-weed without sinking into it. In addition, I had a second outfit, baited with a large crust, which hung straight below the rod-point in the usual margin-fishing style. Both Maurice and I had electric buzzers attached to the lines; but for the margin-fishing outfit I had to rely on the check on the little multiplier I was using on that rod.

At about 3 a.m., without previous warning, the check on this reel shrieked. I struck; there was a splash, a curious lack of resistance; then the line seemed to be leading into the grass at my feet. With the aid of a shaded electric torch I sorted the thing out—a great rat, fairly hooked in the mouth. Maurice, materializing out of the darkness like a ghost—he knows how to move about when he is carp-fishing—fetched it a clout with the handle of his knife, which killed it, then he melted into the darkness again. I put the margin-fishing outfit away.

At about 3.20 a.m., I heard Maurice's alarm go off. Apparently the fish had dropped the bait as I heard nothing more for a few minutes; then the buzzer went off again, was stopped, and a minute later cried out once more. I learned afterwards that there was a series of small pulls, which continued at intervals until 3.30 a.m., when the line began to run out steadily. At that time I was alert, waiting for what happened; the 'whoosh' of Maurice's rod, and the slash of his line upwards out of the water as he struck. Then he called 'Fish on!'

As I got to my feet there was a tremendous, thunderous splashing directly opposite me. I could see, dimly, white water and great ripples spreading along the banks. When I reached Maurice's position, I could not find him; then I heard him call, and could just see him, ten yards out into the lake. Then I saw the reason for the thigh-boots—he was between the fish and the willows, and in a position to scare it away should it attempt to get into the weed-bed on his right. But that was not enough. 'Go and get some big stones,' he said; and I went. It took me perhaps three minutes to find four or five in the dark, and back I came with them.

I did not know where the fish was then; Maurice told me afterwards that several times it tried to pass him and each time side-strain, combined with splashing, turned it back up the lake. My stones were not needed, the fish was now under control; but it seemed an age before Maurice's rod indicated that the fish was coming nearer. I could see the arc of the rod against the sky, but I waited with the net until Maurice said 'Lights!' Then I slid the net into the water—the corrugated iron saving me from wet feet—and switched on the big lamp.

The first thing I noticed was the line. It was festooned with flannel-weed like pennants at a Navy signalling session, and at the end rolled a great mirror carp. Not for long! Maurice had him over the net in short order. I hauled him to the side and got a grip on the net-mesh with both hands, pulling the whole bag of tricks up the bank and well away from the water's edge. Then I bit the monofil, and carried the net and fish over to where our tents were pitched, Maurice following with the lamp. There we removed the hook and weighed the fish roughly—just short of 25 lb. Later in the day the weight was found to be 24 lb. 12 oz., a grand fish and a well-deserved one, which was released to fight another day.

Two days later, Maurice and I went to Dagenham Lake. The lake is shallow and the bottom was covered with silk-weed about four inches deep. I knew that carp frequented the big bay at the upper end of the lake, which was disturbed by a light breeze.

I put a running lead on my 9-lb. line, stopped with a shot inches from the hook, which I baited with a biggish crust. The idea was that the crust would sit on the top of the silk-weed which smothered the bottom, but that line and lead would be concealed therein. With the big fixed-spool reel and Mark IV carp-rod it was easy to throw this well out, about sixty yards from the bank, right into the middle of the bay which ended on my right with a fringe of willows; on my left was the open lake, with its islands some 150 to 200 yards away.

I put the rod in its rests and attached a buzzer, then leaned back against the eight-foot almost vertical bank to watch Maurice's float. Nobody expects big carp to bite at midday, on August 1st, in hot sunshine, so that when the buzzer spoke, and line whipped out, at 1.5 p.m., I was

astonished, and said so. I banged in the pick-up of the
reel, and bearing in mind fish which had rid themselves of
the hook during the past few days, tightened up with as
much force as I thought the tackle would stand. And I
connected! Far out in the lake was something which could
pull—*was* pulling, going for the willows at the head of the
bay—and I was at the top of the bank without knowing
how I got there, and the rod was horizontal, and the side-
strain was telling as it always does, and the fish was turned
and headed out for the open lake.

I went along the bank after him, recovering line as I
could, and when he turned again he was much too far from
any danger-point ever to get to it. A little farther along,
some steps have been cut in the bank, and Maurice was at
the bottom of these with the landing-net. I went down as
far as the one above him and there the battle was fought out.
Twenty minutes it took, and every second of those twenty
minutes I expected the line to go slack as the hook came out
of yet another big one. But this time the hook held, and
at exactly 1.25 p.m., a tired fish came within reach of the
net; and I have never known Maurice Ingham need more
than one chance.

Shortly afterwards, bailiff Reg. Philpot arrived with a
great jug of tea; and he took the fish away to the club hut,
where it registered 22 lb. 12 oz., a common carp in fine
condition. Afterwards it was put into a large net, where
it was seen by several members before being returned to
grow bigger.

That was a lesson in how a breeze can cool and oxygenate
the water sufficiently to cause fish to feed, even under a
brilliant sun. The fact that the fish were feeding well was
confirmed by my catching another carp of 17½ lb. the same
afternoon, in the same spot.

On September 12th, 1952, Peter Thomas and I again
went to Redmire.

We left home in a downpour, but by the time we had
reached our destination the sky had cleared and the stars
were shining brightly. It was very cold indeed, but we
fished until about 2 a.m., when we noticed a bank of black

cloud coming from the north-west, and decided to pitch our tent before it began to rain again.

We chose a spot on the west side of the lake, in deference to a theory I have that when carp have been driven into deep water at night by falling temperature, they usually move out of it again in the early morning on the side which first catches the morning sunshine. Here we camped, pitching the tent with its open end about three yards from the water and directly facing it. Between the tent and the water's edge a large groundsheet was spread.

Looking across the lake, about a hundred yards wide at this point, we could see a line of trees, which appeared as black shadows. To the left, ten yards along the bank, was a clump of weeping willows, whose branches trailed in the water, and beyond them was the tough pond-weed, of which I spoke when describing the capture of Maurice Ingham's fish. This extended about twenty yards out into the lake, as did another bed of the same stuff on the right of our position. Beyond that, forty yards away, was the dam at the end of the lake, which runs at right angles to the bank from which we were fishing. Half-way along the dam were once some chestnut trees, which have long since been felled, but their stumps still live and a tangled mass of writhing roots trails in the water. Immediately to our right, on the bank from which we were fishing, was a mass of brambles hanging in the water and extending to the bottom, concealing an undercut bank hollowed-out to a depth of between three and four feet, a favourite haunt of moorhens and rats.

Having arranged our week-end home, we baited our hooks and cast out to the edge of the deep water, a few yards beyond the pond-weed; Peter's to the left and mine only a few yards to the right of where his bait landed. Both baits consisted of balanced paste and breadcrust on No. 2 hooks which had been carefully sharpened beforehand; mine was whipped direct to a 12 lb. b.s. plaited nylon line, of which I had 100 yards on a fixed-spool reel. Rods were the usual Mk. IV carp-rods, which have never failed us yet—ten ounces of hardened split-bamboo can be made to do surprising things. Electric buzzers were clipped to the lines between butt-rings and reels, and all was ready for the carp to bite; to attract them, mashed bread ground-bait was thrown out. By this time, the sky had clouded over completely, and instead of rain there was a decided increase in temperature, but the darkness was intense. I cannot remember ever being out on a blacker night. It was so dark that even the rats were less active than usual, and all I could see were the silhouettes of the trees opposite. The lake was completely still, its surface unbroken by either wind or the movements of fish; and so it remained, except for one heavy splash far out, and a brief spell of 'flipping' by very small fish on the surface, until some time between 4.30 a.m. and 5 a.m. About that time one of the buzzers sounded, and we were both at the rods at once.

'It's yours,' said Peter. I raised the back of my hand under the rod to feel if the line was being taken, and felt it creep slowly over the hairs, an eerie but satisfactory sensation. In went the pick-up; a pause to make sure the line had been picked up properly, and then I struck hard and far back. I encountered a solid but living resistance, and Peter, needing no telling that a fish was hooked, reeled up his line out of the way. I crouched so that I could see the curve of the rod against the sky—even that was difficult in the extreme darkness—and waited on events. I did not want a fresh lively fish brought too soon into the fifteen-yard wide channel between the weed-beds, and I determined that if possible the battle should be fought in the deep water beyond.

The fish moved slowly and solidly towards the dam. Every few seconds came a tremendous tug; it felt as if the rod had been struck by a sandbag. As the fish neared the dam, I remembered those chestnut roots. Four pounds or forty, it must not get among them, or all would be lost, so I increased pressure. At first it had no effect; then as I bent the rod more, the efforts of the fish became intensified. I knew only a few yards separated it from disaster, and hung on grimly. ·The rod bent as never before—I could feel the curve under the corks in my hand; but everything held for the two or three minutes that the fish continued to fight his way towards his refuge. Then, suddenly, he gave it up. He turned and forged into the weed-bed between me and the roots, and I was only just able to keep the line taut. Presently he stopped, and all was solid and immovable.

Peter said, 'Take it easy. Wait and see if he'll move.' I did. Nothing happened. I said, 'I'll try hand-lining.' Peter said, 'All right, but *take it easy*. That's a big fish, you don't want to lose it.'

I had no idea how big a fish it was. I knew it was a good one, but all I could think of then was: 'Maybe another 20-pounder—I hope!' I pulled off a couple of yards of line, so as to be able to get the rod up quickly if the fish bolted suddenly; then I pointed the rod straight at the fish and began tugging. The first few tugs made no impression; then came a frantic pull, up went the rod, and out went the fish into the deep water again. I let him go well out, and then tightened up firmly again, praying for him to move *left*; and he did. When he was opposite I gave him the butt and crammed on pressure to the limit; and in he came, grudgingly, pulling and boring every inch of the way, but always losing ground, until at last he came to the surface and rolled three or four yards out.

Peter was ready with the net, and as I drew the fish towards it, he switched on the electric lamp. We saw a great expanse of golden flank as the fish rolled. 'Common carp,' said Peter. The fish rolled again, then righted itself, and suddenly, with a last effort, shot towards me and to the right. I could do nothing to stop it, and to my horror it crashed through the fringe of trailing brambles; in the light of the lamp I could see the swirls as the fish tried to thrust even farther under; but though I put the rod-point under water and strained it as hard as I dare, nothing would shift the fish, which eventually settled down into an immovable sulk.

Peter climbed out to the edge of the overhang and put the big net, thong down, over the hole in the brambles where the fish had gone in. Then, feeling carefully down the line with his free hand, he reached the fish's nose and pulled it round, steering it into the net. I saw vaguely a commotion; then Peter began to lift. He stuck half-way and called for me to take his lamp. I slackened line, put down the rod, and went to his assistance. Once I had the lamp, he could grasp the mesh of the net, and with a tremendous heave he swung net and fish up and over the brambles and on to the bank.

We knelt side by side looking at it. I knew it was big, and suddenly it dawned on me it was more than that. It was tremendous! I cut a stick, notched its end, and with this Peter extracted the hook which was only lightly lodged in the roof of the mouth. Then we put the fish in a sack and lifted it on my spring balance, which goes up to 32 lb. The pointer came up against the stop with such a thump that we both knew at once that here was a new record; but we could tell no more; so we tied up the mouth of the sack and lowered it into the water.

Then we re-baited our hooks and cast out again. Peter went into the tent; but I knew I could never sleep, and sat smoking and thinking till dawn. It was then that I resolved that, record or no record, that fish should not be killed. Many, many times I had wondered what I should do if ever I caught a record carp; now I had to decide, and kill it I could not.

At about ten-thirty, I was able to telephone Mr. H. F. Vinall, curator of the aquarium at the London Zoo. To cut a long story short, a van containing a vast tub, and two good fellows, who gave up their Saturday afternoon for the purpose, came and fetched it; and it arrived alive and well. I asked that it should be accurately weighed on arrival, which was done, and the weight recorded at 44 lb. I thought the sack must have been included at first, but the matter was investigated, and it has now been established that the weight really was 44 lb. to the dot, without the sack or anything else.

It is now living in a large tank at the Zoo aquarium, and its photograph provides the frontispiece for this book.

CHAPTER VI

FISHING AT NIGHT

IN summer, conditions are often such that your best chance of catching a big fish is at night. Most anglers know this, but to the majority night-fishing is either untried or remains as a memory of discomfort and entanglement, with little to show for the trouble.

I do a good deal of night-fishing myself, mostly for big carp, and I can see how difficult it would be for novices to the game to be successful, unless they were given some advice on how to avoid the pitfalls. Once the difficulties have been overcome, night-fishing can not only provide wonderful sport, but can show the angler more of the country-side and the wild life which inhabits it than he will ever see in the daytime. Once a half-grown badger came to investigate my bag of boiled potatoes, and there are few outings on which I fail to observe something of interest besides the actual fishing.

At night there are all sorts of queer noises; bushes and trees look different and cast weird shadows; and my first piece of advice to the novice is to go with a friend on his first few night-fishing ventures. It seems ridiculous to say that a man can become very scared indeed at nothing during a night at the waterside if he is alone. Nevertheless, it is true, and there is a good reason behind it. It is not so many years ago in the history of the evolution of the human race that a man had plenty of cause to distrust the black pool of shadow cast by a bush; to be thoroughly alert to a rustle in the long grass; and to be frightened when he heard a twig snap in the undergrowth after dark. Those fears remain as deep-rooted instincts, forgotten completely in everyday life, but liable to come to the surface when one is alone on a night-fishing venture, and to send a man home at a smart pace. I am not ashamed to confess that there have been occasions when I have had to tell myself very firmly that there is nothing to be afraid of! So let the first venture or two be a two-man affair.

Next in order of importance is comfort. Even after a blazing hot day in summer the night can be very cold indeed, and the nocturnal angler should dress accordingly. If he goes clothed as he would be for fishing in January he will not be far wrong; and the addition of an old army blanket or rug which he can wrap round himself and pull right over his head and ears will prove a blessing on nine nights out of ten. Even better is a small tent, if it can be pitched right at the waterside.

Remember that it is inadvisable to walk about when night-fishing, and take care to choose somewhere to sit which will remain comfortable during a long spell. I like, if it is possible, to use a cushion on a groundsheet rather than a stool or basket. The lower one's eyes, the more one can see at night, and if a tree or part of the bank can be used as back-rest the night can be passed with far less fatigue. I have a rucksack which makes a good back-rest, but a special one of wood and canvas is easy enough to devise.

Like the match-angler, the night-angler should see that everything he is likely to want is within reach of where he sits, and that it can be found without showing a light; 9 p.m. to 4 a.m. is a long time, and in addition to tackle, bait, etc., it is important to have plenty of food and at least two vacuum flasks filled with something hot.

You must choose a suitable pitch for night work. A spot which is a good one in daylight may be practically unfishable by night. The first essential is that the bottom should be sound and free from snags. There should be as little in the way of weeds and lily-pads in the vicinity as possible, and the position of what there is should be well memorized. Avoid fishing near overhanging or other branches in which your tackle may be accidentally caught.

Tackle for night work will, of course, depend on the species of fish sought, but it is always advisable to use something a little stronger than one would use in the daytime. It is a good thing to have a really big landing-net, because it is best to land a fish without showing a light, if possible; and the big net makes things much easier. Of course, if you hook a really big fish, you should not hesitate to use a powerful flash-lamp to assist in landing·it; but smaller fish can usually be netted by putting the big net under the disturbance they create when lifted to the surface.

It is desirable to have two lamps; one a small shaded one, giving just enough light to enable one to unhook a fish and re-bait. This should be kept turned away from the water, and the dimmer it is, the less it will affect the angler's night-vision. The other lamp cannot be too powerful. Mine is like a young searchlight, but I only use it when there is no doubt that I have something extra big at the end of my line—something big enough to compensate for possibly not getting any more bites that night.

You can use many methods at night; but for the majority of coarse fish some form of ledger tackle is by far the most satisfactory; this need not involve the use of lead. Float-tackle can be used, if you like, for roach and rudd, which do not seem to be afraid of lights. I have never yet seen a satisfactory luminous float, and for these fish a white-topped one, with the light of a lamp directed on to it, is best. Most fish, however, are scared by lights, and when fishing for them at night it is necessary to have some other bite-warning device. You cannot rely on hearing the check of the reel, and in the case of a fixed-spool reel there is no check to hear when the reel is set 'free.' Rotating-drum reels are very liable to overrun and tangle, even when the check is 'on.'

One warning device consists of a piece of silver paper twisted round the line between butt-ring and reel; line is pulled off until the paper is about six feet from the rod. If a fish goes off with the bait, the silver paper moves towards the rod, and even when it is too dark to see, the paper can be heard rustling across the ground. The best sort of silver paper is one with a fine pattern. It reflects every bit of light available, and on very few summer nights is it invisible. Another method, applicable to fixed-spool reels, is to wind in line after casting until it is reasonably taut, then place the rod in a rest and lean a light, white-painted or silver-paper-covered stick against the line—one end rests on the line and the other on the ground. The pick-up on the reel is then disengaged. If a bite occurs, the stick falls to the ground. You should always spread a dark mackintosh or rubber sheet behind your rod-rest, not only to render these indicators more visible but to avoid the line tangling with twigs or grass.

Perhaps the best of all warning devices is an electric buzzer, complete with battery and switch, in a small box. Contacts are attached to the rod-rest, and to one of them is fixed a length of springy wire, to form an antenna, a little offset from the centre of the rest. Round this wire the line is placed. When it tightens, the antenna wire is pulled over—the least pull will move it, the principle being that of the well-known dough-bobbin. Pulling over the antenna closes the contacts, which are connected to the box containing the buzzer by a length of flex, and the buzzer sounds. It continues to sound only while the line is being pulled and gives you a good idea of what is happening. With a fixed-spool reel, it can tell you if a fish is running fast or slow, because as the line comes off the spool it moves from side to side, causing the buzzer to emit an intermittent bzz-bzz-bzz. The shorter the interval between the buzzes, the faster the line must be running out.

You must not expect warning devices of this kind to wake you in time to hook a fish if you fall asleep, but they do relieve you of the intense concentration needed to watch a visual indicator in very little light.

Casting in darkness is not easy, and it pays to make trial casts in daylight and tie a bit of silk or something similar to your line so you can be sure you have cast the right distance after dark. You can obtain your direction from silhouettes on the opposite bank, or the horizon. If you take your fishing as seriously as you should, you will not grudge time spent in the dark at home, learning to pick up your rod swiftly and efficiently without your line getting tangled or caught up where it shouldn't be.

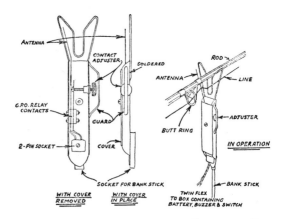

ROD-REST WITH CONTACTS AND "ANTENNA"
FOR NIGHT-FISHING

It is surprisingly difficult at night to tell how far or in what direction a hooked fish has gone, unless it leaps or surfaces. Experience will tell you what the duration of the noise of your ratchet check, when a fish is taking line, means in terms of the distance he has run, while by crouching you can learn his direction by watching the curve of your rod against the sky. If there are weeds or snags it is vital that you should know where your fish is and which way it is going.

The ability to see in semi-darkness varies with different people; but anyone who is going to take night-fishing seriously can improve his night-vision considerably by never going out into sunshine without wearing dark sun-glasses, and by avoiding any kind of daytime fishing which involves watching float or fly in brilliant light. At night, the less one uses lights the more efficient one's eyes become, and the angler who perseveres without lights will soon need them very little.

Finally, do not expect to be a successful night-fisher if you try it after a long spell of daytime fishing. You cannot expect to be successful at a method which is undoubtedly more difficult, if you are dog-tired. Try and get in some sleep during the afternoon or evening before you set out, and do not stay fishing all day after fishing all night. Angling is done for pleasure.

Since the first edition of this book was published, numerous attacks on the use of electric bite-alarms have appeared in the angling Press. The objectors, none of whom could have had experience of night-fishing for carp, if for any other fish, all seemed to be under the impression that the purpose of an electric bite-alarm is to permit an angler to go to sleep and to awaken him in time to deal with a biting fish. This, it is said, is unsportsmanlike.

I suppose that to most people, the ideas of night and sleep are inseparable and they are unable to imagine a night-angler not wishing to sleep, but in fact the experienced carp-angler, when he decides to stop fishing and sleep, finds it difficult to do so. He will most certainly never do so while his bait is in the water, for no bite-alarm will rouse him in time to deal with the majority of bites from what is, after all, the fastest of all our fish, while should he fail to awake, he knows he will probably lose his rod, reel, line, hook and all.

The electric bite-alarm serves the single purpose of indicating a bite. It demands as much knowledge and skill and wakefulness as any other bite-indicator—such as a float.

FURTHER NOTES

Proprietary electric bite-alarms are now available. I have come to prefer a small electric bell to a buzzer, as its noise cannot be confused with any of the natural noises one hears at the waterside after dark.

In addition, I have come to choose more and more a device called the Glowbobbin. This is made of clear plastic and contains a beta-light, which glows brightly, without the aid of batteries, for about twenty years. It can be clipped on the line between butt ring and reel, but where fast runs are expected it is better to fold a strip of PVC over the line, and push the ends of this between the jaws of the clip on the Glowbobbin. Then the line can run freely even if the Glowbobbin goes up to the butt ring.

The comfort of the angler has been revolutionized since this book was written. Warm clothing and bed-chairs, with vast umbrellas, make it much less of an ordeal to spend a night out of doors. Unfortunately, the popularity of still-water fishing generally and of carp-fishing particularly, has led to practices that virtually ensure failure to catch fish. I have visited more than one lake, only to leave early in the night because there were pressure-lamps lighting up the banks like a fairground, portable radios blaring programmes from several stations; bonfires burning, people flashing powerful electric lamps, shouting and tramping back and forth. Not only does this sort of thing destroy any chance of catching carp and seriously reduce the possibility of catching other kinds of fish; it is also apt to annoy local residents and lead to the loss of the fishing rights.

Very recently I have been experimenting with floats having built-in beta-lights. A beta-light rated at about 500 micro-lamberts, about 5 millimetres thick and 25 millimetres long, is ideal for the purpose; it can be easily seen at up to 30 yards.

The beta-light is inserted in a clear plastic tube and located there by pieces of balsa; one constitutes the float body, and can be of any length and thickness, according to what weight the float is required to carry. The other piece of balsa sits above the beta-light when the float is cocked, and must be painted black. The float is shotted so that nearly all the beta-light is above the surface of the water.

The purpose of the black top is to allow the float to be seen in all lighting conditions. As the light decreases in the evening, a time comes when it approximates to that emitted by the beta-light; the internal coating of the beta-light is then illuminated equally both from without and within, and is consequently invisible, on the principle of a grease-spot photometer. It is therefore necessary to provide a black top to the float, which remains visible until the light has decreased

to the point where the beta-light exceeds the natural light
and can be easily seen.

From then on, watching the float is fascinating. With a
calm surface, usually found on still waters from dusk on-
wards, one sees not only the beta-light but also its reflection,
in a continuous vertical line.

When the float is drawn down, this vertical line shortens at
twice the speed at which the float is sinking, since if the float
sinks by, say, a quarter of an inch, its reflection shortens by
the same amount, and the vertical line that you are looking
at decreases by half an inch.

If the float rises to a 'lift' bite, the vertical line at first
separates into two, with a gap in the middle; as the float rises
still further, and begins to keel over, the two vertical lines
assume an angle to one another of less than 180°; the more
the float tilts, the smaller the angle becomes.

How a Beta-Light float behaves after dark:
a. When the float is pulled down, not only does its top apparently decrease in
   length, but so too does the reflection.

b. When the float rises, a gap appears in the bright vertical line; as the float
   heels over, so too does the reflection.

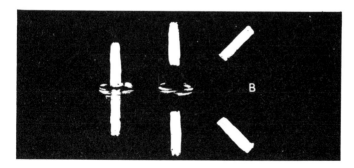

It is true to say that one obtains a better indication of the nature of a bite from a beta-light float used in the dark, than from an ordinary float used in daylight.

At the time of writing, the only beta-light floats made commercially incorporate beta-lights that are inadequate, and only visible at very short range. The cost of beta-lights increases with the brightness and no doubt this explains the inadequacy of the floats now on sale; but to my mind, a float too dim to be practical is expensive at any price; it is worth paying whatever price may be necessary, to ensure a float that really works.

It is not difficult to avoid loss; one simply uses a hook-length that is some 30–50 per cent weaker than the main line, combined with a thoroughly firm and reliable means for attaching the float.

CHAPTER VII

TENCH

THE tench is found in the majority of English ponds and lakes. It is an extremely handsome fish, varying in colour from dark green to deep copper-bronze, according to the locality. The fins are usually dusky in colour, almost black, but in some waters, especially flooded chalk-pits, tench are caught with brilliant brassy-gold sides, white bellies and red fins, while a rare variety known as the Vermilion Tench has greenish sides and a vermilion-orange belly. Whether it is a distinct variety or the result of environment I do not know, but it is a most striking fish. The famous Thornville Royal Tench mentioned in Daniel's *Rural Sports* had this coloration, and I always thought this was due to its unusual surroundings until I was fortunate enough to see a live Vermilion Tench caught in Bedfordshire; the only mystery remaining about this famous fish now is how a fish having the length and girth of a 30 lb. carp could weigh so little!

There is also, of course, that well-known variety, the Golden Tench, yellow-gold with a few black spots, but this is seldom met with except in aquaria.

The tench has a reputation for sliminess, but although it is undoubtedly well-covered with slime, and very slippery to handle, it does not readily part with its slime, and one can handle tench more easily than bream.

Tench grow to a good size, and specimens weighing as much as twelve pounds may exist in some lakes. There are probably more record-breaking tench waiting to be caught than any other fish for it needs very heavily-weeded waters if it is to reach great size, and as it is an extremely powerful fish, this makes it difficult to land even when hooked.

Feeding Habits

It used to be thought that tench were exclusively bottom-feeders; but while they certainly do most of their feeding there, it has now been discovered that on warm nights the fish are at the surface a great deal, and large specimens have been caught on floating crusts designed to catch carp. Further experience is needed before a reliable technique for dealing with surface-feeding tench can be laid down, but the fact that they sometimes do feed at the top should be remembered. Mr. J. G. Roberts tells me that he has caught many large tench fishing at night with floating crusts.

In hot summer weather tench can sometimes be caught on a bait fished at midwater, or allowed to sink very slowly, especially on heavily fished waters. A fuller explanation of this is given in Michael Shephard's book *Come and Fish*.

For the most part, however, it is on the bottom that one expects to catch tench. There is no difficulty in finding where they are feeding at bottom, for as they probe about they send up characteristic bubblings consisting of very fine bubbles indeed—'needle-bubbles,' I have heard them called. These bubbles are easily recognized, and once seen will never be forgotten. They vary very much in volume, no doubt according to the type of bottom and the volume of natural gases contained in it.

Like carp and bream during summer weather, tench feed mostly in the late evening, through the night and in the early morning, except in shallow lakes where the chilling on clear nights may cause them to cease feeding during the hours of actual darkness. Unlike carp and bream, they do not probe very deeply into the bottom and therefore do not stir up much mud, so that, apart from seeing the fish themselves, the angler must look out for the strings of bubbles. Early morning reconnaissance in hot weather will usually reveal the whereabouts of their feeding-grounds, which are seldom far from weed-beds. Tench like being near bulrushes, those clumps of tall, dark-green, circular-section stalks found in most lakes and slow-flowing rivers. Perhaps some kind of insect or organism, which they eat, lives on or in these bulrushes; perhaps the fish like a gravelly bottom, the only place where these bulrushes will grow. Whatever the reason, the fish are very often found in numbers wherever clumps of bulrushes are growing.

It is often necessary to prepare a pitch for tench-fishing, and one of their peculiarities is that dragging operations, so far from alarming them, have a definite attraction. The use of a double-sided rake drag does more to attract tench than any amount of ground-baiting, and anglers commonly hook big tench within a few minutes of having dragged a pitch. Dragging should be done thoroughly and a patch at least ten yards square cleared of weed.

Effects of Vibration and Temperature

Like all bottom-feeding fish, tench are very sensitive to vibration, and while the extreme precautions necessary in carp-fishing may not be quite so important for tench, nothing is lost by approaching a tench-pitch carefully, keeping out of sight, and walking about on the bank as little as possible. It may seem curious that a fish that takes no alarm at dragging operations will flee at a footfall, but it is so.

Although tench are sometimes caught in the middle of the day, especially in slow rivers, in lakes it is not usually very profitable to fish for them on the bottom after 10 a.m. or before 7 p.m. in hot, calm summer weather. They are like carp in their reactions to temperature and the amount of dissolved oxygen in the water, and windy conditions or rain will drive them into deeper water where they may continue to feed all day. Like carp, tench can be caught provided the water temperature *somewhere* in a lake is not too high or too low, and when they refuse to oblige in their usual spots they must be sought elsewhere. Since they are a much smaller species than carp, they take less time to digest a meal; and are thus easier to catch if you can find out where they are; like carp they feed little in water below about 60° F. or above 70° F.

Because really cold weather causes them to hibernate, the end of October marks the end of tench-fishing in still waters, and often it becomes fruitless some weeks before that. In rivers, of course, tench are taken quite often in winter, but in ponds and lakes the chances of catching one then are slender.

Tench have a reputation for being capricious, though I have not found them so. Temperature influences their feeding, but provided its effect is understood, it should not prove difficult to catch them in fair-sized lakes with hard bottoms. It is where they find the bulk of their food in the mud rather than in the weeds that they become difficult to catch. They then become confirmed 'bubblers,' like carp of that habit, and they are equally difficult to tempt. Experiments on the lines suggested for 'bubbling' carp might produce results.

Tackle

Choose tackle to suit the water you are fishing. In open water, of course, fine tackle may be used, 3 lb. b.s. line and cast. But tench are seldom found in open waters, and most good pitches have weeds or other obstructions within ten or twelve yards of where the tackle is to lie. Although they are not given to making long runs, a good fish finds little difficulty in covering fifteen yards or so, and you have to use gear capable of checking it and steering it out of danger. To be on the safe side, where weeds are bad and tench run up to 4 lb. or more, the tackle may well be of 6 lb. breaking-strain throughout. Once a tench manages to get into the weeds it nearly always succeeds in freeing itself: how the fish unhooks itself and transfers the hook to the thickest and strongest weed-stalk in the patch I don't know, but nine times out of ten it does, and Dr. Lewis Smith's advice to slacken line on a weeded fish, so effective with chub, is not, in my experience, of much use for tench.

While I do not myself use a long rod for tench-fishing, being content with something of ten or eleven feet, there is a case for using a longer rod, especially where the pitch is a smallish area cleared from the middle of a bed of weeds or lilies. It is easy enough to advocate the dragging or clearing of a larger pitch, as I have done earlier, but this is not always possible, and even when it is, tench will sometimes not venture more than a few yards into it and must be fished for close to the edge of the weeds. By the use of a rod of fourteen, fifteen or even sixteen feet, it is possible to keep the rod-point right over the fish, so that it seems not to know which way to run. By skilful handling it may be persuaded to keep in open water until tired enough to bring to the net. Where this close control is needed, a long rod made of Spanish reed or bored-out tonkin cane with a not-too-fragile top of spliced-in split-cane and a little more give than usual in the middle is a useful thing to have.

With the long rod, a six-foot handle to the landing-net avoids much stretching and heart-in-mouth as a fish plunges on the rim of the net! Of shorter rods, more modern versions of the well-known Avon rod designed by F. W. K. Wallis are excellent, and have plenty of power to deal with heavy tench; they are also lighter and more comfortable to use than the longer rods, though this is not of primary importance, since in tench-fishing the rod is in a rest for most of the time, while long casting is seldom necessary.

Tench can be fished for from a boat, especially in waters where the fish are used to boats. Nevertheless I would never use one where the fish could be approached from the bank. With a boat, the eleven-foot rod will be long enough, and one even shorter, say eight or nine feet, may be found even better except where the water is more than six or seven feet deep.

Since long casting is not often needed, any reel free from vices and capable of recovering line quickly is suitable for tench-fishing, but you must be able to apply finger pressure to the drum when a fish has to be checked. Even for short-range work, a good fixed-spool reel has many advantages. Its slipping clutch enables one to strike without fear of breakage, and when ledgering, the pick-up can be left 'off' and a stick-indicator used as described for carp. Even when float-fishing it is best to leave the reel thus; often a tench will bolt with the bait and with an ordinary reel will either cause an overrun and tangle, or else feel the check and spit the bait out. Unless the fixed-spool reel is used it pays to coil a yard or so of line on a mackintosh sheet between butt-ring and reel as in carp-fishing.

When the fish are really big and the bait is to be a big lob, try the simple tackle used for carp. Camouflage the end of the line by staining it to about three yards from the hook; a 6 lb. b.s. monofil line and No. 6 or No. 4 hook make a good combination. Tench sometimes swallow a worm without swimming off with it and you will find a float helps to show what is happening down below. In calm conditions, you can use a shot ledger with a very small float; put the shot about three feet from the hook and adjust the float to be about half as far again from the shot as the depth of the water. After casting draw the tackle in a little so that all is taut and any disturbance will be registered. Even when it is windless, however, there is often drift, and more shot and a larger float will have to be used to counteract it. If there is wind or drift you will need a pierced bullet and fair-sized quill and if waves run over an inch or so it is best to use a long antenna float. For rare long-distance work, this arrangement works quite well, though wind and drift usually make a sunken line, and a float attached by the bottom ring only, necessary. With tackle arranged like this you should deal with a bite by a vigorous sideways strike, especially with a big hook and heavy lead.

Under some conditions a plain ledger with a fair-sized lead pays dividends; it is a tackle which is generally used in a lazy way and thus becomes ineffective. When ledgering without a float, carefully draw the line taut and arrange a stick-indicator or something similar; and don't leave your rod!

Everyone who has fished regularly for tench must be familiar with those occasions when the fish appear to be playing with the bait and refusing to take it properly. Nearly every book on coarse fishing describes how the float will bob and dip, travelling round the swim in a maddening way, and never giving a decisive signal for the angler to strike. Various means of combating this have been suggested. One way that often works is to draw the bait slowly away from the fish, which is then supposed to grab it quickly for fear of losing what, when it was to be had too easily, it did not want. I think this presupposes a degree of perversity beyond any fish; but the fact remains that the idea does work on occasions, and the real reason for this may be due to an effect which I will describe later.

Another remedy which sometimes works is to change to finer gut and a smaller hook and bait. This is supposed to allay the suspicions aroused by stouter tackle; what happens in reality may often be quite different.

Before going any further, I must explain that I don't claim to have solved completely the problem of 'niggling' and indecisive tench bites. Tench sometimes do play about with a bait and refuse to take it properly. But it is just as often the fault of the angler, who is fishing so that the hungry tench, eager and willing to swallow the bait offered, find great difficulty in getting it into their mouths or even touching it; it is these frustrated approaches that make the float behave in that curious way ascribed by the watching angler to the tench 'playing with the bait.'

Failure to understand the behaviour of fish when they are feeding is the cause of much disappointment in angling. Anyone who has seen tench feeding on the bottom should have realized why the float so often bobs, dips, moves sideways—does anything but give decisive slanting-downwards movement that almost always precedes the solid hooking of a fish. A tench feeding in earnest stands almost vertically on its head; 'head to hell and tail to heaven,' as a sporting parson once described it to me. In order to maintain this attitude, the fish 'fans' quite vigorously with its fins and specially with the tail.

Now consider what happens when a tench attempts to take a bait offered on the usual float tackle with a few shot on the bottom and the line or cast running almost vertically upwards to the float.

If the bait is fairly close to the shot, either because the hook-length is short or because there is a loop or coil or two between bait and shot which the angler has failed to draw straight, the tench may very likely brush against the line running up to the float. This may or may not alarm the fish; it will certainly result in movements of the float, though the bait has not been touched. Suppose the tench has not been alarmed: it waggles its tail to push its head down to the bait. The eddies thus caused wash the line sideways, the shot and bait are pulled along the bottom, and the float moves to accommodate itself to the new position of the shot. The fish finds the bait is no longer where he thought it was; rises a little from the bottom, spots it, and tries again with a similar result. A really hungry and persistent tench will keep this up for fifteen minutes or more, chasing the bait (followed by the float) all round the pitch; while the angler on the bank says to his friend, 'The tench are not hungry this morning—they're only playing with the bait.'

It may surprise many people that the water movements set up by the waggling of a tench's tail are sufficient to move bait and shot along the bottom. But it is so. A tench a yard from the line can cause enough 'wash' to drag two or three shot; while at closer ranges, a drilled bullet weighing as much as a quarter of an ounce can be moved! I have seen it done.

Now let us return to our angler who has complained about the tench not being hungry. After a time he remembers the advice about drawing the bait away, and tries it. This lowers the angle which his line, between float and shot, makes with the bottom. It draws the gut between shot and bait perfectly straight; and it ensures that the hungry tench that has been vainly chasing the bait, now approaches it from a point directly opposite to where the shot are lying, and as far away from the line rising to the float as it can ever get. This gives the fish the best chance to get hold of the bait without washing it away from itself, and very often it succeeds.

But perhaps our imaginary angler, instead of trying the trick of drawing away the bait a little, decides to try a smaller hook and finer gut. In this case, the reasons for the occasional success of such a change are less obvious. But when tackle is changed, the changes are sometimes greater than intended. They may mean that the shots are now farther from the hook; that the depth, or rather the distance between float and shot, has been increased; quite a lot of things may be altered which, if they all minimize the 'washing-away' effect, may result in an odd fish or two being captured.*

Having described the process, what is the remedy for the trouble? At the very least, two feet between bait and shot; plenty of room between shot and float, so that the line leaves the bottom not too near to the vertical; shot drawn back to ensure that the gut between it and the hook is straight, and, if necessary, the use of a drilled bullet or pear-lead to anchor everything firmly against 'washing-away' by the tails of the tench.

By now many readers will be thinking, 'But I have caught dozens of tench without having the bait more than three or four inches from the shot.' Of course! Tench are not *always* working head downwards over a piece of bottom. Very often they are swimming along normally, spot a bait, and just tilt downwards a little and suck it in. Often, too, they *do* succeed in grabbing at bait in spite of the 'washing-away' business, which is why a 'niggling' bite often develops into a decisive one. Moreover, as I have said earlier, there *are* times when the tench are *really* playing with the bait, and no amount of distance between bait and shot will make them take it.

I am absolutely convinced, however, that much of what is ascribed to 'playing with the bait' is in reality due to the reasons I have given; and the effects I have described are at their height just at the time when the fish are actively feeding, and when, with a little more thought about what goes on beneath the surface, anglers could enjoy the best possible sport.

When the angler is certain that indecisive bites are not the fault of his tackle, a smaller bait may be tried, and if that fails, a change to a bait of another kind.

Bobs and jerks, of course, may be produced by the attempts of small fish to take the bait, but with small fish such as roach and rudd, the bobs and twitches are more staccato, quite different to the slow curtsy, the partial

---

* Success gained through changing to a smaller bait may also be due to the angler having used ground-bait consisting of small particles, with which the fish have become preoccupied.

submersion, and the sidewise swing of a float which indicates the interest of a tench.

Bait

Many baits have proved successful in tench-fishing. Worms of all sizes, gentles, tubifex worms, wasp-grubs, various forms of bread, and water-snails are among the most effective, and of these, large lobworms are probably the best in most cases, though curiously enough all the tench I have caught upwards of 5 lb. in weight have been taken on crust or crust and paste. Far more important than choice of bait is accurate locating of the fish, and fishing for them at the right time and with the right tackle.

Ground-baiting a pitch in advance is well worth while during a spell of settled weather, but no amount of ground-baiting will attract tench into a pitch that temperature has made unsuitable. It is an advantage to ground-bait lightly and continuously while actually fishing. It may be thought that this will attract undesirable small fish, but it has been my experience that when tench are feeding well, one is seldom troubled by small roach and rudd; and even small perch are less prone to swallow one's worm in the presence of a number of good-sized tench.

Not only tench but many other kinds of fish can be attracted to a given spot—provided conditions do not prevent it—by hanging a sack of dead rabbits, or sheep's guts, or anything that will generate an ample supply of maggots, on a branch overhanging the water, or a stout pole driven into the bottom. Maggots will fall into the water, and a bunch of them on a hook cast into the vicinity will be effective. One pays attention to wind-direction before beginning to fish. This is, of course, a very old idea.

Striking and Playing

The tench is a persistent and powerful fighter and while lacking the speed of carp, its big tail allows it to exert a considerable pull on tackle. If weed is near it always tries to take refuge in it, and if successful will often transfer the hook from its mouth to the weed in an uncanny way, hand-lining seldom having any effect.

(*above*) Ken Taylor lands a 3lb perch; (*below*) a brace of perch, 4lb 3oz and 4lb 5oz, caught in successive casts by the author from Arlesey Lake

(*above left*) Graham Marsden with four bream, all over 7lb, taken from a Cheshire mere; (*above right*) George Bebbington (left) with a 10lb 3oz bream. Will Gollins with his 11¾lb fish; (*below*) the author lands a big bream

When first struck, big tench are often slow off the mark and their resistance for a few seconds may be so feeble as to deceive the angler into supposing that a small fish has been hooked. His attempt to haul it to the surface coincides with a sudden powerful rush which accounts for numerous breakages, and for this reason it pays to assume that every fish hooked is a big one, applying only light pressure at first until the fish has declared itself. This rule doesn't apply when a fish is hooked very near to weed or obstructions from which it must be hauled immediately, but stouter tackle should be used in these conditions.

Tench fight to the last, and many are lost through attempts to net them too soon. An angler experienced in playing big tench will be able to judge when a firm application of extra pressure will lead a surfacing fish over the landing-net, but if in doubt it is better to defer netting until the fish is obviously exhausted and on its side.

Need for Observation

While in many waters night-fishing for tench is effective, I have not been very successful at it myself and can only remember catching one large one in darkness, and that accidentally. As I have said, there are times when tench appear to feed at the surface, and this is often during a summer night, when, like carp, they will come very close inshore. No doubt observation of their habits at this time, and the development of appropriate angling methods, would result in the capture of more large specimens than are now recorded. The tench, like the carp and the barbel, has the reputation of being capricious largely because too few anglers take the trouble to study it. This may be because all barbuled fish probably feed by touch rather than by sight, and can feed in darkness when they are difficult to observe and relatively few anglers are about.

Unlike roach, rudd, and bream, tench are easily frightened by lights, and so, probably, are all fish with small eyes and barbules.

A great deal remains to be learned, but now that such anglers as Mr. J. G. Roberts, Mr. John Ellis and Mr.

F. Murgett are attacking the problems set by this species, we may expect the next few years to show better results.

Breeding and Growth

The tench is a valuable fish for stocking still waters, and no water is too deep or too shallow, too clear or too muddy, too large or too small, to suit it, while it seems able to breed nearly everywhere without multiplying to the point of overcrowding. While profusely weedy lakes with hard bottoms and varying levels seem to grow the largest tench, even the most unpromising pools will produce fish big enough to provide sport.

It is curious that while tench will grow to good size in quite small ponds, they are often difficult to catch there, in spite of their activity near the bait. Tench-fishers much more expert than I tell me their experience has been similar. I have never found the same difficulty in large waters, and it may be significant that most of my tench-fishing has been done in lakes with firm hard bottoms.

Practical Examples

The biggest tench I have ever seen live in a ten-acre lake which is very heavily weeded, and full of lily-roots wherever the water is shallow enough for them to grow. On very hot days, the tench rise and bask among the lily-leaves, which do not overlap in a dense mat as in some lakes, but are well spread out. The sight of these tremendous black shapes is breath-taking. I have stealthily worked a boat close enough almost to touch them, and I am certain that many are easily over 10 lb. Attempts to catch them have so far proved fruitless, not because they do not bite but because their haunts are among a mass of crossing and re-crossing lily-roots that form a tangle four feet deep. The tench feed on the bottom; in the early morning they bubble profusely and by dropping a worm straight down it is often possible to get a good bite and hook the fish, only to be tangled-up and broken almost instantly, even with the strongest tackle. One of these days I mean to clear an area of these roots and *then* see what can be done!

There is another three-acre pond in Lincolnshire containing tench that cannot be far short of double figures. They can be seen rolling on the surface among the weeds at spawning time; Maurice Ingham remarked that their dorsal fins are the size of a man's hand. We have rather neglected these particular tench, as there is another pool close at hand containing big carp, and they remain the subject of remarks beginning 'One of these days . . .'

Peter Thomas hooked the biggest tench I ever saw on the end of a line. It had been a disappointing morning: we had fished the water, a Bedfordshire lake, before, and knew fairly well where to expect the tench in good weather or in bad; but on this particular morning, it was 'betwixt-and-between' and we could get no bites in any of our usual pitches. Peter settled down to fish a fairly shallow spot, using a little progressive-action eight-foot split-cane rod weighing between 5 oz. and 6 oz., a trout-size fixed-spool reel, and, because of the wind, a ledger-tackle consisting of a pierced bullet on his 3 lb. b.s. line, stopped by a shot about eighteen inches from his No. 8 hook, which was baited with a big lobworm. I tried another, deeper pitch, and fished there fruitlessly for about an hour, until I heard a whistle from Peter, and looking in his direction saw that he was into a fish. I went along—it is a pleasing thing to watch Peter play a fish, and in this case the pleasure was sustained, for it must have been twenty minutes or more before he reached for the landing-net, and still we had not seen the fish. I knew it must be a very big one from the vortices it caused in the water each time it turned, but I did not expect anything quite as big as it proved to be when at last it came up and showed signs of having had enough. Eventually Peter had it on its side and, with rod well bent, drew it towards the net.

Then, for some reason, the split-shot came off. The pierced bullet shot down the line, straight into the mouth of the fish, and knocked the hook out as neatly as possible.

Peter has always refused firmly to tell me how much *he* thinks that tench weighed, but I am not so hesitant. I do not think it can have been less than 8 lb.

We fished in the same spot a year later, and had a fine morning's fishing, the best I have ever had. We caught six tench each, and for once I had the best two; nine times out of ten Peter beats me at tench-catching, but this morning my best were 5 lb. 1 oz. and 5 lb. 5 oz. and I was very pleased about it. I was using a ·010 inch perlon line with an extra-powerful Avon rod, and had no difficulty in keeping my fish out of the weeds, which were about fifteen yards to our right and extended far out into the lake. We were both float-fishing, and presently I had a bite which took a long time to 'develop.' Eventually the porcupine vanished decisively and I connected. This one took some time to decide what was the matter and at first I thought it was a fair fish only; but then it really began to fight. It made off for the centre of the lake, and though I could stop it, off it would go again before I could recover any line. This went on until it had taken about thirty yards of line off the reel in a succession of powerful rushes, and both Peter and I became excited about it. It never once occurred to me that the fish would be lost; my tackle was sound and of ample strength, and I was quite confident that the fish would be landed and only wondered how much it would weigh. Suddenly it turned and shot inwards to my right, towards the weeds. I applied considerable side-strain to turn it, with the result that it went into the weeds very fast on a tight line, which broke. I have never been more bitterly disappointed since I first began fishing; it was like finding one's house has been burnt down or that one's bank balance (if any) has been embezzled. Peter and I just looked at one another, speechless. His suggestion, made later, that it was only a 4-pounder with the hook attached to the ult. instead of the prox. end of its digestive system, I reject with the contempt it deserves.

No! That was Peter's 8-pounder, with a year's added growth!

Some splendid catches of large tench have been made in pitches baited with a ground-bait containing ox-blood. The substance haemo-globin is common to both bloodworms and ox-blood. Tench feed exten-

*sively on bloodworms : so do carp, some of which were hooked, but not
landed, in the ox-blood-baited pitches. Possibilities seem to lie here.*

*Experiments with tubifex worms as bait have shown that these creatures
rapidly disperse into the bottom mud, even when enclosed in a bag. To
prevent this, a piece of cork in the bag causing it to rise in the water,
with some lead on the tackle limiting the rise of the bag to a couple of
inches, may be used. The tubifex worms then remain together, though
their ends wriggle through the material of the bag, which can well be
made from a piece of fine gauge nylon stocking. A large carp was seen
to take a bait so arranged, and would have been hooked, had the hook
been outside instead of inside the bag.*

*Mr. Terry Augustus recommends as ground-bait a mixture of bread
and the contents of swan mussels, the mixture to be left standing in the
heat of the sun for 2–3 hours. In lakes where the level fluctuates, swan
mussels are often left to die and dry in the sun's heat, and the resulting
scent may well be attractive to fish accustomed, when the water rises, to
finding dead, open-shelled mussels.*

FURTHER NOTES

With the great and continuing increase in the number of
anglers, the problem of fish learning which baits to avoid has
become more acute. I have discussed this when dealing
with carp; it now also applies to tench.

At the commencement of the coarse-fishing season, tench
may be taken successfully with large baits such as lobworms,
bread paste, and crust, but on heavily-fished waters, the
tench learn, within a few weeks, to avoid these baits and it
becomes necessary not only to change to others, but also,
often enough, to use more sensitive methods of bite indication. In addition, there appears to be a tendency on the
part of tench to prefer smaller baits as the summer progresses.

Among the useful baits that can be tried as a change are
freshwater mussel, rush-grubs, maggots, trout pellets as for
carp, puffed wheat, cornflakes, sausage, luncheon meat,
congealed blood used with blood soaked cereal groundbait,
and breadpaste mixed with such things as Bovril, Marmite,
crab paste and various sorts of paste.

Increased sensitivity in float-fishing is often possible by the
use of the 'lift' method, in which the float is attached bottom
end only. The shot or shots are placed, as a rule, within an

inch or two of the hook, and the distance between shot and
float is set at some 20–30 per cent more than the depth of the
water. After casting, the rod is placed in rests and the line
wound in until the float cocks and shows the right amount of
its top, as is shown below.

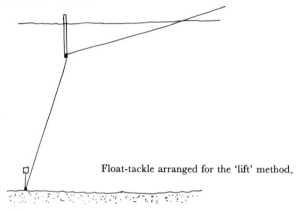

Float-tackle arranged for the 'lift' method.

Bites are usually indicated by the float rising, sometimes
even heeling over and lying flat.

In choosing swims for tench-fishing, it is well to remember
that this species dislikes feeding when the light level is too
high. In darkness, tench often move into very shallow
water.   I have taken big ones in water no more than a foot
deep at night.   But as the intensity of the light increases,
after the sun makes an angle of more than 10° to the water's
surface, the tench move into deeper water.   Where possible
therefore, two or three different swims may be pre-baited,
the angler fishing the shallower swim in the dark, moving to a
deeper one in the early morning and a still deeper one at full
daylight.

On many waters, the use of swim-feeders has proved very
successful for catching tench, especially on heavily-fished
waters where disturbances on the banks scare the fish and
drive them out.

CHAPTER VIII

PERCH

THE perch is a very common fish, and one for which people who have fished from childhood have a special regard. Its appearance is striking: dark vertical bars on its sides, two dorsal fins of which the front one is armed with sharp spines, brilliant vermilion-orange ventral and anal fins and a reddish tail, make it a fish impossible to mistake for any other.

It is found in large numbers in fresh water all over Britain, and appears equally at home in a quick-running river or a small pond, its size depending on the amount of food available. It appears to be entirely predatory, feeding on all kinds of small animals, from the tiniest crustaceans upwards, and of course on fish of all sizes, from small fry—including its own species—to quite large specimens; a perch weighing 3 lb. will attack and consume a roach of nearly ½ lb. The attack of the smaller perch, up to 1½ lb. or so, differs from the pike's; it hunts its prey down relentlessly, grabbing again and again at the tail of its quarry, until it is so injured that its owner is slowed down and eventually overtaken and engulfed by its pursuer. But the *big* perch lies in ambush and only strikes when an easy chance occurs. These different habits are worth remembering.

Perch run up to at least 7 lb. or 8 lb., and possibly up to 10 lb. in exceptionally favourable circumstances, but in the majority of waters a 2-pounder is a good fish and a 3-pounder exceptional.

Habitat

The finest perch are found in large lakes and chalk-streams, and it seems big perch grow best in clear water—understandable when one considers that they hunt largely by sight. Very shallow but extensive lakes are not so conducive to rapid growth as might be supposed. They chill more quickly in autumn and have no depths where perch can feed through the winter; though they favour the growth of fish on which perch prey, they produce fewer fish small enough for the perch to swallow. So though big perch of 3 lb. and over do exist in such lakes, it is in the deep clear reservoirs and similar waters that the extra-large perch of 4 lb. and over are more commonly found.

In these waters big perch are more difficult to catch in summer than anywhere else. Firstly, while small perch shoal all the year round, big ones tend to be solitary after spawning and until autumn. Secondly, they swim at depths determined by the extent of the upper layer of warm water mentioned in the chapter on carp. Thirdly, natural food abounds and there is ample weed-cover from which the perch can launch their attacks. Under the circumstances, the angler's problem is to locate a single fish, in three dimensions, which has probably already filled its stomach without the least difficulty.

After the autumn frosts, however, the upper layer of warm water is chilled and the autumn gales mix it well with the cold water in the deeps, driving the perch into deeper water, where at this time of year they tend to shoal with other perch the same size. The weed dies down, and there is in any case little weed in the depths where the perch congregate at this time. Here temperature never falls below about 39°F. for reasons explained earlier. Since perch feed at temperatures as low as 35°F. they are quite willing to feed at these depths, and on an angler's bait, too; for having no cover from which to attack, and little light to see by, they find their prey harder to catch, as they must then rely to some extent on their sense of smell and ability to detect the vibrations made by small fish.

The angler is now faced with an easier problem. The fish are hungrier, and it only remains to locate them in two dimensions instead of three. Fortunately, this is not too difficult. Shoals of small fish on which they prey tend, at this time of year, to swim at constant depths, near the bottom. Lacking weeds from which to launch an ambush, the perch choose the next best thing, usually some obstruction on the bottom round or over which shoals of small fish must pass, only, perhaps, to round the bend into the jaws of a waiting perch. These obstructions are often ridges in the bottom; ramps running out from the bank into deep water, or something of that kind. Perch will often be found waiting at the ends.

If the angler is able to discover the contours of the lake-bed, he may find where the shoals of big perch are most likely to be. The likely spots are usually some distance from the bank. Where a boat is available, plumbing the depth is comparatively simple, but the bank-fisher, though handicapped, can form a good idea of the lake-bed, first by seeing what signs of shallows there are near the bank; then he can cast out in different directions and time how long his plummet takes to sink. In deeper waters a fixed float cannot be used; fortunately it is unnecessary, since one only needs to know where one place is deeper than another. If, as a matter of interest, the actual depth in feet is wanted, this can be found by using a sliding float.

Tackle and Methods

The technique for perch-fishing in winter is quite different from that used in summer. In winter, assuming the where-abouts of the shoals have been found, they can be attacked in a variety of ways. In shallow lakes no deeper anywhere than fifteen feet or so, the big perch will rove on milder days, attacking shoals of small roach and the like; and spinning or plug-fishing is likely to catch some good fish. It is un-necessary to use strong tackle for this work, a nylon or perlon line of about 4 lb. b.s. being amply strong. Small spoons and plugs should be used, but with a good-sized tail-treble, as the tail-end is nearly always attacked and a small hook either fails to hold, or holds so poorly that after a few kicks the fish wins free and dashes off, often followed by the remainder of the shoal. Make sure that the tail-hook is in line with the axis of spin. Except in special circum-stances mentioned later, spinning is most effective when the big perch are feeding at the surface, and their prey can be seen scattering in all directions to escape them.

In deep lakes, the winter shoals of perch are at great depths and spinning is not so profitable. At a depth of from twenty to fifty feet it is not easy to keep the spinner travelling very slowly, just clear of the bottom. By using a lead hung a foot or so below the trace like a paternoster lead, a spoon—perhaps the best deep-water lure—can be trailed along the lake-bed, by keeping the lead always dragging bottom; but I have not found spinning under these circumstances nearly so effective as ledgering or paternostering with a worm as bait. Even when the spinner is got down to the fish, they often tend to follow it and then sheer off without taking, whereas a worm may be inspected for some time, perhaps tweaked once or twice, but in the end is usually taken. If you are spinning try a big, bright hookless spoon two feet or so ahead of the lure proper as an attractor.

The rival merits of ledger and paternoster have been discussed for many years, and both are effective tackles. With large perch, from 3 lb. upwards, I like to allow a fish to run ten yards or more with the worm before striking. If, while the fish is running, it feels a check, due either to the lead being fixed, or to line not running freely from the reel, it will usually drop the bait. These big perch are much more suspicious and circumspect than their smaller brethren, and more subtle. When you are using ledger tackle, make sure the line runs freely through the lead, there should be no knots or other stops in the line on the rod side of the lead. I like a perlon monofil line for reel line; it slides easily through the lead and rod-rings. The line should either be coiled between butt-ring and reel while you wait for a bite, or a fixed-spool reel can be left with the pick-up off. Such a reel is invaluable for winter perch-fishing in lakes, when you have to make long casts. For this the line must be strong enough to take the shock of casting, and with leads of 1 oz. or so a b.s. of at least 6 lb. is essential.

The running ledger should have its stop-shot at least two feet from the hook, which should be at least a size 6; for big fish a 4 is not too large. Any kind of lead may be used but my own preference is for a special pear-shaped one with a swivel instead of a plain wire ring.* If the tackle becomes twisted as it flies through the air, the swivel allows the twists to come out as the tackle sinks. The line runs easily through the eye of the swivel, no matter what the direction of pull is, and leads of this shape do not catch so easily in snags on the bottom.

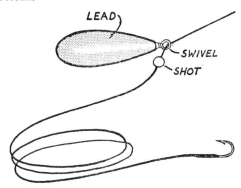

LEDGER TACKLE, SHOWING THE BEST KIND OF LEAD

An alternative to the ledger is the running paternoster. This is similar to a ledger, except that instead of the line running through the lead, it runs through one eye of a small swivel, to the other eye of which the lead is attached, via a piece of nylon monofil just long enough to suit the depth to be fished. The stop-shot that prevents the swivel from sliding down to the hook is put about six inches from the hook, instead of two or three feet as in the ledger. This tackle has all the advantages of the paternoster, besides allowing a running fish to travel without dragging the lead. The bait can be 'jiggled' up and down with it, thus helping to attract the fish.

Casting

Accurate long-distance casting is needed to catch these deep-water lake perch. When you have decided where they are likely to be fix the place by reference to a landmark on the opposite shore of the lake. Then make a search along each side of an imaginary line drawn from the angler

* The 'Arlesey Bomb', now made commercially.

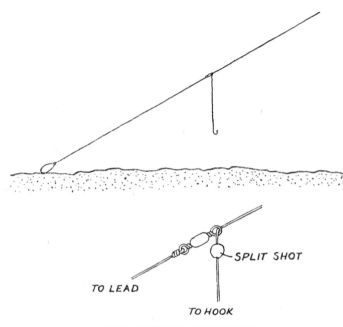

SPLIT SHOT

TO LEAD

TO HOOK

THE RUNNING PATERNOSTER

to that landmark. When the fish are found, their exact position should be noted and aimed at whenever you fish there again. They are likely to be found there throughout the entire winter.

When a lead sinks in really deep water, a strong wind acting on the line before it has had time to sink may bring the lead on to the bottom some distance from where you intended. If there is a cross-wind, aim to overcast slightly, then check the lead in its flight so that it drops in the right place, straightening the line as it does so. Simultaneously drop the rod-point into the water, so as to sink as much of the line as possible right away. I hardly need to say that you may have to aim your cast some distance upwind in order to persuade the tackle to drop in the right place. To avoid the effects of wind while awaiting a bite, set the rod in its rests with the top ring close to the surface.

One does not strike in the normal way when a run takes

place. If big perch are expected, give ample time, then check the line, and, as it tightens, apply a long deliberate pull with the rod-point. Playing the fish is largely a matter of pumping it up to the surface; still-water perch are poor fighters and the big ones especially don't struggle much, except for one or two vigorous jerks and a few easily-frustrated attempts to sheer off the line along which they are being towed. They should be handled carefully, how-ever, as rough handling may easily drag the hook from their mouths, while if the line is allowed to slacken the hook will often fall out or be shaken clear.

Bait

Mr. J. G. Roberts, of Co. Westmeath, Ireland, whose angling prowess and knowledge of fish and their environ-ment are remarkable, tells me that in a lake where he caught numerous perch between 3 lb. and 4 lb., using small live roach as bait, the best time was for about half an hour just after dark, but all my best fish, taken on lobworm, have been caught at times when the amount of light penetrating to the bottom was at a maximum.

Since blue light penetrates deepest, there seems to be a case for using not simply blue, but daylight-fluorescent blue, colourings for artificial baits worked at great depths; but since the vibrations set up by artificials are at least as important as other attributes, and since, for night-fishing, artificials painted completely black have worked well, it is difficult to develop artificials on logical lines.

It may be that while perch can detect a spinner or live-bait by its vibrations and can be caught on such lures at night, they need light to be able to see a lobworm at con-siderable depths. Perhaps when worm-fishing in deep water, we should choose those big, bluish-pink, pale-coloured worms, in preference to lobworms. I caught a 4-pounder on one of that sort of worm, which can be found by digging in chicken-runs.

Although these deep-water perch are congregated in shoals, you must not expect to catch them often one after another, as some angling writers say you can. That individuals from a shoal will follow a hooked fish is well known, and where long casts are made to reach them, this is likely to disperse the shoal when a fish is hooked, whether it be landed or not. If it escapes, some, if not all, of its mates follow it as it dashes away; if it is landed the shoal still follows it, individuals giving up the pursuit at different stages, until they are spread over a wide area. For this reason, after a fish has been caught, it pays to search the line between the spot at which it was hooked and where it was landed, either with a worm on paternoster tackle, or a small spinner.

In fishing at considerable depths, i.e. upwards of twenty feet, I have always found a big lively lobworm on a No. 6 round-bend hook, the most successful bait. No doubt a minnow or gudgeon would be equally attractive to the perch, if either could be presented in 'good order'; but the impact with the water at the end of a sixty-yard cast, followed by a sudden descent into depths where the pressure is high, is not likely to leave small fish in a lively condition. Even if it survived, pike would probably prove a nuisance.

I am often asked how I get big lobworms in winter. It seems to be generally thought that it is only in summer that these big worms come out after dark and lie about on the ground, but actually they are out at any time of the year, provided the ground is moist and it is not freezing, and that there is no more than a little wind. Because the ground is moister then, I find it easier to get lobworms in winter than in summer, and far easier to keep them when caught, in a wooden box filled with damp straw and pieces of rotten sacking.

Despite careful observations, I cannot assess the effect of weather conditions on perch shoaling in very deep water. I am inclined to think that at such a depth, weather has very little effect. My best bag of big perch, consisting of six fish from 2 lb. 14 oz. up to 3 lb. 10 oz., was made in deep water at Arlesey Lake in a biting east wind, and I have caught big ones there over ice-margins thirty yards wide; but bad weather is no advantage, for my biggest fish have been taken in bright winter sunshine. The amount of light, however, may have some effect, for I have never caught these fish on a dull day; and the four hours at midday have always proved best in winter.

Now for summer perch-fishing—a very different matter. Unless the sky is overcast or there is a good breeze, morning and evening offer the best chance. Catching big perch in summer is, as I said, much more difficult than in winter for the fish tend to be solitary, spend most of their time in the weeds, and are well supplied with natural food. You may catch a few by assiduous spinning, but you are more likely to catch lots of small pike, and, when a very small spinner is used, many little perch but few, if any, big ones. Of course it is sometimes possible, usually in the early morning, to spot a big perch attacking a shoal of small fish, and a fish feeding in this way can usually be attracted to a small spoon or a floating plug. Otherwise, summer perch-fishing can be carried out in either of two ways. Search holes in the weeds, the margins of lily-beds, and other likely places with a medium-sized redworm or a live gudgeon or minnow on paternoster tackle, or try collecting the perch in one spot. Various methods have been suggested for this—glass globes containing live minnows, worms sewn to pieces of turf, and other ingenious devices. The only one I have found of much use is ground-baiting continuously with a cloud ground-bait containing sufficient feed to attract quantities of small fry, which in turn attract the perch. Pike will be attracted too, and their unwelcome intrusions have to be suffered philosophically.

It takes time to attract perch by this means. Choose a pitch near to an extensive weed-bed, or drag out a big hole in the middle of one, and ground-bait and fish this exactly as if you were taking part in a match—an 'all-in' match—making every effort to attract and catch small fish, using appropriate tackle. Some of the small fish can be kept for live-bait in case the perch put in an appearance, unless you are provided already with a can of minnows or gudgeon, or propose to attack the perch by spinning. It may take half a day or more to attract perch to the swim, and you will know they are there by frantic leapings of small fish, or, in deeper water, by the sudden cessation of bites on the light tackle; or perhaps a perch will attack a fish you are bringing in. Then is the time to begin the actual perch-fishing, and often one can capture three or four good fish in succession. The cloud-bait should be put in continuously, even after perch-fishing proper has begun.

Inevitably you will come across pike, as worms are not much good for this fishing, and either fish or imitations have to be used. If you should hook a pike it is debatable whether it should be played carefully, or bustled out at the risk of a break; if you do break the pike will probably be sufficiently scared to go off.

In late autumn and through the winter it sometimes happens that big perch and small pike combine to harry shoals of very small fish—chiefly roach and rudd—on the surface. These shoals of small fish are densely packed, and instead of singling out victims, the perch and pike rush into the shoal where it is thickest, grabbing several small fish and scattering the remainder*. They then wait until the shoal has reassembled before renewing their attack. At such times they are most difficult to catch and the situation is most exasperating, especially when, after a long spell of fruitless casting, one succeeds in hooking a fish only to find that it is a small pike of 3 lb. or 4 lb.

I don't yet know how best to deal with this situation. The pike can sometimes be attracted to a surface plug, but it is not the pike we want. We need a lure not to imitate a single fish but a shoal of small ones, and I can only make some suggestions how that might be done.

A clear plastic tube might be filled with bright slips of silver paper, closed at both ends and adorned with a treble hook.

In America, black bass have been caught on a lure consisting of a bunch of bright darning-needles strung together and tied to a single hook. I have tried this on chub and caught several small ones, up to about 2 lb. on it; the darning-needles become rusty very quickly.

I think the likeliest suggestion is to cut from thin sheet nickel a number of willow-leaf-shaped slips about an inch

* Another example of preoccupation with small food-units.

(*right*) Peter Collins
with a good Norfolk
roach;

(*below*) the British
record roach of 4lb
2z caught from a
lake near Nottingham
by Richard Jones

Fred J. Taylor with a fine rudd, taken from a Lincolnshire lake

long and pierce a small hole at one end of each. Two trebles mounted tandem on fine wire—in case of pike—could then be plentifully adorned with them. You could try threading half a dozen slips on a length of monofil nylon, a knot separating each slip from the next, and attaching a string to the bend of each treble, giving thirty-six slips. Several more strings could be attached, one, perhaps, to the eye of each treble, and three or four to the wire ahead of the trebles. That would make quite a respectable shoal! If you put a disc of celluloid ahead of the whole lot, you could retrieve more strongly and probably create a turbulence which would make the nickel slips flutter in a very attractive way. I am sure that experiments along these lines would produce remarkable results.

In clear-water lakes that are not heavily fished, perch can sometimes be seen near the bank where there is deep water and cover such as tree-roots, or near small artificial dams and culverts. They can be caught with careful stalking and the use of an extra-lively worm or minnow on fine tackle; but perch have sharp eyes and are sensitive to vibrations, and great care must be taken not to alarm them.

One hears and reads of catching perch on an artificial fly, usually one that looks like a small fish when fished wet. On some waters you can catch numbers of small perch up to eight or nine inches long in this way, but I have never caught any big ones myself by fly-fishing or come across anyone else who has, though it is obviously not impossible, and it might be worth trying to design special flies for perch.

An interesting account is given in Marshall Hardy's *Angling Ways* of Mr. Wilfred Cutting's method of fishing for the big perch of Hornsea Mere. The bait consists of the entire gill equipment of a small perch, fished on a No. 4 hook beneath a float large enough to drift and drag the bait along the bottom when cast out cross-wind. This gill-bait is bright red when removed from the small perch, but eventually the blood is washed out of it, and it loses its attractiveness.

As an additional attraction Mr. Cutting casts out a large spoon beyond the drifting bait and spins it back towards it, rather as Col. Tattersall in pike-fishing spins a large spoon towards a live-bait. Both methods have caught fine specimen fish. Mr. J. G. Roberts tells me he finds strips of flesh or skin from the sides of roach an excellent bait.*

As with all other fish, much remains to be learned about catching big perch. Every year, a few big perch hurl themselves suicidally on to the hooks of anglers who neither expect nor deserve to catch them. Some people, like myself, have done a little better by catching perch deliberately with a method that is sometimes successful in a water they know well and fish regularly. Perhaps there are anglers who *really* understand big perch; who can go to any water containing big ones and catch them by known methods or by working out new ways to meet the circumstances. They would be entitled to call themselves perch-fishers. I have never met one, unless it be Jack Hargreaves, who understands the mentality of perch better than anyone else I know.

Unfortunately for the perch it is good to eat, especially when it is caught from a clean river or lake. I fear that as a fighter it does not shine, though most angling books praise it in this respect. But its tail is too small for power or speed, and big perch especially seem puzzled at being hooked, rather than alarmed. Nevertheless, no fish looks more impressive when brought to bank—perhaps the number of small perch every angler catches during his career make big ones look even bigger by comparison—but that a big perch does look every ounce and more of his 3 lb. or 4 lb. there is no doubt and his colours are glorious too. I have caught quite a lot of big perch, up to nearly 5 lb., and every one has made me feel very pleased about catching it; and I always return it with regret because I feel it is such a prize I would like to take it home.

I am therefore sorry to have to say that it is of debatable value in a lake. It does not seem to me to have much effect in reducing the numbers of roach and rudd sufficiently to prevent their becoming overcrowded and stunted where they have not enough to eat, but there is no doubt that it is detrimental to the breeding of carp, though where there

---

* Anglers at Croxby Pond have caught large perch using complete heads of gudgeon or small roach as bait.

are many carp the perch hardly ever grow big. In deep clear waters it thrives in company with roach, and where the latter never attain great size but only great numbers, perch often do grow big and are desirable then for their own sake. Bream and tench don't appear to be much affected either way. In coloured waters there are often lots of small perch especially when there are no deep places in which they can take refuge and go on feeding in winter. But many other waters which should be favourable to big perch are said to yield only small ones; the fish are supposed to have bred numbers beyond the capacity of the available food supply. I am convinced that in many of these waters there are big perch that are never caught. Perch eat perch; and in winter big ones may lie in the depths that could be got at with correct angling technique. Vast numbers of small perch inhabit Windermere, but 3-pounders are caught there by those who know how to go about it. There are without doubt many other waters about which the same could be said, if more anglers would try.

One of the first perch I ever caught over 3 lb. was more a matter of luck than anything else. I was fishing a large shallow Bedfordshire lake which is full of mediocre pike, and since these fish congregate mostly on the edge of what passes for deep water, about fifty yards out, I was using a powerful but flexible casting-rod, one of my earliest attempts at designing a rod suitable for carp. With this and a fixed-spool reel bearing a gut-substitute line of about 6 lb. b.s. I was able to cast an average size jointed plug about sixty yards in calm conditions, and on that October morning conditions were very calm; the surface had not the least trace of a ripple.

As I moved along the bank I passed a fellow club-member, Fred Brolia with a live-bait on float-tackle about thirty or forty yards out, and I had only gone a few paces when a shower of small fish burst from the water about thirty yards beyond his float, followed by a swirl on the calm surface. 'That's about the tenth time he's done that,' said Fred, 'see if you can get out to him; I can't, not with live-bait tackle.' We both thought it was a pike of 4 lb. or

5 lb., and I cast out. As is usual with me, the cast was inaccurate, the plug falling a good fifteen yards to the left of the right spot. I worked it in and had just retrieved it when up flew the small fish again; and as the plug flew out once more I saw distinctly a big, prickly fin break the surface. This time the plug fell within a yard of the swirl and beyond it, and it had not wriggled a yard along the surface—it was a floater, green and white with yellow stripes —before a big mouth closed over it and the fish was on.

It did not put up much of a fight and was played to the side and safely netted within two minutes of being hooked; a fine, fat, but rather blackish-looking perch of 3 lb. 1 oz., an example of what may be done with a floating plug when the opportunity presents itself. I have had the same sort of chance several times since, almost always when I have not had the necessary tackle fixed up.

My most successful perch-fishing has been at Arlesey Lake, a water of about fifteen acres which was once a clay-pit, but whose artificial origin has been hidden by the growth round its banks of trees, reed-beds and rushes. It is a deep water, fifteen feet or more within a few yards of the bank, and at fifty yards, as deep as thirty to forty feet. This lake harbours some monster perch; the largest have yet to be caught, some of them I am sure, are more than 7 lb. On very hot days in summer they can sometimes be seen; small shoals form and cruise round the lake, just beyond the limit of the weeds and three or four feet below the surface. Up to the time of writing, no one has succeeded in catching a perch at Arlesey in summer, except small ones up to a pound or so. No doubt the big ones *could* be caught then if the right method could be found, but the usual methods have proved useless. Sometimes two or three big perch can be persuaded to follow a spinner, but they keep well behind it; and other methods, such as the use of small live-baits on fine tackle, have fared no better.

Exasperated at my continual failure to catch them in the summer and early winter of 1950, I began a campaign against them consisting mainly of a careful plumbing of the depth at all points round the lake, up to a distance of

about ninety yards out; I did this by casting out a lead on
a light line and noting how long it took to sink. This told
me where the deepest holes were, and I explored them
with a live minnow on paternoster tackle which I could cast
about sixty yards or more; but it proved fruitless, probably
because the impact with the water and the descent into
depths where the pressure is 30 lb. or so per square inch was
too much for the minnow. Suspecting this, I tried big,
lively lobworms on ledger tackle on January 14th, 1951.
After an hour or two without result in one spot, I moved
to another, and as I was tightening-up after my first cast
there came a tug at the rod-top with which the answering
strike failed to connect. Re-baiting, I cast out again, and
I had not long to wait before another pull came, at which I
struck with the same result. This was repeated five times
in all, till I decided to give the next biter all the time he
wanted: I had begun to suspect eels.

I did not have to wait long. The line ran out from the
fixed-spool reel, with its pick-up set 'free' and I let it run.
I should think I must have let twenty yards go before striking,
and this time something heavy was hooked. I put on
pressure, expecting the heavy resistance soon to change to
the usual wriggle of an eel, but instead I felt decided thumps,
and eventually brought up a fine perch weighing 4 lb. 2 oz.

I had one more bite that day, and hooked the fish, but it
managed to foul some underwater obstacle and after waiting
some time to see if it would free itself, I was forced to break.

In the following fortnight I had two more days after these
perch; on the first another angler had forestalled me where
I wanted to fish; but I had two bites not far away and landed
both fish, alike as two peas and each weighing an ounce
over 3 lb. On the other day I had the best catch I am ever
likely to have; I got the pitch I wanted and had nine bites,
landing six fish from 2 lb. 14 oz. to 3 lb. 10 oz., only one
under 3 lb. I hooked the other three, and lost them on
snags; they felt heavier, and I was unable to pump them up
before they snagged me.

Never since have I had so many bites as I had that
winter; two in a day has been the limit, and I have fished

many days there with none.   But I have caught many more
perch, three of them over the 4½ lb. mark and the best
4 lb. 13 oz.   My friend Bob Rutland had a fine fish of
4 lb. 10 oz., and plenty have been taken between 2½ and 4 lb.
We continue to fish for them in the hope of eventually
landing one of the very much larger specimens we know are
there; some day, that lake will produce a record-breaker.

The fish are big; but after catching a good many of them,
I must admit to finding the fishing somewhat dull; I can
remember, perhaps too vividly, the days when I was de-
lighted and enthralled if I succeeded in catching 1-pounders.

FURTHER NOTES

Since this book was written, the run of very big perch at
Arlesey Lake has come to an end, probably owing to the
disease that went on to kill vast quantities of perch all over
the country.

I caught two more perch over 4 lb. in a small lake at Little
Brickhill, fishing a large lobworm on float tackle near the
mouth of a feeder stream which colours the lake water after
heavy rain.   Both fought extremely well, and one would
have been lost had not Bob Rutland leapt in and freed the
line from an overhanging and partly submerged bush!
Fred J. Taylor also had a 4-pounder from this water.   Thus,
all eight of the perch I have so far caught over 4 lb. fell to
lobworms on the bottom; but there is no conclusion to be
drawn from this about the relative merits of various baits and
lures.

I say that because I have learned from fishing the large
reservoir at Hanningfield, near Chelmsford, that various
types of trout-lure can be deadly for perch.   Hanningfield
is heavily stocked with trout and only fly-fishing is permitted,
but until disease struck, the water held large numbers of big
perch, which we caught accidentally when after trout, usually
when fishing large lures, two-hook tandems, on a high-
density fast-sinking line.

On one occasion I caught twenty-three perch, all over 2
lb. and one or two about 3 lb., plus a 4 lb. 6 oz. trout, in the

space of an hour, from a boat anchored by the valve tower opposite the fishing lodge, over 20 feet of water. I hesitate to guess at the vast catches of perch that might have been made had my friends and I set out deliberately to catch them and spent whole days at it.

The perch took a wide variety of tandem lures and even large single-hook wet flies, but one particular tandem was outstandingly successful, probably because in designing it I tried to include as many as possible of the features by which a large perch may be supposed to recognise a small perch.

This lure was named the Hanningfield Lure, and it has since proved very effective for catching big perch on a variety of other waters. It is somewhat complex to tie, but the results more than justify the trouble. The dressing is as follows:

Hooks 2 No. 8 long shank, front down-eyed, rear preferably up-eyed or eyeless, round bend.

Attachment link Three strands of 11 or 12 lb. b.s. nylon monofil tightly plaited.

Bodies White d.r.f. wool, ribbed fine silver thread.

Throat hackle A bunch of hot orange cock-hackle fibres, overlaid at the front with a shorter bunch of white cock-hackle fibre-dyed cobalt, or fibres from the blue feather of a Vulturine guinea fowl.

Tail A hot orange cock-hackle wound at the rear of the body of the tail hook, clipped to leave the fibres about $\frac{1}{2}$ inch long.

Underwing A bunch of white goat hair tied to lie close to bodies.

Overwing A bunch of fibres from a boldly-marked turkey tail-feather.

Cheeks Two Jungle cock eyes, or substitute made by putting a spot of white enamel on a small black feather.

Head Black tying silk, well varnished.

The procedure is to plait the nylon and bind it firmly to the shank of the rear hook with white silk or terylene thread, using a good water-proof adhesive such as 'Araldite'. Tie in the tail hackle, wind, secure and clip to length. Tie in the white d.r.f. wool and the silver thread, wind the body, wind the silver thread on opposite spiral, secure, whip-finish, varnish whip-finish.

Replace the hook in the vice with the front hook; lay the plaited nylon on the back of its shank and again using adhesive, lash it firmly down with white thread. Tie in white wool and silver thread, wind body and ribbing as on rear hook, and secure, leaving ample room behind the eye for wings, hackle and cheeks.

Turn the thing upside down in the vice and tie in the two throat hackles, with a drop of clear varnish on their roots to secure them firmly. They should not quite reach the point of the front hook.

Again turn the hook in the vice and tie in first the white-goat-hair under-wing, then the speckled turkey over-wing. These should reach, but not extend far beyond, the bend of the rear hook. Apply plenty of polyurethane or PVC varnish to their roots. (Cellulose is not satisfactory. It dries, shrinks and lets the hair and feather fibres slip.)

Change to black tying-silk to tie in the jungle cock or substitute cheeks, and finish the head. Whip-finish and varnish well with several coats to make the head smooth and glossy.

I know this sounds complicated and time-consuming, but each operation is individually quite easy, and I can tie these lures in about 10–12 minutes each.

It is not necessary to fish these lures on fly-fishing tackle. They can be used on light spinning tackle, though I like to use a rod of 10–12 feet rather than a shorter one. Weight for casting can consist of swan shot, or, for long-range work, a barrel lead stopped by a shot, about 3 feet above the lure; or all the lead can be placed right up against the head of the lure when casting into the wind. It is usually necessary to fish close to the bottom. A monofil line of from 4 to 7 lb. b.s., depending on the fishing conditions, will be suitable.

I have described this lure at some length, partly because it has caught so very many perch and partly because it has the advantage over spinners, in that there is no line twist, and neither swivels nor anti-kink devices are necessary in its use. My confidence in its effectiveness is such that if I had to choose one bait or lure only for future perch-fishing, that is what I would choose. Given space in which to fish it, I am sure it would beat spinners, worms, plugs or live-baits.

CHAPTER IX

BREAM

BREAM are fish of slow growth, and they are equally slow of movement. There are two varieties: the Bronze and the Silver Bream. Immature specimens of the former are not easy to distinguish from the latter. Generally speaking, the bronze bream even when immature has darker fins, a smaller eye and generally a more solid appearance than the silver. The silver bream is rather more greenish; its fins are paler and it has a fragile translucent appearance, rather like a deep-bodied bleak to which it is in fact more nearly related than to the bronze bream. Illustrations showing clearly how to identify the two species appear in E. Marshall Hardy's book *Coarse Fish* (Herbert Jenkins).

Both fish prefer still to running waters, and they grow heavier in lakes, especially deep ones, than in rivers. Bronze bream run up to 15 lb. or so; silvers are seldom bigger than 2 lb., the majority being less than ½ lb. Both are plentifully covered with slime. Although they prefer still waters, they seldom thrive in very small ponds.

Bream are almost entirely bottom feeders. On hot days they can sometimes be seen basking on the surface, but it is practically useless to fish for them then, though very rarely they will accept a fly delicately cast over their noses. At times they swim at mid-water, and in the middle of the day an odd fish or two can sometimes be tempted with a single gentle, or a piece of breadcrust suspended on superfine tackle, well off the bottom or sinking slowly; but the only really profitable way is to fish a bait well on the bottom when the bream may be expected to begin serious feeding. This, like most still-water fish, is in the evening, through the night and in the early morning in warm weather; cooler conditions brought about by rain or showers may cause the fish to feed throughout the day, while cold weather makes night-fishing doubtful.

Once you find bream, they are seldom difficult to catch. In large and deep waters the difficulty is to find the shoals. In heavily fished lakes certain pitches get a reputation for harbouring bream, but in relatively unfished waters you will have to use a combination of observation and trial to find out where they are. Bubbles sent up by fish feeding on the bottom in deep water are not easy to identify, and there, regular ground-baiting on a heavy scale is the best plan.

In shallower waters the fish are easier to find. You can follow the progress of a shoal, particularly in the evening, by watching the odd fish or two rolling over on the surface; the main body of the shoal will be below and ahead of these surface-rollers. In clear and shallow water, large patches of stirred-up mud with rising bubbles are practically certain to be caused by bream-shoals. The bubbles they send up when feeding on the bottom are quite different to those produced by carp or tench, and consist of bursts of four or five pea-sized bubbles, with sometimes a like number of smaller ones, coming up at closely-spaced intervals along the line the fish is taking. In shallow water the shoals move round considerably, and each will be found to have a favourite 'beat,' a fact you can make use of. The same thing probably occurs in deeper waters, but observation is more difficult. Bream will feed in very deep water and you will hardly ever see surface-rolling in such lakes.

The surface-rolling of bream, like the leaping of carp, seems to be partly due to changing water temperature, and, as with carp, is often a preliminary to feeding. Still-water bream seldom feed in water below 45°F. I don't know what their upper temperature limit is, but I should guess about 70°F. As explained in the carp chapter, the effect of weather on the water temperature and amount of dissolved oxygen it contains is important and can be of much help in determining where and when fish will feed, though bream will feed in a much wider temperature-range than tench or carp.

A bream's stomach is small for the size of the fish, and though a shoal will clear up a great deal of ground-bait, the quantity each fish eats at a 'sitting' is not large. Having eaten its fill, some time will elapse before it feeds again, depending on the size of the fish and the rate of digestion; the colder the water, the slower digestion will be, I think.

When a shoal is found, quite often a bait will be refused though conditions are suitable for feeding, especially where extensive ground-baiting has been done and the whole shoal has begun eating at about the same time. This is probably due to the fish digesting what they have eaten, and it pays to continue fishing, as even the largest fish only take an hour or so to finish digesting their food, and if you are willing to wait you are likely to make a heavy bag when they do begin feeding again.

Shoaling is by size, fish of similar stature swimming together, and the larger the fish, the smaller the shoal. In a shallow lake I know well there are four main shoals, each with its favourite beat which crosses and recrosses other beats but does not coincide with them. The largest shoal consists of fish up to about 1 lb., and besides the bronze bream there are many silvers in this company of five hundred or more. The next shoal, about one hundred and fifty strong, consists of 1½ to 3½-pounders. Then there is a shoal of perhaps fifty fish, running from 2½ to 6½ lb. Sometimes we see the grandfathers, fish of from 6 lb. to 10 lb. or so; there are not more than a dozen or so of them. Perhaps one day we may see just two fish together weighing 15 lb. each, and catch one of them.

Bream are both shy and stupid. They are easily alarmed by vibration in or rocking of a boat at all near to them; and they appear to have keen eyesight. But they are not hard to tempt if not alarmed, though they prefer reasonably fine tackle, especially in the daytime. Fortunately, perhaps, they put up such a poor fight that you never need to use tackle stronger than about 6 lb. b.s. even in the worst conditions, while the heaviest fish can mostly be dealt with on tackle of half that strength. Hooks sizes 10 to 6

are suitable and the forged type, well sharpened, is preferable. For shallow waters a rod of ten to eleven feet suffices,
and the versatile Avon rod or a modern version of it is
excellent; not that its full power is necessary, but its long
casting is valuable. Long casting is the secret of success
with big bream, especially in shallow waters. Anyone
who fishes the Broads knows this well enough; river anglers
are sometimes apt to forget it. The Avon type of rod,
with a small fixed-spool reel carrying a hundred yards of
4 lb. b.s. monofil line, is a fine outfit, and with a light
ledger tackle or a medium swan quill float carrying six shot
or more, great execution can be done. For exceptionally
long-range work, the use of a Mark IV carp-rod, or something similar, and a 1 oz. lead, will be needed.

When bream are feeding greedily the only advantage of
a float is that it shows the position of the tackle. When
they are nibbling or taking the bait without moving far
with it a float is almost essential unless you use a tackle
that will register small movements, for bream will sometimes swallow the bait without a decisive pull and the dis-
gorger will have to be used on a fish which could have been
struck a good deal sooner and hooked in the mouth.

The difficulty of using float-tackle with long casting is
that drift will either pull the float out of position or else
beneath the surface. This is overcome by attaching the
float by the lower ring only and sinking the line, not as
great a disadvantage as might be thought, for rapid striking
is unnecessary in bream-fishing and a sidewise pull is all
you need to stick in the hook.

When you are making very long casts the best float is
the type with the centre of buoyancy low. A goose-quill
with a cork or balsa body beginning two inches or more
below the top of the quill, is ideal, and the top should be
painted conspicuously: yellow or orange, with a black top,
is a good combination. It is a mistake to use floats with
slender tops for this sort of fishing; visibility comes before
sensitivity when the quarry is a 7 lb. or 8 lb. bream fifty
or more yards away.

Such long-range work is not always necessary, but I

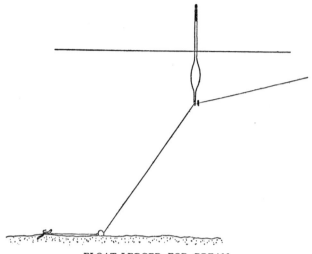

FLOAT-LEDGER FOR BREAM

would never use a boat if I could possibly reach the fish
from the bank. One of the greatest mistakes that can be
made in bream-fishing is getting too near the fish. With
a fixed-spool reel and fine line one need never approach
nearer than thirty yards. It must be remembered that
unless very heavy ground-baiting has been done the shoals
of bream will be constantly on the move; and when one is
forced to use a boat, as on some of the Broads where the
banks are impossible to fish from, the approach should be
made very carefully. The angler who knows the water
and the usual beats of the bream-shoals will take care to
moor his boat well away from where the fish *are*, and sufficiently far away from any point to which they may eventually travel, and bows-on to the spot he intends to fish : never
broadside.

In deep waters, float-fishing is difficult. By deep waters
I mean reservoirs and the like which may be as deep as
twenty to sixty feet or more in places. Unless fairly heavily-
weighted tackle is used, the sliding float is ineffective, and
with long casts it is a troublesome device. In waters deeper
than ten feet it is probably better to dispense with the float;
even with only six or seven feet between float and hook

long casting is beginning to be difficult; but without the float the depth of the water has no effect on one's range. For ledgering, a lead can be used when the bait is worm or gentles, though a ball of mud, not too stiff, on the cast or round the bait itself is probably better. With paste no lead is needed, as a fair-sized ball of paste will have sufficient weight in itself for long casting. The throw should be made with a long swing, of course not a flick.

Bream-bites are usually, but not always, decisive, both on float and ledger-tackle. The text-books say that the bite on float-tackle causes the float to lie flat; I seldom find this, probably because I place my shot at least three feet from the hook. A bream would have to lift the bait a long way to register a flat-float bite on this tackle. Usually there is a preliminary dip and bob and then the float sails away, submerging as it goes. On ledger-tackle, there are perhaps a couple of preliminary twitches of the line, followed by a steady run-out. With large balls of paste, the preliminary twitchings may go on for some little time until the bream has succeeded in getting the bait into his mouth; the steady run-out is the signal for striking. With a mud-enclosed bait the same considerations apply as with paste. In using ledger-tackle, where it is suspected that the fish are holding the bait without running off with it, that old-fashioned but very efficient indicator, the dough-bobbin, can be used. If the rod is put in the rest with the butt high so that the rod points straight at the lead or bait, the dough-bobbin can be placed between butt-ring and reel where it is easier to manage.

Although bream are poor fighters, their broad side offers a good deal of resistance to the water and with light tackle over-energetic striking is likely to result in breakage. With fixed-spool reels this can be avoided by setting the slipping-clutch at a light tension, but with rotating-drum reels care must be taken not to strike too hard, especially at a fish thirty or forty yards away. One still sees anglers striking with the reel-line held in their free hand, or even worse, grasped against the rod-grip. Striking should always be done from the reel; in the case of rotating-drum reels, a finger on the flange of the drum will prevent overrunning after striking, and one is prepared for whatever the hooked fish may decide to do. When using ledger-tackle, or float-tackle with a sunken line, a long dragging pull is better than a sharp strike.

In shallow waters, heavy ground-baiting is not necessary, and where the movements of the fish can be followed easily, it is hardly worth while ground-baiting at all. But in large deep lakes, ground-bait is a big advantage. The method I find best is the one I described for carp-fishing: fix a convenient mark on the opposite side of the lake and make a line of ground-bait. The usual bread-and-bran mixture is as good as anything; it is worth mixing in some redworms and gentles. In deep waters a cloud-bait is not recommended; sub-surface drifts and currents may draw it elsewhere along the bottom. It is better to use a mixture that will sink fairly quickly. The numbers of bream accidentally caught over an in-line ground-bait designed for carp is ample evidence of its effectiveness.

Boiled wheat or barley, gentles, caddis, cheese, potato, and worms of all kinds are accepted at times, but in my experience bream are usually to be caught on paste, gentles or worms, or not at all. Gentles often result in much annoyance from small roach and the like: this can be partly overcome by enclosing the baited hook, bearing half a dozen gentles, in a ball of soft mud, and the same can be done with small redworms or brandlings; in any case the mud-ball technique should always be tried when bottom-feeding fish of any species are sending up quantities of bubbles but ignoring baits fished in the normal way.

The less a lake is fished, the more likely it is that worms will be preferred to paste. Large lobworms are recommended by some authorities, but I find these are only taken when the fish are well on the feed. At other times I have done better with small redworms or marsh worms. The much-belauded brandling I have never found of much use for any species of fish.

Gentles need no explanation; five or six on a No. 10 hook are sufficient. Paste should be fished in quite large lumps;

for some reason bream, even ½-pounders, appear to like a piece of paste the size of a big hazel-nut better than a pea-sized piece, and it is really amazing how large a lump they can absorb. I have frequently caught bream of from 1 lb. to 3 lb. while carp-fishing, on pieces of paste the size of a golf-ball. I imagine they must nibble and nibble until they have whittled it down to a more manageable size, but however it is done, the bream have eventually found themselves hooked, landed and returned with some unfavourable comment. In fact the number of bream caught in this way—many after dark—is so large that I think this must be considered as a definite method of fishing for them, using, of course, tackle more suited to the bream, not the outfit which one would normally choose for carp-fishing at night. To adapt the technique to bream-fishing, it would probably be best to use a piece of paste about the size of one's thumb-nail and to surround it with a ball of ground-bait, no float or lead being used. In any case, when fishing from the bank after dark, long casting is not so necessary. Like carp, bream come inshore during the hours of darkness, and there is seldom need to fish farther out than five or six yards, unless of course, with a view to daytime fishing as well, the ground-bait has been put well out from the bank.

When a bream is landed, you must be prepared to deal with quantities of slime. It will be all over the landing-net, the grass, the line—everywhere. I find the best way is to use a wet cloth in one hand and a small pair of long-nosed pliers in the other. I don't take the fish out of the landing-net, but hold it down with the wet cloth while I remove the hook with the pliers. Then I can tip the fish out of the net back into the lake, unless it is of a size for weighing, when it can be slid from the landing-net into a keep-net.

Like carp and tench, bream in lakes are summer and autumn fish, and few are caught after the first autumn frosts. They spawn in the late spring and assemble in large shoals in the vicinity of reed-beds, bulrushes, etc. When introduced into a water they usually maintain their numbers, though they often take a long time to grow up to a reasonable size, even in lakes where there appears to be ample feed. I think very little of the bream as a fish for stocking still waters; to establish a head of big fish is a long-term policy and even a big lake-bream is a poor fish from a sporting point of view. In a river where the current against its side aids it a big bream is capable of putting up a reasonable fight, but in lakes and ponds it is a feeble antagonist.

It is popular with some anglers largely because it is easy to catch and because owing to its shape it looks bigger than it really is. In my district the cry is always for re-stocking with bream, and when this has been done many waters no longer contain the good roach they used to. Whether this is due to the bream I can't say, but if the biologists eventually discover that you cannot have good roach and good bream in the same water, I shall not be surprised—and my vote will go to the roach.

Nevertheless, I should be sorry to see the bronze bream exterminated. It is a favourite with a great many anglers, and has happy associations for many, myself included. There are Walton's amusing instructions for catching it, and memories of week-end expeditions with good friends in pleasant surroundings, when fish after fish of 4, 5 and 6 lb. were landed one after another; all these endear the bream to me far beyond his deserts.

Most of my bream-fishing has been done in the Bedfordshire Ouse, where a bream hooked on fine tackle sometimes puts up what might almost be called a fight. Very often I have caught and cursed bream which have taken baits intended for carp or tench, and it was while in search of carp that 'B. B.' and I came across a private lake, in which the alleged carp turned out to bream of fair size—very much bigger than I can catch in the Ouse now that indiscriminate restocking and other things have done their evil work. So, when we wanted to catch some big bream for the *Daily Mirror* Club contest, which requires large fish of many species to win it, an expedition was organized.

We chose a week-end in August, and one of our Club members, Trevor Lockhart, who was willing to give up

some of his holiday time for the purpose, went in advance
to locate the bream and to do any necessary weed-clearing
and ground-baiting. The remainder of the party, consisting
of Maurice Ingham, Peter Thomas and me, arrived on a
Friday evening, complete with tents and provisions.

Trevor had discovered that there were several shoals of
bream. He had already caught several, the best of which
weighed 6 lb. 2 oz. The lake was roughly in the shape of
a letter Y, the tail of the Y running from north downwards
to south, with the deep water at the dam at the bottom.
On my previous visit I had seen big bream in shallow water
in the eastern arm, but Trevor's fish had been caught near
the dam, and it was there we began fishing.

Only one bream, a fish of 3½ lb., was caught that evening;
and the following morning none at all. But we did catch
a succession of fine, hard-fighting tench up to nearly 4 lb.,
which treated us very fairly in that each of us caught
several. They continued to bite until after midday, when
the weather turned colder and it began to rain.

By evening the rain had abated somewhat, and I pushed
through wet, tall grass until I reached the southernmost
bank of the eastern arm. The water looked leaden and
depressing, and a westerly breeze made casting difficult, so
I fixed up a ledger-tackle and made a long cast of about
fifty yards, then crouched under a gas cape, hoping that if
anything took the big lobworm with which my hook was
baited, it wouldn't be an eel. It wasn't. In the gathering
dusk, some hours later, the rod-top bent downwards, and
on striking I found myself attached to a dull, dragging
something, which was not long in coming to net and proved
to be a bronze bream of 2 oz. under 6 lb.

The next morning was sunny and bright, and the party
arrayed itself in a line along the eastern arm, with a spacing
of about twenty yards between us. Furthest east was
Trevor, then Maurice, then Peter, then me. Trevor had
the first bite, shortly after lunch, and landed a 5-pounder.
Next, Maurice got a better one, 5 lb. 12 oz. We were float-
ledgering, and a water-lily leaf became attached to Maurice's
float. When he struck, he thought at first he had hooked

some tough weed, but on winding in, he found it was the bream, and his comment sums up its fighting ability beautifully: 'I felt something flapping,' he said, 'but I thought it was that lily-leaf!'

Things were evidently working out in a nice, orderly manner, because Peter got the next one, $5\frac{1}{4}$ lb., and the one after that was mine, $4\frac{1}{2}$ lb. Then all was quiet until after tea. Maurice and Trevor had to leave then, but Peter and I stayed on, and in the evening the fun started again. Peter got one of 6 lb. 6 oz. first cast, and I had one $\frac{1}{4}$ lb. less within a few minutes. We caught about twenty upwards of 4 lb. in weight that evening. The fish had evidently found the ground-bait, for bubbling was visible all over the area we had baited-up during the morning and again before going off to tea. The last fish caught that day was a baby of $2\frac{1}{2}$ lb.; not another touch did we have after landing it. We threw out more ground-bait before leaving the two pitches we were fishing, having decided to start early the next morning.

We might as well have slept late. We put out two rods each, and between 5 a.m. and 12.30 p.m. there was one bite, a horrid little eel. But at 12.30 precisely, all four floats disappeared together. I picked up the nearest rod, struck, felt the fish, opened the reel pick-up and put the rod back in its rest. Then I took up the other, hooked the fish and landed it. Peter had already landed a fish on one rod and was reaching for the other, but the fish had gone. The one I had first struck was still there, though, and I landed that one too; and before I had weighed the three fish, Peter was into another; and for the next three hours we caught fish as fast as we could bait our hooks, cast out, and bring the fish to net. We were each using a landing-net with a polished duralumin ring, and at first much time was wasted in landing fish that bolted directly they saw it. Peter eventually got over the difficulty by stirring up the mud, so that the fish did not see the net until it was too late. Joe, the keeper, sat on the bank behind, keeping the score, but in the end even he lost count, and we shall never know how many we caught before we ran out of worms. But we weighed the biggest, 6 lb. 6 oz. (Pete's!), 6 lb. 2 oz., 5 lb. 8 oz., 5 lb. 6 oz. and half a dozen others over 5 lb. None were under 4 lb., and I should think we must have caught about forty fish. The week-end total gave us ten fish between 5 lb. 6 oz. and 6 lb. 6 oz., and averaging 5 lb. 15 oz.; five topped 6 lb.

Those are not, I suppose, *big* bream; expert bream-fishers only talk of big bream when they reach double figures; but I have yet to catch bigger ones, and, as I do not find bream tremendously exciting fish, I probably never shall. It was an interesting experience, though, and subsequent visits to this and other waters inhabited by bream have taught me a little about them. There is no doubt a great deal more to learn.

A characteristic of bream is the way in which a shoal will suddenly commence feeding, and, after an interval, as suddenly cease. One's bait may lie in the middle of a shoal for hours and then be taken, fish after fish being subsequently caught one after another. Then the biting will stop. For this reason it pays to be patient and to persevere with a bream-shoal that has been positively located.

FURTHER NOTES

I am glad to say that since I wrote the above, I have managed to catch bigger bream, up to 8½ lb. The bream is now the mainstay of the match-fishing fraternity, who have devised various cunning means of detecting bites on leger tackle. There are springtips, swingtips, quivertips and various indicators placed between butt ring and reel, and they all work. In fact they are so highly praised that I often wonder how I ever managed to make hundredweight catches of bream without their aid.

To be fair, the matchmen have to catch bream from very heavily fished waters, usually during the least productive hours of the day, and often fishing under the handicap of large numbers of spectators. The small hooks, fine tackle, and ultra-sensitive indicators they use are necessary in such conditions, though one reads so often, in reports in the angling press, that so-and-so would have won, had not three or four bream been lost through failure of the hook-hold. The moral is that if you want to catch big bream, fish at the right time in the right place, and then you can use hooks of sensible size and lines of adequate strength.

In the first edition I said that in relatively shallow waters, large quantities of ground-bait are not necessary. It is true that bream can be caught without it, but if you want a really good catch, and are fishing a water where bream are numerous, you cannot carry too much ground-bait.

I have learned a great deal about ground-bait; Fred J. Taylor and I were commissioned by F. G. Goddard & Co. of Balham, to investigate what ground-bait does, and how best to formulate it. For lake and pond fishing, it is important that a proportion of the ground-bait, when soaked, should be freely suspended in the water, spreading out widely from the baited pitch so as to attract fish from a wide area. Ground rice and ground semolina have this property, and in combination with other ingredients such as sausage rusk, wheat flour and breadcrumbs, can make a ground-bait that is incomparably superior to random mixtures or any single ingredient. The mixture we decided upon is sold under the name of 'Pomenteg'.

Large bream sometimes eat small fish, and as I write, news has come from Grafham water of two bream, each weighing over 10 lb., caught in mid-October by a trout-fisher, using a large white lure on a sunk line. This reinforces earlier evidence from Peter Stone, of Oxford, about the predatory tendencies of big bream. Dead minnows might prove excellent baits for outsize bream, and now deep-freezers are so widely used, there is no problem about the provision of such baits for use at any time of the year.

CHAPTER X

ROACH

THE *small* roach is without doubt the most popular quarry of the majority of anglers. The reason is that it is the easiest of all fish to catch. It exists in enormous quantities, and the methods of catching it have become so well known and so much a ritual, that even the clumsiest and most unintelligent novice can achieve some sort of success. It has cast such a spell over the angling world that the basic methods used in fishing for it have been applied to practically every sort of freshwater fishing except trout and pike. Moreover, as I have already said, for many years the so-called 'general' rod has been made to catch roach—and small roach at that: if it doesn't catch small roach it doesn't sell.

In fishing for small roach, especially in heavily fished waters, it has long been known that more fish are caught by fishing fine and striking fast: small baits result in more bites, because relatively few fish find a tiny bait too small to take. Thus the tendency to use small baits, tiny hooks, very fine tackle and rods designed for faster and faster striking has resulted in anglers getting better at catching little roach at the expense of being able to catch big ones.

They are handicapped by using very small baits, because though a big roach is not averse to taking a small bait, he cannot if a small roach takes it first, which is likely to happen for several reasons. Firstly, a little roach is quicker 'off the mark' than a big one. Secondly, the modern angler has done his best to attract all the little roach in the neighbourhood by using a slow-sinking ground-bait. Thirdly, the bait is kept off the bottom, and is also arranged to sink as slowly as possible. A big roach cannot compete with the small ones in trying to grab it first; he keeps to the bottom and picks up what the small ones miss.

Occasionally it does happen that a good roach takes the bait. The following lightning strike either breaks the gut or pulls the tiny hook in and tears it out in one motion. If the hook is able to take a hold, the rod and tackle—the one by its inflexibility beyond the first few ounces of pull, the other by its fragility—often succeed in losing the fish which the angler was not, in any case, expecting. On the rare occasions when a big roach is landed, it is held up as an example of the efficiency of the method used to catch it.

Because these methods produce bites at frequent intervals, the angler feels that any method which produces fewer bites is dull. Since he believes that the next bite may mean a big fish—despite the previous thousands which resulted only in small ones—he wants the next bite as soon as possible. It is difficult to convince him that he should persevere with methods which provide far fewer bites but bigger fish.

It is worth considering the experiences of two men who have caught really big roach. Mr. W. Penney, during his day's fishing on September 6th, 1938, had three bites. One produced nothing, the others a brace of roach weighing 3 lb. 1 oz. and 3 lb. 14 oz. Mr. Wilfred Cutting, fishing Hornsea Mere, caught only one roach on August 15th, 1917. It weighed 3 lb. 10 oz.

I am not a specialist roach-fisher but it seems clear to me that of all fish the roach, if you want him big, must be fished for with the idea of avoiding small roach, and that failure to do so explains the unsuccessfulness of many roach-fishers.

The majority of roach I have caught weighing upwards of 2 lb. were taken quite accidentally while I was fishing for some other kind of fish. I take no pride in their capture, which at the time was nothing but a nuisance. Either they had taken monstrous lobworms meant for a specimen tench or perch, or else they had succeeded in absorbing a walnut-sized ball of paste intended for carp. The tackle was too stout to allow even the biggest roach to put up any sort of fight. But one thing was very noticeable about these roach; they needed no rapid striking. When a float was in use, it disappeared decisively and the line ran out after it. On ledger-tackle, there was always a clear run-away, the sort that gives one time to light a cigarette before striking. All this made me think; and when the opportunity came to fish for roach in a water where lots of them run to over 2 lb., and an incentive, in the shape of a club competition for specimen-fish, run by the *Daily Mirror*, lured me away from carp-fishing, I tried disregarding the usual roach-fishing techniques in favour of carp-tactics, suitably scaled down in strength of tackle and size of bait and hook—though they remained big enough to cause the average roach-fisher to rock with mirth.

I caught a quantity of roach; not one was under the 1 lb. mark and five were twice that weight or over. There was never any need for rapid striking.

Soon after that, I tried a deep clear lake I occasionally fish to see if there were no roach larger than the seven-inchers usually caught there. All my attempts failed, so I asked Bill Penney if he could give me any tips. He wrote: 'I suggest you fish in deep water, twenty feet if your lake is as deep as that, and try and fish always with the wind in your face. The rougher it is, the better. I fish with a No. 9 hook at this time of year (October) on 4x; in the summer when it is bright and clear, I use a No. 10 on 6x. The style I use is float-ledgering, which enables one to get out to any depth with ease; I use a sliding float, attached by the bottom ring only. Don't throw in ground-bait, but cup it round the hook-bait all the time. I think bread-crust is the best bait, a cube about a third of an inch square. *Don't strike at the first movement of the float, only when it is going away.*'

The fact that scale examination later showed that there were no big roach in that lake is unimportant. Here was a letter from a first-class still-water roach-angler—one of the only two men, I believe, who has caught three roach over 3 lb.—telling me that he agreed with what I had long suspected, i.e. in still waters, big roach do not need rapid striking; it pays to use a good-sized bait (a ⅓-inch crust will swell to nearly twice that size in the water), ground-bait should go to the bottom quickly and not form a cloud; and tackle, except under extremely bright and clear conditions, should be proportionate to the size of fish, both in thickness of gut and size of hook.

In passing, it will be observed that Mr. Penney is well aware of the effect of wind on the deep, extensive waters he fishes and knows that fishing in the teeth of the wind is the way to get results.

Later, Mr. Penney was kind enough to send me a specimen of the tackle he uses, ready made-up on a winder. It consists of a ledger used with both lead and float sliding; the lead looks as if it would weigh about $\frac{1}{8}$ oz. and has an ample hole through it. It is prevented from running down to the hook, a No. 8 short-shank spade-end gilt crystal, by a split-shot about twelve inches from the hook. The float has a bottom-ring made from a tiny loop of nylon monofil, and the line is threaded through this, its only point of attachment, so obviously no attempt is made to make the line float, which would be a disadvantage in rough water. The float is of the antenna type, a spine six inches long with a small pear-shaped cork body, five-eighths of an inch long and half an inch in diameter, in the middle. A tiny piece of rubber band, clove-hitched to the monofil line, limits the distance between float and lead. The whole thing is neat and practical and thoroughly effective, as Mr. Penney's catches prove.

This tackle would allow a crust to rise a foot above the bottom, but for crust-fishing, a dust-shot is pinched on about two inches from the hook, which will circumvent silkweed.

Mr. Penney usually uses a sixteen-foot Spanish reed rod with a split-cane top, but he tells me that when there is no wind and the water is of that amazing clarity sometimes seen in summer, with every grain of sand visible on the bottom fifteen feet down, he uses a nineteen-foot rod and a fixed float, and replaces the running lead with two shots. This reduces the splash of the cast and the long rod enables him to fish at a good depth and allows him to sit well back, out of the sight of the fish. I expect Mr. Penney has found, as I have, that it requires more than a few split shot to make a slider-float work satisfactorily. Of the nineteen-foot rod, he says, 'It is hard fishing!' Anyone who wants to catch big fish might note that the fact that it is hard fishing does not prevent him from using it.

Nevertheless, I have wondered if a floatless tackle might not be as good, used on a shorter rod with a dough-bobbin on the line between butt-ring and reel as a bite-indicator. In fishing into the wind on large lakes where a considerable wave is running it often pays to set the rod in rests with a good foot of its top (whose varnishing must be beyond reproach) under water, and if there is much of a swell, to sink the line thoroughly by wrapping a tiny ring of lead wire round the line above the rod-top, after the cast has been made. If the rod is held well up, this will run out along the line and sink it more deeply when the rod is replaced in its rests.

The famous roach of Hornsea Mere were fished for in a completely different way. Hornsea Mere is a shallow lake, and its roach were nearly all caught by boat-anglers using lobworms as bait. The technique was to fish with a fairly substantial cork-bodied float and two-hook tackle arranged so that one hook dragged bottom while the other hung a few inches above it. The hooks were often as large as No. 4, and baited with the largest lobworms that could be found. J. H. R. Bazley said that Hornsea roach were indifferent to paste or breadcrust and preferred above all else an outsize lobworm which they invariably attacked at the head end, where Hornsea anglers arranged for the hook to await them. Most roach like bread-baits, but a penchant for large lobworms is not confined to the roach of Hornsea Mere; and I believe that with increasing size roach become more and more interested in meat rather than veg. as an article of diet. It has been known for a long while that big roach eat a good deal of their own newly-hatched fry and probably that of other kinds of fish; and now from Holland comes news of the capture not only of some enormous roach but also bream on light spinning tackle, during June and the first half of July. It may be that the tendency to eat small fish then comes from some deficiency of protein or other necessity caused through spawning.

Almost every year we find anglers writing letters to the Angling Press reporting that they have caught big roach on live-baits or spinners. It has happened so often that no one need be surprised at it. Yet anglers nearly always are. 'Omar' (O. M. Reed) considers that roach-bream hybrids are predatory in character, and has seen shoals of them chasing small fry in reservoirs. The habit is not by any means confined to hybrids; true roach, bream, and rudd all eat quantities of small fry when they have the chance.

In Holland a definite technique has been evolved, and tiny spinners developed for fishing the shallows, where in the early part of the season big roach and bream are often found. A very light split-cane rod with a fixed-spool reel carrying a monofil line of about 1 lb. b.s. is used. The tiny spoon has a single split-shot nipped on about eighteen inches above it and is retrieved rapidly about six inches below the surface. At times, however, big roach will take larger spinners and the largest caught to date was taken on a pale gold spoon $1\frac{1}{4}$ inches long and $\frac{3}{4}$ inch wide, with a single triangle behind it, plentifully adorned with brown and white feathers and red wool.*

I doubt if these methods will ever replace the more usual ones but they should not be overlooked, and it may be that their use in this country would produce bigger roach than are now thought likely to exist.

Margin-fishing for carp has shown that in summer big roach will come to the surface and to the bank for bread-crust, provided they are not alarmed and that water-temperature is sufficiently high. More than once a roach of well over 2 lb. has done its best to take my matchbox-sized crust at dusk or during the night, and I am sure that with margin-fishing principles and tackle and bait scaled down to a suitable size, big roach could be caught on most waters, given peaceable fishing without the thumping and stamping about that many anglers seem unable to avoid. Because little roach are comparatively bold I suppose fishermen think that big ones are hard to scare too. This is

* Scale examination of many of the large 'roach' taken in Holland on spinners has revealed that these fish were, in fact, roach-bream hybrids.

not so. A big roach is one of the shyest and most timid of all fish and the only reason why carp and chub are rated more shy is because their departure is more easily seen. I do not think the roach, however big, is nearly as intelligent as some other species of fish, but of his extreme sensitivity to alarms there is no doubt.

More different baits must be known for roach-fishing than for any other fish. Ted Ensom ('Faddist') has a tremendous list in his *Baits and Groundbaits* and some good advice on their use in his most comprehensive work *Roach-fishing*.

Men have always searched in vain for the irresistible bait, and many roach-fishers place more faith in bait than in effective angling. Somebody reports that the roach in such-and-such a water are taking wheat because he has just caught some; whereupon everyone who goes there promptly stews up some wheat and confirms the original report, after which roach-fishing in that water is hardly thought worth trying without a plentiful supply of the stuff. This continues until, unable to get wheat, some enthusiast falls back on, say, pearl-barley. He catches roach, and the news spreads. Soon, pearl-barley alone will do. So it goes on, when plain bread paste would probably be equally effective all along, and more attention to keeping quiet and inconspicuous, and to choice of swim, etc., would have doubled the size of the catch.

I am all for experiment in baits or in methods, but there is a world of difference between thoughtful experiment and thoughtless switching from one bait to another. One often sees a man fishing with a well-known bait but catching nothing, perhaps because he is in the wrong place, or the fish are off feed, or, most commonly, have been thoroughly scared. Presently he tries another bait which proves equally useless, but which would have been equally good if the fish had been there and feeding. The second bait is, however, often condemned through its single failure and never used again. Or it may be an inferior bait, but tried at a time when the fish are just coming on feed or returning after having been scared. It then proves partially successful, but henceforth the angler will consider it vastly superior until something happens to change his mind.

My own experience has been that when roach are feeding and don't know you're there, it is seldom they cannot be tempted with paste, crust, or worm; but they will also take many other things, though most of them are small enough to be too easily taken by smaller fish. It might be helpful to try more natural baits like snails, freshwater shrimps, alder and mayfly larvae and the larvae of sedges, especially the great red sedge whose caddis-case is made of weeds.

Roach bite well at night and seem not to fear lights, so a white-topped float can be used and the beam of an electric lamp focused on it. They will feed at quite low temperatures, down to 40°F. and sometimes even lower, but they are soon put off if the temperature is too high and become difficult to catch on hot summer days, in common with most fish except rudd and chub. Much effort has been wasted on attempts to catch roach at the wrong time, but the man who wants to catch big roach is content to wait until his chances are at least reasonable.

Shoals of roach travel about a great deal, like bream, and seem to follow definite 'beats,' but unlike bream give little indication of their whereabouts, so that it is often difficult to find where they are. In a large water a trail of ground-bait will help, lying along the bottom and leading to the baited hook. Fishing for roach at long range may be done as for bream, and a running paternoster with hook-link and lead-link nearly equal in length can be effective, the lead being hidden in a ball of stiff ground-bait, alongside which the hook will lie when the line is pulled a foot or so after casting. If the angler cannot find the roach, he can only dispose his hook-bait and ground-bait in an intelligent way and hope *they* will find *it*; at the same time doing his best to ensure that they do not first find *him*.

On suitable tackle a good roach can put up a splendid fight and needs skilful handling. I am not ashamed to admit to having been broken by big roach, a much more sporting fish than the bream. It prefers gravel to mud and thus is not often found near the worst kind of vegetation such as

reeds, reed-mace, and water-lilies, so that it is seldom
necessary to use very stout tackle, and 3 lb. b.s. monofil
should ordinarily be strong enough to land the biggest
roach.

Unfortunately, few waters contain big roach. There
seems to be a sharp distinction between waters which will
and will not grow roach to specimen size. Some lakes and
reservoirs grow fine roach, 2-pounders being caught in
numbers each year, and 3-pounders being an ever-present
possibility. Other waters produce quantities of fish up to
half a pound, but nothing over; and between these extremes,
there is very little at all. It seems that there is some essential
to their growth which some waters possess and some do
not; I don't know what it is. It is said that they become
overcrowded, small, and stunted without sufficient predatory fish to keep the numbers down, but I doubt if this is
so. There are plenty of waters, with lots of predatory fish,
in which the roach never reach any size, and others containing big roach but no predatory species at all. I have
come to the conclusion that the essential is either an ingredient in the diet of the fish, or a suitable chemical com-
position of the water, or both, because the second may
affect the first. Inbreeding cannot be blamed, as intro-
ductions of roach from waters in which they attain good size
seem to have no effect.

I think that in cases where the roach never attain worthwhile size, *and where the water is clear*, it is a good thing to put
in perch rather than pike. They may thin out the roach
and improve their size thereby, but even if they fail in this,
they are at least likely to grow to good size themselves, since,
to a perch, even a four-inch roach is a good meal.

Some years ago the Freshwater Biological Association, at
the request of the National Federation of Anglers, investigated the biology of 'coarse fish,' and among other things
produced a table showing the rate of growth of the average
roach in the Norfolk Broads and the River Cam. The
figures given seem to have been taken to be representative
of roach everywhere. They have even been quoted in
support of the mistaken idea that given time, a little roach

will always grow into a big one. Actually, they have proved most misleading and all they show is the rate at which some very small roach managed to grow. It would be more useful to have figures giving the growth-rate of some *big* roach, with a biological survey and analysis of the water they came from, thus helping us to assess the maximum size to which small roach may grow in similar conditions, and showing what those conditions are.

The more valuable parts of the Freshwater Biological Association's report, made by Mr. P. H. T. Hartley, appear to have been largely overlooked by anglers. He said that at the start of the discussions with the N.F.A. it was assumed that 'deficiencies of numbers and poor qualities of stocks were alike to be made good by the straightforward policy of restocking.' I have seen no indication that this view has been changed, as far as the N.F.A. and many River Boards are concerned, and while good quality fish cost money and useless stunted ones can be got much more cheaply and in vast quantities, and while those who provide them can maintain their popularity among anglers by doing so, no change seems likely.

At the present time, the introduction of roach into a still-water fishery is a decided gamble, with the odds against success.

The question of hybrids is one which puzzles many anglers, and though this is not intended to be a book on ichthyology, a few remarks may be helpful on how to distinguish hybrids.

Hybrids, as far as we know, are the progeny of parents of different species and are themselves sterile. It is therefore impossible for a fish to be, say, three-quarters roach and one-quarter bream, or 'a roach with a dash of bream blood in it' as I once heard a fine specimen of a true roach dubbed, simply because, like most big lake-roach, it was deep-bodied and rather dark in colour compared to smaller specimens.

The only hybrids one is likely to meet in still waters are roach-bream and roach-rudd. Hybrids between roach and bronze bream are fairly common in some waters, and while I have yet to see a cross between a roach and a silver bream,

(*left*) May Berth-Jones is attached to a large pike; (*right*) the landing net that landed the record carp is more than adequate for May Berth-Jones's big pike

(*above*) Gerry Berth-Jones lands a big pike; (*below*) a catch of pike from Slapton Ley

I expect they exist. A true roach can easily be distinguished from either hybrid by counting the number of rays in its anal fin, i.e. the fin nearest its tail. If this fin has more than twelve branched rays, the fish is not a true roach. Actually an experienced angler can spot a hybrid roach-bream at a glance.

The other hybrid, the roach-rudd, is more difficult to distinguish. One feature of the lightning-strike procedure is the number of tiny roach which are deprived of their top lips early on, making their mouths distinctly rudd-like. MacMahon says the roach-rudd hybrid will have 42 or 43 scales in the lateral line; true roach have 40 to 46 and rudd 39 to 44, so that this test tells us little, except that a fish having 44 to 46 lateral line scales, and which looks like a roach, *is* a roach and not a roach-rudd hybrid; a fish of similar appearance with 42 or 43 lateral line scales could be either. MacMahon further says that in a roach-rudd hybrid 'the *beginning* of the dorsal fin is in a direct line above the middle of the ventral fins or over the tip of the little loose scale bordering these fins.'

If the presence of 42 or 43 lateral line scales and the position of the dorsal fin lead one to suspect a fish of being a roach-rudd hybrid, the best plan is to send scales to someone who knows how to read them; the absence or otherwise of spawning marks will show whether the fish is a hybrid, while other indications will also help to determine its identity.

FURTHER NOTES

Hybrids

Since this book was first written, the problem of identifying roach-rudd hybrids has caused much confusion, and now we have a roach-rudd hybrid, caught near Stamford in 1964 and weighing 3 lb. 14 oz., accepted by the Record Fish Committee as a true roach equalling Mr. W. Penney's record fish.

Here are the identifying characters:

	Roach	*Rudd*	*Hybrid*
Scale colour	Silvery sides, tinged with copper in large fish in some waters	Except in very small specimens, brassy yellow or golden sides	Pale brassy yellow sides
Eye colour	Crimson iris	Yellow or golden iris	Yellow-orange iris
Fin colour	Lower fins crimson to blood red	Lower fins orange	Lower fins orange-red
Mouth shape	Top lip overhangs bottom lip	Bottom lip projects beyond top lip	Lips level
Abdominal keel	Absent	Present	Present
Pharyngeal teeth numbers	One row of 5 or 6 teeth each side	5 large, 3 small, each side	5 or 6 large, 1 or 2 small each side or on one side only*
Pharyngeal teeth appearance	Smooth or very lightly serrated	Heavily serrated	Definitely serrated

* In some examples of roach–rudd hybrids, these small second-row teeth are absent, probably because they are extremely fragile and easily broken. Examination of the pharyngeal bones will, however, reveal their roots or sockets.

In addition to the separate characters, there is the general appearance. With experience one can distinguish the hybrid at a glance. It is more heavily built, the mouth shape is obvious, and the yellowish or brassy colour cast in scales, eye and fins, most noticeable. Yellow or brassy pigmentation is characteristic of rudd that exceed about 1 lb. in weight. Even in the variety in which red pigment is absent, the yellow remains.

In recent years good catches of big roach have been made with the aid of swim-feeders. Of these there are two types, open-ended and so-called 'block'. With the open-ended type, samples of hook-bait mixed with dry ground-bait are held inside a simple clear plastic tube with plugs of dampened squeezed ground-bait. In the water, the dry stuff swells and ejects the plugs.

The 'block' feeder has one end permanently closed, while the other has a lid. Maggots or other hook-bait samples are kept in by the lid during the cast, but escape through the holes or slots in the sides when the feeder is on the bottom.

Having regard to the difficulty many anglers experience in

placing both hook-bait and ground-bait in the same place, the swim-feeder can be most helpful, though the quantity of hook-bait samples or ground-bait that it can distribute is severely limited.

Where greater quantities are necessary, one can improve ground-baiting accuracy by throwing out a marker buoy, consisting of a very large brightly coloured float attached to a heavy lead by a length of strong nylon, a foot longer than the depth of the water. This can be cast out with rod and reel, or simply chucked out by hand and retrieved at the end of the day by casting over it.

These expedients are not, of course, confined to roach-fishing, but can also be used for bream, tench, crucians and rudd, where the last species is likely to feed at the bottom.

CHAPTER XI

RUDD

RUDD are among the most beautiful freshwater fish. There are four varieties. The commonest has brilliant red ventral and anal fins and a red tail. The back is greenish and the sides are silver in an immature fish. As it gets older the sides become more and more tinged with brassy gold. Fish of 2 lb. and over are quite coppery in some waters, though the depth of colour varies with the water. The eye is brassy-yellow.

Another variety, not very common, is identical except that its fins, instead of being red, are bright lemon-yellow. This is not an environmental variation, the yellow-finned fish being found in the same water and among shoals of the common sort.

There are also two varieties of rudd which are practically limited to aquaria, or ornamental ponds, the 'red' rudd and the golden rudd.

The rudd reaches weights of from 4 lb. to 5 lb. in exceptional cases, but specimens over 2½ lb. are uncommon. They are by no means formidable fighters, and nothing very stout in the way of tackle is needed to deal with them. Equipment for rudd-fishing should be on similar lines to that used for bream, for rudd delight in shallow water and must not be approached too closely; you will therefore want an outfit that will cast a good distance. Since rudd are largely surface-feeders, it is worth while adding a fly-rod and tackle to the other equipment. A tackle-strength of 3 to 4 lb. b.s. is strong enough except where the rudd are very large and weeds or snags numerous. Hooks can be gilt crystals, sizes from 12 to 8, according to the type of bait used.

The methods depend largely on temperature. In warm

weather the shoals feed at or near the surface and should
be fished for there; it is seldom, if ever, that water temperature in Britain is too high for rudd to feed. Where a boat
is available, or the fish can be covered from the bank, a
deadly way of fishing is to use a fly-rod with a hook-to-gut
instead of a fly, carrying a bunch of six or eight gentles. The
fish will take an artificial fly, especially one with the well-
known white kid tag, and they are very partial to gold-
bodied patterns, but I have always found the gentles more
effective. Get out as long a line as you can cast comfortably.
It must be well-greased and so should all but the last link
of the cast. Strike on seeing the line pulled along the
surface. Ground-bait can take the form of crusts of bread
anchored to the bottom, or you can throw in loose crusts
and follow them down-wind in a boat, keeping as far away
as you can cast.

In many cases, however, the rudd are well away from the
bank and no boat is available. Then you must use tackle
that will cast a much greater distance than the twenty
yards or so which is as far as most anglers can throw a
fly continuously. With a split-cane rod of the right design,
a fixed-spool reel, and a fairly heavily-loaded float, it is
possible to cast forty or fifty yards; in extreme cases sixty
yards or more can be covered by using a big fixed-spool reel,
loaded with fine monofilament, and a fairly powerful rod.
I have on occasions succeeded in throwing a big stream-
lined balsa float, carrying a barrel lead, well over sixty
yards, using 0·006-inch perlon monofil line, a big, fixed-
spool reel and a ten-foot casting-rod. You have to use
fifteen feet of stronger monofil above the lead to take the
shock of casting. Usually, however, a forty-yard cast is
sufficient to cover the fish, and the Avon type rod and small
fixed-spool reel is adequate.

Floats for rudd-fishing near the surface should always be
fitted with a piece of valve-rubber at the top through which
the line passes, otherwise the hook will frequently catch
on the line above the float. For long-distance work, well-
varnished paper or thin celluloid vanes, painted a good
colour and fixed to the top of the float, help to keep the

lead ahead of the float during its flight and make the float easy to see.

If the vanes are made semicircular, they have the appearance of a little ball sitting on the surface, yet the pull needed to take the float under is not in the least increased. Such floats are excellent for long-distance work in calm conditions, for all kinds of fish, but in a wind they drag badly.

SIDE VIEW   END VIEW

FLOAT WITH VANES FOR EXTRA VISIBILITY AT LONG RANGE

Ground-baiting can be done by the usual floating crust method; if you can arrange to fish downwind, the crusts can be ground to a coarse powder and thrown high into the air. If this is repeated at intervals, the shoals of rudd will be attracted upwind for a considerable distance. Avoid attracting them too close or they may catch sight of you and take fright. Alternatively, crusts can be allowed to drift against weeds or reeds, or moored in hair-nets to which a stone is attached by a length of string or monofilament.

Baits for fishing just under the surface include cubes of breadcrust, paste, maggots and small worms. Rudd are greedy feeders and will take any of the above baits; since maggots are less likely to be detached from the hook in casting, they are probably the best thing to use; indeed, I have never known rudd show a preference for anything else. Sometimes, however, one can use a lump of paste, or an outsize lobworm, large enough to keep off the small fish and catch larger ones.

Where the water is no deeper than two or three feet, you can catch rudd on light ledger-tackle, the bait being allowed to lie on the bottom. Ground-bait can be the usual bread and bran and should be mixed stiff enough to allow it to be thrown a good distance. Where there is a carpet of silkweed or very soft mud use breadcrust and set the distance between ledger-lead and hook so that the latter is an inch or so above the bottom weed. You can also fish bread crust by using a float made of heavy wood which only just floats, and no lead, the float remaining horizontal on the surface about two feet from the hook. For big rudd, a piece of crust about $\frac{1}{2}$-inch across is not too large.

In colder weather rudd are more difficult to catch. They feed best in temperatures upwards of 45°F. and, like the majority of still-water fish move into deeper water as temperature falls; but instead of hugging bottom, they often move about in shoals at a depth of six or seven feet giving no sign of their whereabouts. The best plan is to use a slowly-sinking ground-bait and to fish at a depth of six feet or so in the hope of attracting these roving shoals. Sometimes they will feed at greater depths but I have only once caught rudd actually feeding on the bottom in deep water, and that occasion was a contradiction of the usual rule, for it was a warm summer day. The rudd were feeding on the bottom in twelve feet of water alongside a dense bed of yellow water-lilies, and I was float-ledgering for tench. Rudd after rudd seized the small worm, and I caught ten weighing 16 lb.; nowhere else were sizeable rudd caught in that lake on that day. Why they were there I don't know, but it was an exceptional case; apart from this instance all my best catches of rudd, including one of forty fish weighing 64 lb., have been made fishing not more than two feet deep.

Anglers who do much margin-fishing for carp will know that large rudd may be caught in the same way, using suitable tackle. The best way to catch a number of fish is to fish along the bank with a long rod pointing left or right as the angler prefers. A hooked rudd can then be steered round and away from the large crust which will have been moored to the bank to attract the fish, so that the rest are not scared by the struggles of the hooked fish.

In some waters, rudd develop predatory habits and may be caught by spinning; a light outfit such as is used in spinning for trout is suitable, except where there are fringes of reeds or weeds to cast over when a long rod is much better. Small spoons are effective. It may be that much remains to be discovered about rudd; for though they are sometimes most difficult to catch, they usually respond so well to well-known methods that anglers have little incentive to work out better ways of catching them. As with roach, natural baits would almost certainly be effective, but there is no need to spend much time in catching caddis and other larvae when the rudd are equally willing to take maggots.

In late autumn rudd can usually be found on the *edges* of the shallows, in three or four feet of water. I have seldom succeeded in catching rudd in winter, though a spell of mild weather may bring them out and into their summer and autumn haunts. Then they are inclined to feed on the bottom in shallow parts of the lake rather than on the surface.

Rudd grow best in lakes where the level alters. Wherever a water changes its level from year to year, exposing considerable areas of bottom at intervals, both rudd and tench thrive and grow big. Unless, however, a water contains predatory fish, the rudd are said to increase so that they outrun the available food supplies, resulting in vast numbers of small, stunted fish. That such small fish do exist in many waters is beyond doubt. Whether the introduction of predators has much effect is not yet fully proved. As with stunted roach, introducing perch may at least produce big perch, even if it has little effect on the size of the rudd.

Rudd are so easy to catch at times that they will even take a bare gilt hook devoid of bait. They are extremely prolific and, given sufficient food, grow quite quickly. In shallow lakes their presence is usually an asset; being surface-feeders, they do not interfere too seriously with baits fished on the bottom for tench and carp; and where they grow to a respectable size can provide very good sport themselves. It should be remembered, however, that unless ample feed is available they will remain small and be a nuisance to anglers out for large species, since small hungry rudd feed at all depths.

Rudd are not suited to all waters, and I know of two in which the large quantity originally introduced seem to have died out, though fish of other species, including roach, have increased in numbers. They seem to feed largely on such forms of insect life as is found in weeds and marginal sedges, etc., and unless there are large areas of surface weed they seldom grow large.

I have always thought it a pity that some of the best rudd-fishing in Britain is inaccessible to the angler, because it is in reservoirs which are stocked with trout and controlled by trout-fishers, who, though they complain bitterly that their waters are overrun with large rudd, will allow no one to make any attempt to remove them by angling.

FURTHER NOTES

In some waters, usually extensive, clear, and reed-fringed ones, rudd spend most of the daylight hours in the reed-beds. Traditionally they may be enticed into open water by ground-baiting or by drifting floating crusts, loose or enclosed in hairnets. In practice this is only occasionally successful; more often it is necessary to fish close up against the reeds, or in spaces between reed-clumps. This is done from a boat, except where one can cast from the bank across to reed-beds opposite.

The secret is to use a float attached by pieces of rubber tube at each end, and to put the bulk of the shot touching one another, right up against the bottom of the float. The tackle can then be cast to strike the reed-stems. When the float drops in the water, it remains close to the reeds and the baited hook swings down and underneath it.

Now and then the hook catches on the line above the float, and one has to retrieve, unhitch and re-cast, but despite that, the method is very successful. A difference of a foot or two in the distance between the bait and the reeds can have a very great influence on the number of rudd you catch.

CHAPTER XII

CHUB

WE seldom consider chub as inhabitants of still waters and I had never intended to deal with them here until I came across a shoal in a Lincolnshire lake I fish for carp. A number of alleged record roach caught in still waters have now been divided into hybrid roach-bream and chub respectively, and it seems that still-water chub are more common than I had supposed. Lt.-Col. G. Lawton Moss, the pioneer of the amateur rod-building revival of recent years, tells me that Lake Vyrnwy teems with big chub which are quite easy to catch, and I have promised myself that I shall investigate them one day.

My limited experience of chub in still waters has given me a healthy respect for them. I have caught a great many chub in rivers, including some big ones, but never found them more difficult to catch than in that Lincolnshire lake. River chub are shy; often they seem to have eyes in their tails, and they feel vibrations easily. Those Lincolnshire chub probably have eyes in their tails, too, but since they lie in a shoal facing in all directions, they can use the eyes in their heads, and anyone who can get within thirty yards without alarming them has my respect.

An additional difficulty is that the shoal lives on the outermost fringe of the branches of two large chestnut trees, that overlap and trail in the water about fifteen yards out from the bank. These cover a length of about thirty yards of bank and of course the chub are at the exact centre: to reach them means a cast of at least seventy yards from the opposite bank of the lake. If the fairly large lead necessary to achieve this does not overshoot and land in the chestnut branches its descent will certainly disperse the chub, and leaving the bait for them to find when they return has resulted only in the capture of eels or insignificant bream.

The size of individuals in this shoal ranges from one to five pounds, at a guess. So far, I have succeeded in catching just one of them, which, needless to say, was a 1-pounder. John Ellis had one a little bigger while carp-fishing at night at a spot as far from their daytime haunt as it is possible to fish. And one morning before sunrise an elder of the community neatly removed the crust from Maurice Ingham's hook where it had been placed to attract a big, margin-patrolling carp. That is the total of success, if it deserves any such description.

With such limited experience I cannot offer much advice about catching still-water chub. Those at Vyrnwy are caught by fly-fishing, usually by accident, I imagine, and where it is possible to come within range, in the daytime, the well-known technique of fly-fishing for river chub would probably be equally effective on lakes; as with chub everywhere, the approach is more than half the battle. There may be circumstances where the chub could be reached with a floatless, leadless line bearing only a hook with a lobworm or a small floating crust on it. I have seen the Lincolnshire chub take a crust without hesitation whenever they were not alarmed but I have not yet been able to get a crust to them with a hook in it. A crust floated up above a lead might do the trick if the chub came back before it had been broken up and consumed by small roach.

There seems no doubt that these chub roam far and wide from dusk to daylight, and at various depths, and no doubt a bait placed to intercept them would be effective, if we had any idea of the paths their goings and comings take. Fly-fishing in the dark with a big floating sedge might bring one of them up, and any persistent angling with baits attractive to chub would account for a few over a long period; but that is not a very positive approach.

These still-water chub present a very difficult and challenging problem, one that requires a great deal more study and experiment than I have been able to give it as yet.

Chub are at least semi-predatory, and spinning, or the use of plugs, might prove effective in catching them. Ken Sutton suggests that a frog, with or without a lead would be worth trying. The whole business of chub in still waters strikes me as most interesting, and the experimental stocking of a virgin water such as a gravel-pit with chub only might result in an extension of our knowledge and some excellent sport, for the chub can be caught in a variety of ways and will put up a splendid fight if sufficiently light tackle is used. If the lake in Lincolnshire is any criterion, it does not need running water for chub to grow big, nor for them to breed successfully, and as they will feed in very cold water, they would provide sport in winter when most other species except roach, perch and pike, are more or less inactive.

Edward Fitzgibbon (*Ephemera*) was emphatic that the chub is a pond fish and his experience was not small. Certainly stream-fed lakes breed and feed fine chub and we may find them a great asset to some still-water fisheries.

FURTHER NOTES

After twenty years, I have learned little more about how to catch still-water chub. I caught one of 5 lb. 6 oz. at Redmire Pool, on a balanced paste-and-crust bait put out for carp, and I have taken a few others up to $4\frac{1}{2}$ lb. from still-water fisheries in various ways, mostly by accident when fishing for some other species. The only ones I have taken by design were caught either on an artificial daddy-long-legs fished with a fly-rod, or on balanced crust-and-cheese baits, arranged to sink very slowly indeed.

I found the chub would only take these baits while they were actually sinking. Once they rested on the bottom, the chub would have nothing to do with them. I should think an inflated lobworm that just, but only just, sank, would be equally effective.

CHAPTER XIII

PIKE

ALFRED JARDINE showed that it is possible to understand pike and how to catch them; unfortunately he failed to pass on his knowledge through his writings, for he painted only the details of the picture instead of the background. It is difficult for a man to put into words his understanding of what passes for the mind of a fish, but that he possessed that understanding Jardine's results clearly prove. Perhaps the best modern advice on pike-fishing is contained in Norman Hill's *A Fisherman's Recollections* (Herbert Jenkins) which every pike-fisher should read.

I do not understand pike. My pike fishing has been mainly done on text-book lines by going through a ritual without properly understanding its deeper meaning, and as always when one fishes in that way, the results have been poor. That is probably because I do not like pike; whenever I hook one I feel as Jorrocks did towards his horse when he said 'Come *hup*, you hugly brute!'

My contribution to the reader's knowledge, if I can make any, must therefore be on methodical or mechanical lines rather than the more intimate approach.

There are a number of theories about the feeding of pike, of which two are worth considering here. One is Maurice Ingham's, and I think he would wish me to say that he is in no way dogmatic about it, but he thinks it worth going into.

He points out that days when pike are feeding ravenously are as rare as days when none are feeding at all; that on most days a small proportion of the fish are feeding at any given time. He further suggests that on these 'average' days those pike which are not feeding, are abstaining because they have had enough, for the time, of the most readily available food. Most animals find any food unpalatable after they have eaten enough of it.

Maurice suggests that these 'fed-pike' are more likely to be tempted by a bait which is unlike their natural food and he cites the fact that a fish strange to the water is usually a better live bait than one to which the pike are accustomed. An example is the deadliness of dace as bait in lakes where dace are not found. It is also possible, he thinks, that the well-known tendency to attack injured fish or hooked fish as they are being drawn in is due to their giving the pike's rather limited mind the idea, not that they are injured or tethered, but that they are *different*.

A further suggestion Maurice makes is that pike may have an instinct to attack anything which moves violently. One frequently sees a pike lying quite still with small roach all round it, yet if one of them is hooked and struggles the pike will have it like a shot.

Naturally, a *hungry* pike will attack anything which appears edible.

If these ideas are correct, it means, says Maurice, that the bait or lure should be one which either imitates the pike's natural food behaving in an unnatural way, or makes no pretence of imitating anything but moves violently in one way or another.

This is the broad outline: he qualifies it by saying that it disregards the question of colour, which should be considered as well as the other points he makes; he says that the effectiveness of plugs painted and shaped to imitate baby pike, and the deadliness of baby pike as live-baits, must not be overlooked.

I believe that experiments along the lines of these ideas would be well repaid.

The other theory is the 'profit-and-loss' idea. According to this theory, the natural feeding of wild things is governed by the balance struck between the energy-value of a food and the energy required to get it. There must always be a surplus in the food-value obtained for a given expenditure of energy. This surplus is necessary to make good the natural wastage of body-tissue in fully-grown creatures; in growing creatures, a greater surplus is required. Anything over and above these requirements would be stored as fat, and it is probable that this is prevented from becoming excessive by the unpalatability-mechanism mentioned by Maurice Ingham.

As a pike—or any other fish—becomes larger, the energy it requires to propel itself at a given speed becomes greater; not only greater in proportion, but greater per pound. The weight of a fish increases in proportion to the *cube* of its length; its tail-fin area only as the *square*.* As a pike grows larger, therefore, it will have to concentrate more and more on meals that are easily got—meals that give an increasing return of energy compared to the energy spent in getting them. Injured fish will appeal, but injured fish are relatively uncommon. In practice, no matter what its size, a pike will prefer the biggest fish it can comfortably swallow, other things being equal, and as it grows it will tend to feed on bigger and bigger fish. Its prey will largely consist of fish that swim in shoals and, as shoals usually contain individuals similar in size, the pike will go for shoals with fish of a size best suited to its needs. The growth of pike will therefore be governed, broadly, by the size of the fish on which it preys, excepting those such as carp that rapidly grow too big for pike to swallow.

The immediate objection that big pike often take little baits can, I think, be met. It is not suggested that a pike will always refuse a bait smaller than that which at the time forms the bulk of his food. Whether he will or not depends on the amount of energy it takes to get it, which means that he will probably take it if it is nearer, or slower than, or otherwise easier to get than fish of his 'favourite size.'

The fact that a pike often takes a small spinner or plug—*any* artificial lure is small compared to the 'favourite size' of a really big pike—may be because the disturbance caused by the majority of artificials, specially spoons, is greater than that caused by a swimming fish of double or treble

* I know that scientists say that it is not the tail-fin which propels a fish. I do not believe them. My whole experience goes to show that those fish whose tail area is greatest, pull hardest and accelerate fastest. In the pike, anal and dorsal fins are near the tail, and assist also.

the size. The theory that vibration in the water is one of the primary attractors of pike seems to be proved, and once the pike has expended the energy needed to overtake a spinner he cannot replace it, and even when he sees that the 'fish' is much smaller than its vibrations made it seem, he will probably make the best of a bad bargain, unless he decides that it is not edible, or the reek of formalin puts him off.

This would explain why my own experience has been that the clearer the water, the less effective are those artificials which depend mainly on vibration for their success.

Perhaps, however, this all assumes that pike are more intelligent than they really are!

One other objection to the theory remains: pike of all sizes up to very big ones—Norman Hill mentions one of 22 lb.—have been found full of fish as small as an inch long or even less. I think this occurs when there are concentrations of these tiny fish, as explained in the chapter on perch. Then, a pike may be able to grab quite a large number at one mouthful, and since these densely-packed shoals are collectively slow, little energy is required to take toll of them.

There is one other feature of the theory, which is, simply, that a fully-grown pike needs less food than a growing one and will therefore feed less, needing only to replace wastage of body-tissue.

If this 'profit-and-loss' theory is correct, how does it affect pike-fishing? I think we can draw the following conclusions, if we are careful to treat them as generalizations rather than hard-and-fast rules:

(1) To catch bigger pike we should use bigger baits, or lures which give the impression of being bigger fish.

(2) The nearer a bait is to a pike the more likely he is to take it; the fact that he sees it or feels its vibrations may not be sufficient to make him attack it unless it is near; and this, of course, puts a premium on the most careful searching of the water.

(3) A lure should be drawn along as slowly as is compatible with its deceptiveness and the requirements of (2). Obviously we have a difficulty here; the faster we cover the water

(*above left*) Fred J. Taylor (left) and brother Ken with a morning's catch of bream, tench and rudd, taken on a Lincolnshire lake; (*above right*) four big eels from Woldale Lake; (*below*) a pike lure made from a muskrat skin for Fred Buller by the author

(*right*) Barrie
Rickards with a
10lb 6oz zander;
(*below*) Barrie
Rickards returns a
zander of 13¼lb

the more likely we are to put our lure near enough to a pike
for him to take it, but we are then less likely to offer it
slowly enough to make him go after it.

(4) Anything which imitates a wounded fish will be
attractive for it will seem to the pike an easy meal. This
point, it should be noted, occurs in Maurice Ingham's
theory, though for a different reason.

It may well be that these two theories are far from correct;
but I would always prefer to fish to some plan than to none,
and, with due regard to other matters affecting pike, of
which I shall say more later, I think methods that fit in with
either or both the above theories might catch big pike. They
would involve the use of a bait or lure which appeared to
the pike as a big, wounded, slowly-moving fish of a species
strange to, or uncommon in his water, and as near to him
as possible.

All those requirements are met by fresh herring on
wobbler tackle—but please note that I have *not* said that
a fresh herring on wobbler tackle is the best bait for a
big pike!

It has a number of other advantages. It is cheap and
easily got, and lasts well in use. It is soft and pike hang on
to it; if allowed they will usually swallow it—they seem to
like its flavour. It is as big as can reasonably be cast, but
not too big. The best pike I have taken to date, a poor best
of 17½ lb., was taken on a wobbled fresh herring.

Too little attention is paid nowadays to the use of natural
baits. I seldom see a natural of any size used on waters
where I fish. Everyone is using artificials of one kind or
another, mostly spoons which all look too small and too
flashy to me. If I had to use a spoon for big pike I should use
one like Jim Vincent's Broads spoon, which is nearly six
inches long. All plugs seem too small but I have caught a
lot of small pike, up to 8 lb. or so, on plugs painted like baby
pike: olive back, silvery sides crossed by diagonal bright
primrose stripes, and a white belly. One home-made
jointed plug, long and thin, has done very well with these
smaller pike. It is a floater, but dives when pulled. I have
another big jointed plug, also home-made, about seven

inches long, with an action and colouring like a wounded rudd; this, too, has done well on the smaller pike, and I rather fancy its chances of catching a big one some day unless I lose it first. But I think the natural is normally best, and failing a fresh herring, I would use a roach or dace at least eight inches long, mounted quite simply by threading a two-foot single-wire trace-wire with a No. 2 treble attached to it, from mouth to vent. If I wanted to fish very deep I should thread a barley-corn lead or two on the wire and shove them down the fish's throat. There would, of course, be a swivel and an anti-kink lead between the line and the trace.

These natural baits are heavy. To use them, you need a fairly powerful double-handed rod of the type suggested for live-baiting in the chapter dealing with tackle. For the specialist in big pike probably a multiplier is a better reel than anything else. But nothing can save this sort of outfit and this kind of bait from being a strenuous combination to use, and you may very well emulate the pike in balancing the value of what you get against the energy expended in getting it. You may be consoled to think that you need less energy to use modern tackle than the gear recommended by Alfred Jardine!

To avoid exertion, recourse may be had to live-baiting, which may also be necessary where vegetation or snags make spinning impossible. It often fails when it is used as a "second string" and the angler's attention and interest are mainly occupied by some other kind of fishing. It fails even more often owing to the cruel way in which the bait is attached to the hooks. That shudder the bait gives when the hook is stuck into its back means it is badly hurt, and setting aside moral considerations, a badly hurt bait does not remain a live bait very long. Dead baits suspended off the bottom catch few pike. See note on page 241.

But it is possible to live-bait in an intelligent and reasonably humane manner. We have mentioned rod and reel; the line ought to float when needed and for that reason, I think, should be a plaited one. For ordinary float-fishing, the commonest and the worst kind of float is the *Fishing*

Gazette type with a slit body and wooden peg. By saying this, I intend no discourtesy to the fine angling journal from which this relic received its name!

This anachronism loses its peg, and thus itself, at the least provocation and especially when you strike. If you force the peg in hard in an attempt to prevent this you break the body in two. The peg catches weed whether the float is coming or going, the body is a poor shape and usually a bad colour, and the whole thing prevents you from fishing any deeper than the length of the rod except by the use of curious devices or contortions.

The best pike-float I know of consists of a thin whole bamboo with a small hole right down its centre, covered with a cork body shaped like a slim aerial bomb—a 'Tallboy' bomb, if you know what that looks like. The upper third, the *pointed* end, please note—is painted with a colour made by mixing yellow and deep pink; this gives a salmony-orange colour, the best I know for visibility under all sorts of varying conditions. There is a similar colour, even easier to see, in the range of daylight-fluorescent paints. The size of this float can be what you like; mine just goes under with a 2 oz. lead.

To use it, you simply thread the line through the central hole and set your depth by fixing a small piece of rubber-band with a clove-hitch to the line. Or you may tie across a plaited line a two-inch length of cuttyhunk, which does not slip too easily though you can push it up or down when you wish.

Since either of these stops will go easily through your rod-rings, you can fish as deep as you like, for the float is a free slider. When you strike, you strike *through* the float. If you want to use pilot floats, let them have holes large enough for the stop to pass through readily; a very small pilot with a wire ring is good.

The spiral lead with the little brass corkscrews at each end cannot be too strongly condemned. Its advantage is that it can be easily put on: its disadvantage, the ease with which it comes off. Spinning loses it for you more quickly than live-baiting, but that it will escape sooner or later you may be certain. In the larger sizes it will usually bring home some weeds first.

For live-baiting an ordinary, simple barley-corn lead threaded on the line is much better. It rests against the swivel between line and trace which should always be there to avoid the trace-wire cutting the line.

I do not use a separate trace; I make up a tandem tackle on eighteen inches of single wire with a swivel at one end, and at the other the *original* Jardine snap with the upper treble hook fixed and not movable. I carry three of these tackles with varying distances between the hooks to accommodate different sizes of bait, finding it very much easier and quicker to change the tackle than to fiddle about with the adjustment on the usual kind of Jardine snap, which kinks the wire badly and in any case can't be got on the single wire I prefer—the proper place for a hawser, to my mind, being in shipping rather than fishing.

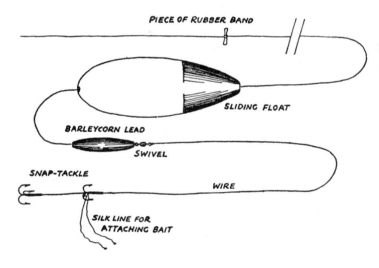

In passing, beware of the Jardine snaps in the shops nowadays. Too many hooks snap at the least provocation.

Since a live-bait does better without hooks stuck into its heart or its spine I catch the small hook of the end triangle in the top of the gill-slit, as advised by Jardine; *not* in the root of the pectoral fin; and I *tie* the upper treble to the back of the fish, just in front of its dorsal, with a piece of 2 lb. b.s. white silk line which goes twice round the fish, crossing between the ventral fins. It takes longer than sticking-in the hook; but the bait not only stays on during the cast, but remains a live-bait.

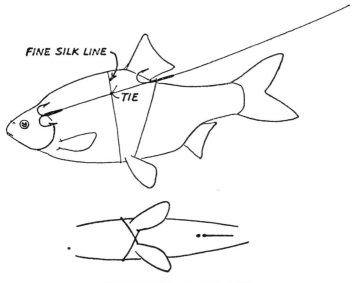

ATTACHMENT OF LIVE BAIT

Live-baits may be fished on ledger or paternoster, with or without a float, using the same arrangement of hooks and I do not think any explanation is necessary for either of these methods, which, in still-water fishing, need only be used when you want to tether the bait. They should not be used purely because the water is *deep*; the slider float provides for that.

Unless a pike is known to inhabit a definite place, or weeds and snags make it impracticable, the live-bait on float-tackle is probably preferable since it covers much more ground by making use of wind and drift. When one is using a paternoster at a distance it is as well to use a cork or a bubble-float a few feet above the junction of line and trace, otherwise an excessive length will be needed between trace and lead to keep the bait off the bottom.

Fishing for pike is largely a winter pursuit. I think the commonly held idea that in winter the pike, especially the big ones, are near or on the bottom in the deepest water, is generally correct: and it is necessary to spin close to the bottom, or display a live bait there, to catch them. Attention should be given to underwater features of the lake-bed which the pike can use as an ambush. The rule about fishing deep is disregarded by far too many pike-fishers, mainly, I think, owing to the ubiquity of the fixed float making deep-water fishing difficult. But there are exceptions to the rule. The temperature of lakes that are shallow all over will be much the same everywhere, especially in winter, and on mild winter days the pike may be found anywhere, often in water no more than eighteen inches deep. In such conditions a floating plug is probably the best thing to use, preferably one which will dive to an extent controllable by the rate of winding and the height at which the rod-point is held. This can be worked near the surface in the shallower parts and, by lowering the rod-point and winding more quickly, be made to dive down into any holes or deeper water.

Floating plugs are also useful where the bottom is very snaggy, irrespective of its depth. By using a two-foot wire trace between reel-line and plug, and attaching to the junction a foot or so of monofil rather weaker than the line, with a lead attached to its end, it is possible to work the plug very slowly indeed, the lead dragging along the bottom. If it is hung-up, only the lead will be lost.

Floating, or perhaps more correctly, *buoyant* plugs seem to be universally damned with faint praise by anglers in this country. I would always prefer floaters to sinkers, because it is easy to make the floating type sink simply by adding lead. You cannot persuade the sinking type to float. Much, however, remains to be learned about the design and use of plugs, and in shallow waters, in autumn and on mild-winter days, there is no doubt that floaters have great possibilities. Pike attack them in the most vicious way, their rush often taking them feet up into the air.

The frequency with which pike attack and eat moorhens is well known. Most anglers at one time or another will have seen a moorhen vanish with an anguished cry in the middle of a mighty swirl. Peter Thomas and I once hatched a heroic plot for the catching of a very big bird-eating pike whose whereabouts we knew. The idea was to shoot and skin a moorhen and to sew its preserved hide over an artificial body built mainly of balsa wood, with a lead keel. Artificial green legs were to be arranged, each bearing a substantial treble hook, others being also attached at strategic points. (We decided to try it out first before including a mechanism with internal pendulum to make the legs kick alternately!) The line was to be attached to the front of the neck, well above water-level, and with the aid of a lead weight on the line, it was thought that a very realistic bobbing motion could be given to the thing.

To use it, one would put it into the water and then, paying out line, walk round the bay in which the pike lived. At a point where angler, 'moorhen' and pike's lair were in line, the 'moorhen' would be worked across. Failing an attack, the angler would return to his starting-point and repeat the process.

This particular floating plug has not yet been constructed, but in the U.S.A. attempts to imitate such things as frogs, swimming rats, and the like, have been quite successful. I still incline to the moorhen idea, however, because it will make such a magnificent angling story when the 40-pounder for which it was invented is caught on it.

Boat-fishing is a possibility; pike are not easily scared. Apart from the more usual methods of fishing, snap-trolling with a big fish—a herring is as good as anything—might be tried, especially in deep water. The bait has a leaded spike pushed down its throat and a couple of trebles arranged along its side, so that it hangs head-downwards. It is allowed to dive to the bottom, is then pulled up fairly slowly for several feet and allowed to dive again. Trolling is becoming a lost art, but it accounted for mighty pike in its day.

Many anglers confuse *trolling* and *trailing*. *Trailing* means dragging a spinner, natural or artificial, or a plug, behind a moving boat. This is illegal in some areas though I could never understand the objections to it; it is certainly a lazy way of fishing, but many other methods of fishing could be condemned on those grounds, too. Trailing is useful in fishing very large areas of water where the fish are hard to find, and it has taken some big pike. One has only to bear in mind the same considerations that apply to other ways of spinning, and to find out the most likely areas.

I need only add that two swivels, one at each end, are sufficient for any trace, and swivels about half the size fitted by the tackle-makers are strong enough for any pike that ever swam. 'Alasticum' wire makes cheap reliable traces less subject to kinking than those of most other single wires. Spinning leads may be half-moons made of thick sheet-lead, folded over the reel-line just above the trace: doubling the reel-line here is of benefit. There is no point in having swivels above the lead.

Alternatively a good spinning-lead can be made by making an eye at one end of a piece of 22 or 24 swg brass wire, and threading the other end through the right-sized barleycorn lead. Attach the end as neatly *and shortly* as possible to a swivel or a link-swivel, and bend the lead firmly to nearly a quarter-circle, making the twists in the brass wire disappear into the lead.

If the sharpness of hooks for other fish is important, for pike it is imperative. A pike has an extremely hard mouth, and only the sharpest hooks will penetrate it.

Towards the end of the last century, Francis Francis, or Cholmondeley Pennell, I forget which, did some experiments with hooks of different shapes and gave figures for the force required to bury them over the barb. The conclusion reached, which was that the sneck hook was by far the best, does not impress me. I think some factor other than the bend of the hooks, such as length of shank, thickness of wire, height of barb or sharpness of point, must have come into

it. If two hooks have the same shaped point and barb, are
the same size, and have the same angle of penetration, any
difference between the parts behind the barb is irrelevant;
that being so, we may as well use the strongest shape,
namely, the round bend. Keeping hooks dead sharp has
far more effect than shape on penetration.

Because the mouth of a pike is so hard, he needs firm
striking. There are many different views about striking pike,
some advocating a firm tightening, others a sharp strike,
others repeated striking. For my part, I believe in tightening gently until I can feel the fish and then hitting him
as hard as I can. With the right relationship between line
strength and rod-action breakage on the strike is almost
impossible. In spinning and plugging, of course, the preliminary tightening-up is unnecessary. In live-baiting we
have the vexed question of *when* to strike. With fairly small
baits on snap-tackle I think it as well to strike almost at
once: if you miss it usually means the pike was only a small
one anyway. But with a good big bait you should give
the pike time to turn it, and you can guess when he has by
keeping the line almost, but not quite taut as he runs off.
After he has stopped and the line has jerked a few times,
you may strike with reasonable certainty.

Playing pike is a matter of good hands and cool head, as
with any other fish, but there are a few points to watch. If
you put on too much pressure—and sometimes even when
you do not—a pike will come to the top, put his head out of
the water and shake it violently at you. Everyone tells me
you should drop the rod-point to slacken the line if this
happens. I do not believe them. The pike will shake out
the hooks quite readily enough, especially if they have a
heavy plug attached, without your assisting him by giving
slack. Drop the rod-point by all means—put it right in the
water—but *tighten* the line as much as you can.

A very big pike can be deceiving. I have never landed a
big one, but I have hooked several that stayed quite still for
as long as a minute before making off, making me think I
had hooked a snag. Having decided it was a snag I lowered
the rod-point to get a straight pull and was broken by a

terrific pull from the fish. Bernard Venables, who *has* caught some big pike, tells me that this imitation of a snag is a sure sign of a big one.

For a reason I cannot explain, while I detest gaffing all other species of fish, I have no compunction about gaffing pike. A gaff on a five-foot bamboo handle, firmly lashed on with varnished twine, and with a turned-up tang to avoid slipping is every bit as good as a more expensive one; two and a half inches is large enough for its gape, and it should be kept very sharp. Its point can be protected with a length of hollow cane tied to the shaft by a piece of strong line; this is much better and more durable than the usual cork.

The best place to gaff a pike is under the chin; but if there is any difficulty, put the gaff under the water, point up. As the fish comes, or is led over it, press the shaft up against his belly, a little forward of his point of balance, and at the same time snatch the point in, continuing the movement well back.

If you have a friend playing a big pike, and neither you nor he has a gaff or a large enough net, you can land his pike easily enough by cutting from the hedge a forked stick; leave about a foot on one arm of the fork and make the other about four inches long and point it. This point is stuck into the pike's chin, in the continuation of the gill-slit, and the fish can be dragged ashore easily enough. It has to be good wood, though: willow is useless.

Pike-fishing is at best an uncertain business. A big pike eats a big meal and takes a long time to digest it, especially if the water is cold. This, and their comparative scarcity, make it unlikely that a casual angler will catch them. When the big ones *are* feeding, the small ones keep very much out of their way and I am never encouraged by catching small pike: rather the reverse. Whenever I have seen big ones feeding or caught, there have been very few small pike about. I well remember a day when I hooked only one fish despite hours of arduous spinning, and that on a water which usually produces a dozen pike averaging 4 lb. or 5 lb. The one I hooked could easily have eaten any pike of the average size for that lake, which was probably why there were none about. Not one of the dozen other anglers fishing that water on that day caught a fish, either. Needless to say, my patriarch made good his escape; with me, they always do.

I have come to regard what might appear a 'dead' day more optimistically than I used to, because I tell myself that if I catch a pike at all it will probably be a 20-pounder at least.

Before leaving the subject it may be as well to consider the value of pike in a fishery. The popular assumption is that by keeping down the number of other fish and eliminating the sick and weakly ones, pike improve or keep up the standard of other species in a water. Examples are quoted of waters containing big pike and big roach; the roach, it is alleged, are big because their numbers are kept down by the pike. I think this idea is mistaken, and that the roach are not big because of the pike, but the pike are big because of the big roach. I further believe that the roach would be big, in many cases, whether the pike were there or not and that there might be a lot more big roach if the pike were removed. I know waters containing roach up to 2½ lb., where there are not and never have been any pike.

Carp reach great size without pike being there and the biggest carp I have ever seen live in a lake containing no other species with the exception of a few smallish eels.

I also know of quite a large number of cases where, in spite of frequent restocking with pike, the roach remain small and numerous, while the pike don't get very big either. In fact, most schemes of introducing pike to thin the numbers of stunted rudd or roach result in waters containing stunted rudd and roach, and stunted pike. A pike of five or six pounds may not seem a small fish to an angler, but stunted is the only term to apply to it if that is as big as it will ever grow.

The pike is certainly a most uneconomical fish, for to add a pound to its weight, a pike must eat at least 5 lb. of other fish.

I don't hope to convince many anglers that pike are undesirable fish, nor am I convinced that they always are. In some waters, evidence is conclusive that the presence of pike is essential to prevent roach from breeding too rapidly and deteriorating in size as a result. The pike is a fish liked by many anglers, and it would be a great loss if it became extinct: fortunately there is no danger of that, as the species is well able to take care of itself. Anyone in charge of fisheries, however, would do well to go into the question very thoroughly before preserving or introducing pike, particularly in the smaller waters of a few acres only, where it is more likely to be a liability than an asset.

The biggest freshwater fish ever caught in Britain was a pike. Among a mass of tales and legends of monstrous pike, this fish is beyond doubt. When you consider the time when it was caught, it is a matter for wonder that any record exists at all, but not only are the details of its capture fairly complete, but the jaws of the fish still exist.

At some period between the Jacobite rebellion in 1745 and the death of Bonnie Prince Charlie in 1788, John Murray, gamekeeper at Kenmure in Galloway, caught in Loch Ken a pike that weighed 72 lb. In 1910, its skull, still preserved in Kenmure Castle, was measured by no less an authority than Dr. Tate Regan, who found that it measured nine inches across the back and eight-and-a-half inches along the jaw. Nothing more was heard of the relic until 1952, when Malcolm Logan made a search for it. In an outhouse attached to a cottage at Kenmure, he found a case with most of its glass missing, and in it was all that was left of the skull of a mighty pike—little more than the great jaws. These, he found, were six inches wide, and the teeth were a full inch long.

I have measured the jaws of two stuffed pike, of 21 lb. and 23 lb. Both were less than three inches wide, and none had teeth as long as *half* an inch.

Doubts about the weight of the Kenmure pike have been expressed, an alternative weight of somewhere between 60 and 70 lb. having been given, though by whom, I could never discover. It is worth remembering that through the Stuarts, Scotland has associations with Holland, and in Scrope's accounts of salmon-fishing on the Tweed, and elsewhere, we constantly find references to salmon having weighed so many lb. 'Dutch weight.' Now, the Dutch *pond* weighs about ten per cent more than our lb.; so that the Kenmure pike *would* have weighed about 65 lb. 'Dutch weight.'

Away with these Doubting Thomases! Of course the Kenmure pike weighed 72 lb., and that isn't all the story. Draw a pike's head in chalk on the floor, nine inches across the back, and then draw in his body in proportion. If he was six inches across the jaws, double as much as a 23-pounder, wouldn't he be double the length, and that forty-two inches? Didn't the Gordons of Kenmure say he was seven feet long, and isn't that eighty-four inches? Didn't John Murray's master complain that the loch contained nothing but 'parr,' by which he meant small trout, because Murray, whose job included catching trout for the table, had for some time been able to produce only small ones? Isn't it likely that the great pike was finding it as difficult to get enough for his own belly as Murray was finding it to get enough for the Laird's? When you consider the tackle that was used in the 1760's, do you think, if that tremendous fish had been in his full prime and power, that Murray could have landed him? Do you think a fish like that would have moved himself after a bunch of peacock feathers, if he hadn't been near starved to death? I believe he was so starved that when he snapped the fly, in his hunger and desperation, he was too weak to upset the boat, or bite the hand clean off his captor, and so save himself, as a pike of that calibre ought. And if he weighed 72 lb. when he was thin and weak, wouldn't he have weighed 100 lb. and more, when he was in his glory? And isn't it likely that his descendants in Loch Ken, and pike in other lochs in Scotland, weighing 100 lb., are swimming about now, waiting to be caught?

During the last few years, largely at the instigation of Fred Taylor and his brothers, of Aylesbury, a good deal of investigation has been made into the willingness or otherwise of pike to pick up dead, inert fish from the bottom. It is now perfectly clear that there are times when a dead fish used as a bait cast out to lie motionless is even more attractive to pike than a live bait, a spinner or a plug. What has not yet been fully determined is the question of how to recognize when this is the case.

However, such has been the success of dead baits that it is safe to say that more pike upwards of 20 lbs. in weight are now taken annually in Britain on inert dead fish than by any other means of pike fishing. Most of these pike are taken on herrings, but whether this is due to some particular attraction herrings have for pike, or to their size, which is rather larger than the average small roach that pike fishers are inclined to use, or if it is simply a matter of herrings being easily obtainable, convenient to use and thus fished far more often than other types of dead fish, I cannot say.

The method of fishing a dead herring is quite simple; a tackle is made up consisting of two trebles and a single hook mounted on wire about eighteen inches long and terminating at the line end in a swivel. The herring is attached to hang head downwards, the hooks being arranged along one side, the end treble is stuck in next to the gill cover; the next treble in the middle of the side and the single hook, which is attached to the wire at the appropriate point, is put in at the tail. Where long casting is contemplated, a few turns of thread around the "wrist" of the tail and the single hook will greatly assist in preventing the bait being thrown off with the force of the cast.

These herring baits are heavy and casting them demands rather a strong rod and an appropriate line. It has to be admitted that tackle strong enough to cast a full-size herring becomes rather oppressive on any pike that may be hooked, even a big one, and among the many instances of pike over 20 lb., and in some cases over 30 lb. that have been caught in this way, I cannot recollect any account of a spectacular battle; usually the fish has been brought to gaff without having much to say about it.

It has been found that to follow the usual procedure of allowing the pike to run off after it has taken the bait, and give it time to turn it, as is usually done in live baiting, almost always results in the pike having swallowed the bait

completely, and this one prefers to avoid. We have, therefore, developed a technique of striking directly the line is
seen to run out, with no delay whatever; and with dead
fish bait it is seldom that one fails to hook the pike.

For those who like to watch a float, there is no reason at
all why one should not be used when fishing with dead
baits, and as the bait does not have to be held off the bottom
as does a live bait, a simple small float is entirely adequate;
I use a very small circular cork float with a little peg in it.
With herrings no lead is, of course, necessary, as the weight
to be cast is already too heavy, but when sprats or small
fresh-water fish are used some weight can be added to
increase casting range when needed. I do not think it
necessary to make this a running lead; pike in a feeding
mood seem not to worry at all about dragging $\frac{1}{2}$ oz. or so of
lead, and the pike that picks up a dead bait only does so
because he means to eat it, unlike the pike that, as so often
happens, attacks a live bait simply to kill it and then, having
done that, lets it go, leaving the frustrated angler to strike
at nothing.

When using dead fresh-water fish, remember to prick the
swim-bladder, otherwise the fish will float. For a pike to take
a fish that is dead and floating is, in my experience, unusual
but not unknown. I once saw a pike come up from deep
water and take a roach that, to my certain knowledge, had
been dead for ten days and which had become covered completely with white fungus. This incident convinced me that
pike are not very fussy about whether their food is alive,
dead, or even decomposed. The fact is they will eat anything that can provide them with nourishment. I am told
that floating dead fish have been tried successfully on some
waters, and since a pike can see upwards better than it can
downwards, it seems likely that in clear water this method
may be well worth trying.

FURTHER NOTES

Because I believe that live-baiting is a practice that large
numbers of the general public, uninformed as they are about

the biology of fishes, can easily be persuaded is extremely cruel, I have now abandoned its use.   In common with other field sports, angling is assailed by members of anti-blood sport organisations, and I think anglers are unwise to provide such people with so convenient a weapon as live-baiting.

That imposes no handicap because pike can be caught well enough with dead-baits and artificial lures of various kinds.   Professor Barrie Rickards has shown that dead herrings can attract pike over great distances, and more recently, he has decided that mackerel are considerably more attractive than herrings.   If only large mackerel are available, tail-ends can be used.   Now that many households have deep-freezing facilities, a pike-fisher can ensure a supply of suitable dead-baits for the entire fishing season.

Where large numbers of big eels are found, a dead herring lying on the bottom is quickly consumed.   On Loch Lomond we found they were eaten up completely in from 15 to 20 minutes.   Mackerel last much longer but where eels are nuisances, harder dead-baits such as roach, rudd, etc., or small trout, are preferable.   Pike are particularly fond of trout; I have often seen a dead trout taken within a minute or two of being cast out in a place where a dead roach had lain ignored by the pike for hours.

I have now altogether discontinued the use of Alasticum wire, since if it becomes kinked, only a small sharp jerk suffices to break it.   Stranded wire is much better.   Unfortunately no tackle manufacturer offers live- or dead-bait tackles ready-made that are acceptable and you have to make your own.

What sort of tackle is the best is a subject that has been debated for centuries.   I continue to use tandem trebles on 30 lb. b.s. stranded wire, their size and spacing being determined by the size of the bait.   The wire should be a foot longer than the longest pike you expect to hook.   I prefer taper-shank trebles, and make up tackles by bending the end of the wire back on itself so that it goes down one side of the shank, between the bends, and up the other side of the shank, which is smeared with 'Araldite'.   I then whip the wire tightly to the shank with touching turns of fine copper wire, wipe off surplus 'Araldite' with a damp rag and let it set. The upper hook has its shank wound with open turns of copper wire and smeared with 'Araldite', after which the wire is laid alongside and whipped with the copper wire. The open turns of wire on the shank prevent slipping. When the 'Araldite' is well set, the bindings are given two or three coats of polyurethane or PVC varnish. I do not favour adjustable hooks, but prefer to carry a number of tackles with different hook sizes and spacings to accommodate baits of various sizes. Hook sizes include 2, 4 and 6.

Bill Giles has shown that dead-baits may be fished successfully off the bottom. The first time I saw him using this method, with a dead herring, on Loch Lomond, he very quickly had it taken by a fine fighting pike that weighed 25 lb. It avoids the attention of eels, and covers more water if a big float and a floating line are used, and a good breeze is blowing. He attaches the bait by the back so that its attitude in the water is approximately horizontal.

Fred Buller, in his book *Pike*, puts forward the theory that the largest pike are to be found in waters where indigenous fish grow well and where there is also a run of migratory species, usually sea-trout and salmon. I find his arguments totally convincing. Migratory species are growing on sea-food, and consequently provide pike with far more food than the lake or loch in which they live could produce.

In Loch Lomond there is not only a large population of indigenous roach, perch, trout and eels, supplemented by migratory trout and salmon, but also another species, the powan, whose ecological niche is different from that of other species, so that it still further supplements the food supply.

It may be significant that Loch Ken has a run of salmon and sea-trout. Loch Lomond holds vast pike. Despite its rejection by the Record Fish Committee, there is absolutely no doubt of the authenticity of the 47 lb. 11 oz. pike caught from Loch Lomond by Tom Morgan in 1947. I have talked with the late Jackie Thompson, who was Morgan's boatman when this great fish was taken. Jackie rowed me to the exact spot where the fish was hooked, and described in detail what happened subsequently. If ever an account had the ring of absolute truth, that one did. Subsequently, I was present when Fred Buller hooked, but unfortunately lost, another monster pike. That fish came within 5 or 6 feet of where I sat in another boat, with most of its back out of water. My estimate of its size made at the time, not less than 50 lb., was, I think, conservative.

Finally we have the evidence of the dried head of a pike found stranded on the banks of the Endrick, one of the rivers that feed Loch Lomond. I have measured and photographed this head, which must have belonged to a fish not less than 50 lb. in weight, and which could have weighed as much as 70 lb., especially when one realises that Lomond pike have exceptionally small heads in relation to their body size.

I believe that Loch Lomond holds pike as large as and perhaps larger than those anywhere else in the world.

CHAPTER XIV

EELS

Eels are regarded by most anglers as a nuisance; and certainly they seem so when they take a bait carefully arranged to ensnare some mighty carp or tench. There are people, however, who specialize in eel-fishing, and there is no doubt in my own mind that a big eel is a worthy quarry.

A big eel will put up a fight that will surprise anyone who has not previously experienced it. By 'big' I mean upwards of 2 lb.; but no one really knows how big eels grow in this country. I have seen the body of a 9-pounder but this is probably nowhere near the limit. Now and then an angler live-baiting or ledgering with lobworm has a tremendous bite, hooks something he can't cope with, and is eventually broken in a most devastating way, or finds that he has to break since whatever is attached to his hook has become immovable. Sometimes stout wire traces are severed as if by wire-cutters. Ducklings, moorhens and even cygnets are pulled under screaming, and not always with the splash and swirl one associates with big pike.

If a number of good anglers, properly equipped, were to investigate the question of how big eels really do grow, we might learn a lot. There would undoubtedly be great battles and eel-fishing might come to be regarded with more respect. For myself, I lack the necessary resolution to pursue eels with the concentration they deserve. But sometimes on a blazing hot day I find myself beaten and baffled by carp, or tench, or whatever it is I am fishing for. When this happens I turn with an unholy glee to the business of catching a big eel. This is how I go about it.

First of all, I catch a few small fish—almost any kind will do, but a roach of about five inches long is hard to beat. I kill it, and thread it with a baiting-needle on to a monofil line that goes in at the root of the tail-fin of the bait, and is brought out from its mouth. The end is then tied to a No. 3 or No. 4 ring-eyed, black-japanned eel-hook, which is drawn back into its mouth until only point and barb project. Then I pinch one shot on the monofil, as close to the tail as possible, so that it cannot slide back up the line, which ought to be at least 9 lb. b.s., and is best used with a carp-rod, or something of that kind, and a fixed-spool reel.

If I have only small baits and want to throw a long way, I put on a barrel lead of the right size before attaching the hook so that the lead disappears down the bait's throat; but as far as possible I avoid lead except for the single shot.

If no lead is used, the swim-bladder of the bait must be deflated by squeezing or pricking its abdomen, otherwise it won't sink. Many would-be eel-catchers make the mistake of using dead-baits of this kind on a running ledger, usually with a large coffin lead, so that the bait rises from the bottom, perhaps pulling line through the lead, and they fail to catch anything because of not deflating the swim-bladder.

The purpose of the shot at the bait's tail is to prevent it being pushed up the line when the eel tries to eject it after being hooked. A small roach gags an eel and he cannot close his jaws sufficiently to bite the tackle through unless he can rid himself of the bait.

I then cast out the bait as far as I can. Especially in the daytime, big eels seem to prefer to keep well away from the banks, perhaps because they are the favourite food of herons and otters. Whatever the reason, I believe in making a long throw and I am never satisfied with less than forty yards, unless the lake is less than eighty yards across. The rod is then put in its rest and the pick-up of the reel put in the disengaged position, after having just tightened the line so that it is reasonably straight from rod to bait.

If I am using a rotating-drum reel, I coil at least fifteen yards of line on a mackintosh, for a big eel will often run quite as far as that when he first grabs the bait. First signs of a bite are gentle twitches; then the line runs out steadily for some distance. If the eel looks like taking more line than has been coiled, it must be pulled off the reel by hand so that he feels no check. Then nothing happens for a minute or two, save perhaps an occasional twitch. Finally, the line begins to run out smartly again; now, and not before, is the time to strike. Nine out of ten eel-runs follow this pattern.

I don't use a conventional ledger because it tends to catch the tackle on snags on the bottom and the running eel is likely to feel a check and so let go the bait.

Formerly, when I fished in the usual way, I found that half my runs were abortive owing to the eel dropping the bait, and I am sure it is as important with eels as it is with other fish to avoid checking them in any way when they run off until one is ready to strike.

Playing an eel is a simple business and its success depends on the anglers not caring in the least whether he is broken or not. There is no place for finesse in playing eels. If you play them carefully, they will either tie your tackle in knots or get their tail round a snag, or both, and a big one firmly coiled round a sunken branch is a tough proposition. Speed, therefore, is the essence of the contract, and wherever possible I walk backwards, winding and pumping as fast as I can, until the eel is at the edge of the water; then I point the rod straight at it and pull hard, so that it slithers up the bank. The slipping clutch on the reel is screwed up tight all the time. It is useless to try landing a big eel with an ordinary landing-net or gaff. I remember a veteran eel-fisher showing me a gaff he had made specially for big eels: it was a cod-hook on about a yard of snare-wire. The snare-wire was passed through two wire-netting staples driven into an ash-plant, and then looped round it. The loop was drawn up until the cod-hook shank went through the staples; then when it was stuck into the eel it slid out again, and the eel was unable to use the shaft to lever itself off the hook.

I never saw it work, but I can imagine how successful it was.

Your fight is not over because you have got your eel on to the bank. Indeed, the harder struggle is yet to come. You have now to *assault* the eel, and if you think you can hold it with your hands you are welcome to try. If it is a big eel—and those from still waters usually are—you can forget that clever finger-grip, guaranteed to hold the most slippery eel, that someone showed you. The best plan is to go for the brute bald-headed, armed with a newspaper, a stick and a stout knife. First try to get the eel to roll itself up in the newspaper. You will probably succeed, and if you do, the eel will lie more or less still. This is your chance to get in a blow with the stick, either on its nose or about three inches from the end of its tail. Your next move depends on how you feel about eels. If you intend to eat it—and many think there is no better freshwater fish—you can stick the knife through it just in front of the pectoral fins, aiming to sever its vertebrae; this kills it. It may writhe and kick from muscular reaction, but it is dead. If you don't want to kill it, cut the gut or nylon and put the eel back in the lake. An eel thinks nothing of a heavy blow or two and will swim away to digest the hook at leisure. Since eels, however, are so inimical to every other kind of fish, and even to waterfowl, it is probably best to kill every one caught. Don't bother about the recovery of your hook yet; you can get it back when you cut up the eel for cooking. Put on a fresh bait and hook, and try for another!

While a dead fish is the best bait for big eels, everyone knows they will take a variety of others, such as lobworms, pieces of meat or offal, frogs, skinned mice or birds, etc. I have even heard of quite large eels being caught on paste and have caught them myself on cheese. They will take a live-bait, but a dead one is just as good and less likely to get hung up on a snag or hidden in weeds.

I always prefer a freshly-killed bait. Sea-fishers after conger eels say that a fresh bait is essential. I have, however, met anglers who swear by a really 'high' dead fish or mouse, saying that eels hunt by scent (which is quite true) and will go for a stinking bait rather than a fresh one. The point is whether, having smelt it out, they are equally ready to eat it. I have two bottles of salted roach that I mean to try sometime; while pieces of kipper are said to be deadly.

Where eels run very large, a wire trace with a swivel at each end may help to avoid trouble. I have often had quite stout wire severed by big eels without ever being able to decide whether they have actually bitten it through or whether it has been twisted and kinked until it has broken.

I don't think it matters much whereabouts in a lake one fishes for eels, providing the bait is well out from the bank. Eels are able to smell a dead fish a long way off and will find it sooner or later if given time.

Weather conditions are said to have a great effect on eels, but my own experience is that provided it is not too cold eels will bite under all conditions. I have never found them deterred by hot weather. Like many other still-water fish, they are seldom caught after the first autumn frosts, though they continue feeding later in deep lakes than in shallow ones.

Although I have usually fished for big eels in daytime there is no doubt that eels move and feed more freely at dusk and in darkness, and it is only the prospect of having to deal with a monster eel in the dark which deters me: the struggle I had with one while fishing for carp one night has given me a wholesome respect for them.

Any angler who wants to specialize in a branch of angling that isn't overcrowded, and offers scope for experiment and discovery that may produce extraordinary results, could do worse than choose eel-fishing.

FURTHER NOTES

In weedy or snaggy waters, it is not possible to allow an eel that has taken a bait to run as far as it likes before striking, otherwise the eel will take refuge in a place from which it cannot be extricated.

The remedy for this state of affairs is to use fresh fish-liver as bait, cutting off only enough to nicely cover a No. 4 or No. 2 hook, which should be attached to a short wire trace. Fish liver does not discriminate against small eels as well as a dead whole fish, but it does attract big eels as well as small ones much better than worms. Your sea-angling friends will save you some fish-liver if you ask them, and you can deep-freeze it.

In waters that hold crayfish—and some still waters do—eels will readily take a crayfish. Whether they will do so where crayfish are not found, I have not discovered. They will take boiled prawns anywhere.

I have found that eels of all sizes often patrol the slope of a lake bed, quite close to the bank, after dark, and if one is fishing then, it is not necessary or desirable to cast very far.

Avoid the temptation to use more than one rod when you are eel-fishing. I don't believe that any man is competent to deal with two eels simultaneously!

CHAPTER XV

WELS

THE European catfish, or wels (Silurus glanis) is found in some British waters, and is capable of reaching weights upwards of 40 lb., perhaps very much more. Many people find its appearance repulsive; it resembles a monstrous tadpole with a cavernous mouth surrounded by long feelers.

Wels have been caught in daylight but there is no doubt that they are mainly nocturnal, bottom-feeding scavengers. Suitable baits are dead fish, bunches of lobworms, pieces of raw liver, congealed blood and other meaty concoctions, fished on tackle similar to that which one would choose for large carp.

These fish are powerful fighters, and it does not do to underestimate their tackle-breaking abilities. Anglers at the Tring reservoirs have occasionally hooked unseen fish that have run off 150 yards or so of line and then broken away; large wels were almost certainly responsible.

Not many people will wish to catch these fish, but for those who do, the only real problem is the avoidance of eels and possibly other fish that are likely to take the bait. Otherwise, straightforward fishing at night should produce results from any water in which wels are present in good numbers.

CHAPTER XVI

ZANDER or PIKE-PERCH

Barrie Rickards

THE zander is a species which, until the late 1960s, was more or less restricted to a few lakes, such as Claydon and Woburn, in the Great Ouse River Authority area, and because of this restriction was fished only by a few anglers. In 1963, however, a highly-successful introduction of ninety-seven zander was made in the Great Ouse Relief Channel, which flows from the non-tidal Ouse gates at Denver down to King's Lynn. The official responsible for the stocking was the then head of the G.O.R.A., Norman McKenzie, a man who was to a large degree behind the development of superlative pike-fishing in fenland. He was assisted by Cliff Cawkwell one of the best-known and best-loved fenland bailiffs, and Cliff tells me that they originally put in 100 fish in the 6–10 inch bracket, but that within a short time three of them floated belly upwards and were taken from the water: the other ninety-seven swam away quite happily. Three years later vast numbers of sizeable zander could be caught on the Relief Channel, and by the late 1960s and early 1970s they had successfully spread to many other connected waters such as the Great Ouse, the Wissey, the Lark, the Little Ouse, the Cam, and the drains Old Bedford and Delph.

At this time they attracted a great deal of interest, and anglers now come from all over the country to fish for them, using a variety of techniques which I shall outline later. The zander also became the centre of a burning controversy, those of us closest to the fish and its development insisting that the population explosion was akin to that of rabbits in Australia, whilst others further afield calmly asserted that nothing unusual was happening. However, the details of the debate form a vast and most interesting subject in their own right, and it would be out of place to spend much time discussing them here. Suffice to say that whilst zander-fishing was not readily available until the late 1960s, and whilst it did not at first attract much interest, the opposite is the case today. Zander are widespread, as I shall describe, they are present in considerable numbers in these 'new' waters, and they are a really worthwhile quarry in the sense that they grow big, are active predators and make fine eating.

Perhaps I should emphasise most strongly at this point that zander are NOT a cross between pike and perch: they are not hybrids in any sense but a distinct species in their own right, perhaps much more closely related to perch than to pike. They look like an elongated perch, with more stripes, generally paler colouring, and with transparent pectoral and pelvic fins. They also have a savage-looking mouth, with a distinct set of stabbing teeth in the front of both the upper and lower jaws.

On the Continent there are other species which might be confused with the zander (*Stizostedion lucioperca*) including the eastern pike-perch (*S. volgense*) and the zingel and streber (*Z. zingel* and *Z. Streber* respectively), but in Great Britain the zander is probably now the only representative of this rather odd group of fish. Having said that, it must be pointed out that the American walleye (*S. vitreum*) was introduced in the G.O.R.A. area in the distant past and a fish of $11\frac{3}{4}$ lb. was caught from the River Delph in 1934 by Mr. F. Adams, who now holds the record for that species. It is highly doubtful whether this species still exists, but it is supposedly distinguishable from the zander by the position of the two dorsal fins: in the zander they very nearly touch, whereas in the walleye there is a gap between them approximating to one-sixth the length of the two dorsals added together. There are additional differences in the number of scales along the lateral line and in the presence or absence of scales upon the gill covers, but these facts need not worry us in the presence of a good fin-position feature. It is highly unlikely that anglers will catch any more walleyes, although

I have heard of a few recent and probably spurious claims; but I suppose it is just possible that the American walleye now occupies a similar diminutive rôle in the fishy world to that of the burbot.

The zander, a name used in preference to pike-perch since the Woburn era, occurs in a number of still waters in addition to those in the Claydon and Woburn areas. Landbeach Lakes just north of Cambridge has a few, but they have never bred extensively there, nor have they put on much weight; the heaviest I ever saw there being 3½ lb. There is a small number of fish in a private lake several miles to the north-west of Cambridge and here, although the species has not overbred, I have seen fish up to well over 5 lb. in weight. Some of the river-board stock-ponds have a head of zander, and I suppose it was only a matter of time anyway before they escaped or were illegally placed into the river system. A few other privately-owned lakes also have zander, but I suppose the angler's only *real* chance of a still-water zander is to fish the Woburn Park waters. Happily for the ardent zander-angler, the Great Ouse river and drain system now abounds in the species, and I would particularly mention the Great Ouse Relief Channel, the G.O. Cut Off Channel, the River Delph and the lower Great Ouse itself as waters worthy of attention.

The nature of the fish itself and its habits pose several problems and points of interest for would-be enthusiasts. In the first place they are predators that eat just about anything that moves, and a good deal that doesn't, including zebra mussels and dead fish. They are not powerful swimmers and have a small mouth, and in both these respects may be contrasted with the other big predator, namely the pike. It is not surprising therefore that zander tend to eat *mostly* small fish, and that they tend to hunt during the hours of darkness or under coloured water conditions. Both habits offset the fish's lack of power, since in the dark they can creep up on their prey and if the prey is small they have a better chance of overhauling it and devouring it. Since they are just as happy as pike at low temperatures, they fill a previously unfilled niche in the ecology of the fishy world, to wit,

winter night feeding. Whether the members of the carp
family are happy at being harried during the day by pike
and during the night by zander is another matter!

The zander's enjoyment of dark conditions makes for a
nice contrast between still waters such as lakes, and the
sluggish rivers and drains of the fens. Although the latter
are often all but still waters, they do have floodwater conditions and coloured water conditions fairly often, so that
anglers may take good zander catches during the day,
whereas in the clear lakes such as Landbeach the zander
almost always wait for dusk before feeding. The term
'walleye' used by the Americans for their version of the
zander refers to the peculiar opaque-looking eyes, a feature
also shared by the European zander: I am certain that there
is something about the eyes of zander which gives them
extraordinary vision at night or in dirty conditions. All the
zander I saw from Landbeach were caught during the first
three hours of darkness.

Having said *where* to find zander, and before going on to
deal with the practicalities of their capture, it may be as
well to say *when* you catch zander. Until very recently if a
lake in the G.O.R.A. area (now Anglia Water Authority
area) was not connected with the river system, then anglers
could fish for any species at any time of the year and at any
time of day or night. This applied as much to zander as to
other species and the only restrictions were placed by the
club or the owner. Whether this applies under the present
(1974) confused situation I would not like to say, but as far
as the rivers and drains are concerned the situation is quite
unambiguous. No zander-fishing is allowed before September 1st. I suspect this also applies to still waters. In
addition night-fishing is banned on those two great zander
waters, the G.O. Relief Channel and Cut-Off Channel:
elsewhere the local club rules must be adhered to, and some
of these *also* ban night-fishing. There is quite a ridiculous
size limit on zander, all fish under 18 inches being returned
to the water. It would be infinitely better for the general
ecology of the waters if fish *under* 22 inches could be taken for
eating, and fish *over* that length be returned to the water.

However, those are the rules in 1974.

From the foregoing it is clear, I hope, that the zander is an interesting fish. The mystery, folklore, and fable that surround it are just as intriguing, and when you begin fishing for them I am certain that the element of interest and novelty will be maintained. When anglers such as Peter Frost and his colleagues fished Woburn with great success in the 1960s, many of their good fish and good bags were taken on ledger tackle, usually a leadless ledger rig and with the 7–8 lb. nylon

monofil tied direct to the hook or hooks. Although zander have a mouthful of teeth it was found that wire traces were not necessary at Woburn. Continental zander-anglers take the same standpoint, but it must be pointed out that at Woburn most of the zander caught were well under 10 lb. weight, and my own view is that if zander over 10 lb. are wanted then a fine-wire, dark-coloured trace is essential, because the array of dentistry of a *big* zander really is impressive. It is inconceivable that they cannot bite through nylon monofil and, of course, they are more likely to do this the bigger they get.

The bait at Woburn was usually a small dead-bait, and small dace, gudgeon and rudd were successful as they are elsewhere. The rig, as can be seen from the illustration, is very similar to that used by eel-anglers. The rods to go with the 7–8 lb. line were Mark IV carp rods, and the reels might just as well be fixed-spool reels.

The same technique, simple weightless ledgering, works well on the slow rivers and drains, but with the added factor

of current to contend with, sliding leads are often employed. Personally I would also use a wire trace, dark in
colour, of about 7 lb. breaking strain, although wire of this
strength is becoming increasingly difficult to obtain. Some
of the finer sorrel-coloured wires, for example, 'Tidemaster'
made by Efgeeco, are good even in the heavier breaking
strains.

An interesting point about dead-bait fishing for zander is
that the bait does not have to be small. If the angler is not
fussy about the size of his quarry then small, say 4–6 inch,
baits are probably best, but big zander have on several
occasions been taken on whole herrings intended for pike.
If large deadbaits were adorned with small hooks, about
sizes 8 or 10 trebles or singles, then probably more big
zander would fall to large baits. As it is they tend to chew
between large treble hooks and the bait is retrieved with a
chunk of flesh missing but no real sign of a take. One of the
few valuable pieces of information obtained during the
G.O.R.A. research into zander was that the stomach
contents of some zander contained bream scales from bream
which must have been *considerably larger than the zander
themselves*! It is probable, therefore, that they scavenge
more effectively than do pike: and I know from my own
experiences that zander will attack and kill, often hunting in
packs, much bigger fish than they can actually swallow. It
is tempting to suggest that they later chew at leisure upon the
fish they have killed, and the above research results tend to
support this idea. Generally speaking a smallish dead-bait,
with or without sliding lead as the occasion demands, and
with or without small snap tackle as the angler prefers, is a
good basic technique with which to begin.

A zander take can be a problem. At the peak of Woburn
fishing it was common to reel in and find that the bait had
been chewed, particularly if wire traces were in use on the
outside of the bait. Alternatively, upon retrieving the tackle,
a zander would be found hanging on the end with the hooks
well down its throat. Similar experiences have occurred on
the fenland drains and rivers. Avoidance of chewing seems
to be best achieved by using hooks and traces which are as

small and inconspicuous as possible, and the problem of fish swallowing the bait is probably best solved by using sensitive float tackle, whether the method is dead-baiting or live-baiting.

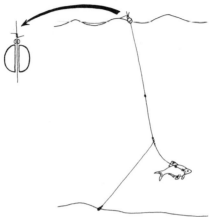

One of the best all-round float tackles is shown above, and it is essentially a scaled-down version of a good pike rig. The line is 7–8 lb. breaking strain, and the snap tackle is of size 10 trebles to fine wire. The float is about one inch in diameter, a slider with a simple ⅛ inch hole through the middle, and it is stopped by a small bead against a standard Billy Lane sliding stop knot. The paternoster line can be 4–5 lb. monofil and the paternoster lead is chosen to suit the occasion. Of course it can be dispensed with if a more roving live-bait or drifting dead-bait is preferred.

The small size of the treble hooks cannot be over emphasised. In 1966 when the Channel first came 'on' as a red hot zander water, we missed up to thirty runs in an evening either through use of a single hook or too big trebles, and I only solved the problem by making tiny snap tackles of size 14 trebles tied to thick monofil and by using 4 inch live- and dead-baits. Once this was done zander were caught at the rate of up to six per hour on each and every swim tried over several miles of water. Few runs were missed, and it was obvious that the small hooks were slipping neatly into the mouth of the zander along with the bait, whereas the larger trebles were pushed to one side by the jaws of the zander.

I have already mentioned the difficulty of finicky runs, but perhaps even more of a problem are the very fast runs. Here the lines run off the spool at an astonishing rate, much faster than a fast carp run. There is no check whatsoever, so that the angler has no idea when to strike. If he lets it go without striking, the float usually pops up about 60 yards away from the point of the take, with the bait gone, for zander are experts at removing baits from hooks. Given enough time, such as a 60 yard run, they'll manage to do this even if small hooks are in use. Therefore the angler has no choice with a take of this kind: allow the line to tighten right up to the rod, having put in the pick up, and then strike hard.

Spinning and plug-fishing for zander was employed extensively in the days of Claydon and Woburn, but has been markedly less productive on the fenland drains in winter. They will, of course, fall readily to lures on occasions, and probably to flies too, but I am far from certain when these occasions are. No, the most successful way to catch a zander is to fish at dawn or dusk, or at night if this is allowed, with a good 3–5 inch live-bait fished float paternoster style. The bait should be set perhaps three quarters of the way to the bottom or a little deeper at times. For float-fishing at night on Landbeach lakes I dispensed with the paternoster, greased the line, and fished in the top 2 feet of water, allowing the live-bait to roam widely. On the fen drains the standard paternoster rig at dawn or dusk seems to pay most dividends.

Coloured water should be greeted with delight by the ardent zander man. By coloured I mean really dirty, filthy brown, with a strong current carrying all the usual objectionable items. A good trick under these conditions, which incidently seem to put off all other species in the fens, is to find an eddy, even a tiny one, at the back of a common reed-bed. I once watched Laurie Manns extract a netful of 5 lb.-plus zander from the swim depicted below. Technique was standard paternoster rig, and small live-baits. Under such dirty conditions zander *can* be caught in open water, but of course fishing there with effective tackle control is most difficult.

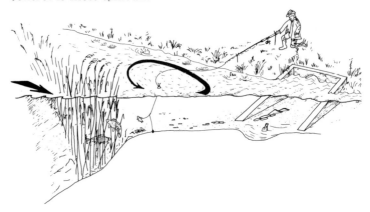

Landing zander is easy, and if your landing net is not to hand they can be beached or picked out with no trouble at all. For a start, unlike most species, zander are not slippery but have a really rough, clean feel to them caused by many tiny spines on the scales. Any ordinary landing net will do. Unhooking zander and subsequent handling of them should be done with care, for they are not the most robust of species. If the angler intends eating his catch, then it's probably best to knock it on the head before unhooking. The mouth is quite small so that gags are not easily used and are largely unnecessary. Usually I lay the fish on its back, pull back the lower jaw with a gloved left hand (taking care to avoid the stabbing teeth), and use artery forceps to remove the small hooks. Using the paternoster outfit described, it is unusual for a zander to gorge the hooks.

Personally I would not recommend putting zander in keepnets, for they do not seem to last very long. Unlike other fish they seem to need space to recover their faculties. I have not yet said anything about fighting ability. I do not rate zander at all as a fighting fish, and if this were the sole criteria for fishing for them then nobody in their right mind would bother. But a big zander is a nice-looking fish, smaller ones are plump and good to eat, and they are not really *bad* fighters, so there are some reasons for fishing for them!

Sorting out big zander from small ones is tricky. I've had four over 10 lb. myself, two of which were British records at the time of capture, and one of which weighed 13¼ lb. I've had plenty of others over 5 lb., as have my friends. It seems to me that the best way to get the big ones is to use good live-baits, say dace, in the 4–6 oz. bracket, rather than small ones. Obviously you fish waters, or stretches of waters, where big ones are thought to be. Then fish at the right time of day or night, and look for the best conditions with some colour in the water. And good luck.

FURTHER NOTES
by Richard Walker

Readers will have noticed that much of what Doctor Rickards says, refers to zander in the Great Ouse Relief Channel and other East Anglian waters. These are not, strictly speaking, still waters, but for much of the year, their current is negligible or non-existent.

Experience has shown that the behaviour of zander in truly still waters, such as the lakes at Clayden and Woburn, is exactly the same as in the waters where Doctor Rickards has done most of his zander-fishing, and his advice is therefore fully applicable.

INDEX